SMALL PARTIES IN WESTERN EUROPE

Small Parties in Western Europe

Comparative and National Perspectives

edited by
Ferdinand Müller-Rommel
and Geoffrey Pridham

SAGE Modern Politics Series Volume 27
Sponsored by the European Consortium
for Political Research/ECPR

SAGE Publications
London • Newbury Park • New Delhi

© editorial arrangement Ferdinand Müller-Rommel and
   Geoffrey Pridham 1991
© Chapter 1 Ferdinand Müller-Rommel 1991
© Chapter 2 Gordon Smith 1991
© Chapter 3 Peter Mair 1991
© Chapter 4 Geoffrey Pridham 1991
© Chapter 5 Mogens N. Pedersen 1991
© Chapter 6 Paul Lucardie 1991
© Chapter 7 Kris Deschouwer 1991
© Chapter 8 Jorgen Rasmussen 1991
© Chapter 9 Yannis Papadopoulos 1991

First published 1991

All rights reserved. No part of this publication may be
reproduced, stored in a retrieval system, transmitted or
utilized in any form or by any means, electronic, mechanical,
photocopying, recording or otherwise, without permission in
writing from the Publishers.

SAGE Publications Ltd
6 Bonhill Street
London EC2A 4PU

SAGE Publications Inc
2455 Teller Road
Newbury Park, California 91320

SAGE Publications India Pvt Ltd
32, M-Block Market
Greater Kailash – I
New Delhi 110 048

British Library Cataloguing in Publication data

Small parties in Western Europe
   1. Western Europe. Political parties – (Sage modern
   politics series; v. 27)
   I. Müller-Rommel, Ferdinand 1952– II. Pridham,
   Geoffrey 324.24

   ISBN 0–8039–8261–5

Library of Congress catalog card number 90–62332

Typeset by Photoprint, Torquay, Devon
Printed in Great Britain by Billing and Sons Ltd, Worcester

Contents

Preface	vi
1 Small Parties in Comparative Perspective: The State of the Art *Ferdinand Müller-Rommel*	1
2 In Search of Small Parties: Problems of Definition, Classification and Significance *Gordon Smith*	23
3 The Electoral Universe of Small Parties in Postwar Western Europe *Peter Mair*	41
4 Italian Small Parties in Comparative Perspective *Geoffrey Pridham*	71
5 The Birth, Life and Death of Small Parties in Danish Politics *Mogens N. Pedersen*	95
6 Fragments from the Pillars: Small Parties in the Netherlands *Paul Lucardie*	115
7 Small Parties in a Small Country: The Belgian Case *Kris Deschouwer*	135
8 They Also Serve: Small Parties in the British Political System *Jorgen Rasmussen*	152
9 The Decline of Small Parties and the Emergence of Two-Partyism in Greece *Yannis Papadopoulos*	174
References	203
Index	221
Notes on the Contributors	231

Preface

Small parties exist in all Western European party systems. Their political function and legitimacy vary, however, across countries. Although small parties play an important role in some European political systems, little systematic research is available that highlights the relevance of these parties in comparative and national perspective. This book seeks to fill the gap in the current literature by presenting theoretical approaches and by providing a comparative framework for analysing small parties in Western Europe which is applied to selected national cases.

All chapters in this book are based on the following assumptions: First, the concept of a small party is a relative one. Secondly, small parties are by definition distinct, on the one hand, from third parties and, on the other, from minor or fringe parties. Thirdly, the analysis of small parties starts with numerical variables and then progresses to consider political variables. Fourthly, there are different possible comparative approaches in studying small parties, but these are accommodated by the framework adopted by this study.

This volume is the outcome of a workshop on 'Small Parties' at the ECPR Joint Sessions at Amsterdam in April 1987. We are grateful to all those who participated in the workshop and revised their papers for inclusion in this book. Apart from the authors in this book the workshop at Amsterdam also benefited from the participation of others – Emile François Callot, Robert Harmel, Christian Haerpfer and Thomas Poguntke – whose contributions to the workshop have been published elsewhere.

Very special thanks are due to Christel Amirmontaghemi, Christiane Adlung and Bettina Krüger from the University of Lüneburg for their valuable help in preparing the final version of this book.

Ferdinand Müller-Rommel   Geoffrey Pridham
Lüneburg   *Bristol*

1
Small Parties in Comparative Perspective: The State of the Art

Ferdinand Müller-Rommel

The role of small parties in Western Europe is an area that to date has not been examined in any systematic or comprehensive way. Small parties have existed in virtually all Western European countries, whether these have recognized multi-party systems or may be said to possess literally the 'geography' of a multi-party situation; but their individual and collective importance has yet to be defined. The common but unreasoned assumption that small parties are simply politically unimportant has tended to be widely held, although the increasing impact of small parties over the past decade has begun to challenge this view. Familiar criteria of size have usually buttressed such an assumption, while the political and societal functions of small parties have often been ignored.

In the interests of comparative politics, there is now a strong case for a study that takes to task such an assumption and develops a viable approach to small parties, drawing together the somewhat diffuse expertise on the subject. This introductory chapter performs two necessary tasks. First, it surveys the comparative literature on small parties in Western Europe and draws lessons from this. Secondly, it outlines four conceptional approaches that channel the discussion on a cross-national framework for analysing small parties.

The universe of small parties in past and contemporary research

Comparative research on political parties has tended to be concerned with the analysis of major parties in European political systems. There is a bulk of literature on Christian democratic and conservative parties (Hahn 1975; Hartmann 1978; Horner 1981; Irving 1979; Layton-Henry 1982; Morgan and Silvestri 1982; Pridham 1976) and on larger communist, socialist and social democratic parties (Blackmer and Tarrow 1975; Lange and Vannicelli 1981; Oberndörfer 1978; Paterson and Campell 1974; Paterson and

Thomas 1977; Pelinka 1980; Rühle and Veen 1979; Tannahill 1978; Timmermann 1979; Waller and Fennema 1988). However, comparative studies on small parties are still a rarity. Even without a clear definition of what 'small' really means, recent research findings have stated that there are at least fifty small parties which have operated in postwar Western European party systems (Merkl 1980; Pedersen 1982). In a cruder way, Mair (in this volume) has identified 157 parties which gained between 1 and 15 percent of the national vote in Western European countries between 1947 and 1987. Given these empirical facts, the lack of information on small parties is even more astonishing. According to Fisher (1980: 609–12) the lack of research on small parties can be traced back to at least three reasons:

First, small parties are often seen as politically unimportant because of their size and the low electoral turnout they command. Once a small party becomes more prominent in public opinion, for example by introducing new issues into the political system, the attention given to such a party increases. Up to the end of the 1960s, for example, this led to discussions about the role and the function of the right-wing National Party (NPD) in the Federal Republic of Germany (Dittmer 1969; Klingemann and Pappi 1972). In Denmark it was asked why Morgans Glistrup's anti-tax party (the Progress Party) could receive – all of a sudden – 15.9 percent of the vote in the 1973 national election. In Great Britain, there was in the earlier 1980s an intensive debate about the chances for success of the newly founded Social Democratic Party (Crewe 1982; Curtice 1983; Denver 1984; Pridham and Whiteley 1986). Recently, research has been conducted on the continuing political impact of green parties in Western Europe (Kitschelt 1989; Müller-Rommel 1989).

Secondly, most scholars perhaps inevitably focus their research on political parties for which information is more likely to be available. Studying small parties obviously encounters some unique problems especially when it comes to gathering information for a cross-national analysis. In most cases there are clearly language problems. Although it is relatively easy to collect information on party programmes, manifestos and party statutes, it is notably more difficult to read these brochures since (in most cases) they have not been translated into English or another international language. Moreover, there is hardly any systematic information available on processes such as intra-party democracy, leadership selection and intra-party decision-making within small parties. Most of these parties have not even a statistical picture of their own membership development and their financial situation. Furthermore, there is generally no clear evaluation of the voters of small parties.

Normally, the number of small party adherents in a national survey is so low that even very simple statistical analyses cannot be conducted. In addition to this lack of basic information, it is rather difficult to identify exact electoral results. In many official election statistics, small parties receive only marginal consideration. They are often categorized under the label of 'other parties'.

Thirdly, the scant attention given to small parties results from their low political impact on government policy. Many small parties, especially those which are not represented in the national parliament, have no measurable political effects on national policy-making.

In order to help to overcome these and other theoretical and practical problems, this book brings together a team of 'country experts' who have worked together with 'comparativists' along a common and comprehensive framework. First, however, the existing literature on small parties in Western Europe was identified. In this context, it should be noted that research on small parties is not as poor as has sometimes been assumed (Herzog 1987: 317). There are in fact numerous studies on small parties available. However, it is also evident that a systematic mapping of current research findings and of the 'occurrence of the various types of minor parties is lacking' (Pedersen 1982: 14).

There are numerous ways of classifying or mapping small parties. As a first step, however, it seems most appropriate to introduce the existing types of small parties. In contemporary Western Europe we find eight different types of small parties which we refer to as 'small party families' (Mair in this volume; Steed and Hearl 1985). These 'party families' are as follows:

Communists Communist parties exist in nearly all Western European countries. They were founded in the early twentieth century and are all members of the Comintern. With the exception of the communists in Switzerland, all the parties have the word 'communist' in the party label. Except for those in Italy and France, they have usually been small parties.

Socialists Small socialist parties are independent from larger social democratic or labour parties. They can be identified on the basis of a common left-wing ideology and – sometimes – radical viewpoints. Quite often, small socialist parties split off from social democratic and communist parties.

Liberals Liberal parties were founded in practically all Western European countries. However, not all of them belong to the prototype of small parties. They sometimes have been in positions where they played indispensable roles in Western European party systems, for example as coalition partners in government.

Christian This party 'family' includes small religious parties which are often allied with conservative parties. Christians may be identified by programmatic demands located in the political 'centre' rather than on the 'right' side of the political spectrum.

Extreme right Most extreme-right parties originated from or are in the tradition of fascist parties of the inter-war years. Some of the extreme-right parties also have a 'poujadist' character.

Regionalists and nationalists These small parties are difficult to place on an ideological left–right spectrum. They represent the interests of various minority groups in European party systems.

Agrarian Small agrarian parties exist predominantly in Nordic countries. Their programme is oriented towards rural political traditions which are difficult to accommodate by larger established parties.

Greens Green parties have emerged in many Western European countries over the past decade. Their political profile is related to 'new' issues and the new style of political participation and communication.

Given this classification of 'small party families', we can summarize the existing studies on small parties essentially under three headings:

(a) national case studies of small parties by different party families;
(b) cross-national studies of small parties by party family;
(c) studies of small parties in national systems including several party families.

In the contemporary literature many *national case studies* on small parties are available. Most of them are, however, published in the native language, which makes it often difficult for English-speaking researchers to understand literally the major findings of national studies. In spite of this problem, the general knowledge on small parties is substantial though it varies across party families. For instance, much research has been conducted on small communist, liberal and green parties. In addition, small socialist parties in France, Ireland and the Netherlands as well as small Christian parties in Belgium and the Netherlands were studied more often than any other small party type. Only little is known on the extreme right, on regionalist and on nationalist parties in single European countries. Much of the research on 'small party families' in single countries is listed in Appendix 1.1.

Most of these national case studies are purely descriptive. They consider either the historical development or the programme, the organizational structure and/or the electorate of small parties in the respective country. Despite the fact that most of these studies are based on empirical evidence, systematic conclusions on the role and the function of small parties in Western Europe cannot be drawn at this point.

Moreover, it is still unclear from these studies how far the 'political relevance' of small parties is affected not only by the size of the party but also by the political culture, and in particular by the degree of fragmentation of society. Several studies suggest that such cultural variables may play a considerable part in determining the 'political importance' of small parties in their respective party systems. Herzog (1987: 318), for instance, argues that small parties are relevant in the process of negotiating political norms and the rules of the political game. As such, small parties can help in measuring the boundaries of the political culture of a party system. In other words, small parties can be viewed as a testing ground for new political ideas which then might be adopted by major political parties (Fisher 1974: 31). Although this argument is rather plausible, too little empirical research has been conducted that focusses on these questions in a systematic manner across countries and over time.

Although there is considerable knowledge of small parties in national countries, hardly any systematic *cross-national studies* of small parties exist. As shown in Appendix 1.2, there is some cross-national analysis of small communist parties (Kellmann 1988; Sparring 1966; Upton 1973) and of green parties (Müller-Rommel 1989). All these studies are organized in a descriptive format. The authors examine the distinctive characteristics of the small parties in each country under the following topics: development of the small parties, highlighting the institutional and constitutional setting in which they have developed; organizational structure, looking at the decision-making process, the leadership role, the parliamentary group, the membership and finance, etc.; electoral support, that is, the percentage of votes obtained in elections as well as the analysis of the characteristics of the small party's voters; programmatic profile and the future of small communist and green parties in their respective party systems.

Another set of cross-national studies is also based on the 'country by country' approach but does not use a rigid format for analysis. Rather, the authors deliberately stress certain aspects which are important for explaining the functions of small parties in the national context (Baumgarten 1982; Gollwitzer 1977; Nullmeier et al. 1983).

A third set of studies uses a systematic cross-national approach to explain the differences and similarities of green parties in Belgium and West Germany (Kitschelt 1989), small socialist parties in the Netherlands and Denmark (Müller-Rommel 1985a) and the centre parties in Norway and Sweden (Elder and Gooderham 1978). However, studies of this sort are still a rarity.

Although, in some countries, small parties have profound effects on larger conventional parties, for example, in challenging traditional institutional patterns and party policies, little is known about the most decisive question concerning the political impact of the various *small party families in national systems*. It is absolutely amazing that there is hardly any systematic country study available of small parties in multi-party systems such as in Finland, France, Denmark, Italy and the Netherlands. Exceptions are Daalder's study of small parties in the Netherlands (Daalder 1965-6) and Lagasse's analysis of small parties in Belgium (Lagasse 1968). On the other hand, it is most striking to find several country studies on small parties in those party systems where various small parties have neither a 'coalition' nor a 'blackmail potential', for example in the Federal Republic of Germany, in Great Britain and in Ireland (see Appendix 1.3).

In sum, Appendices 1.1-1.3 show that the bulk of literature is considerable, though uneven in scope and method, and largely descriptive. Quite often, the various publications date back to the mid-1960s and 1970s without covering the significant recent development of small parties. In addition, the national case studies are often based solely on a compilation of detailed empirical findings. Hardly any of those studies which are listed in the appendices can actually claim to have combined the empirical findings with a theoretically justified approach. While the literature on small parties in national countries as a whole may be extensive, systematic comparative analyses are few. This poses some serious problems for comparative studies. The great need for research on small parties at present is for approaches which provide a framework for analysis on the basis of which it will be possible to summarize, incorporate and interrelate the various characteristics or functions of small parties' 'structure' and 'life' in comparative and national perspectives.

Approaches for studying small parties

Approaches for analysing small parties have to be both thematically comprehensive and systematically cross-national. They need to develop a viable framework that channels the discussion of small parties, so that both arbitrariness in their selection and looseness in the treatment of them are contained.

Most studies of small parties in single European party systems implicitly or explicitly adopt Sartori's definition for relevance over size and use his two criteria of 'coalition potential' and 'blackmail potential' as one possibility for dealing with political variables (Sartori 1976). However, the chapters in this book generally recognize that some combination of numerical and political criteria is necessary for analysing small parties from a national and a comparative perspective. It is suggested that – in addition to the conventional 'Sartori approach' – four approaches might function as a framework for analysis:

(a) *a conceptional definitional approach* that deals with the question of what small parties are and how we classify them in European party systems;
(b) *a numerical and party family approach* focussing on postwar electoral trends and looking at the electoral results of the different 'small party families';
(c) *a diachronic approach* that analyses the cycles of small party development, their formation, their success and (possibly) their death;
(d) *a systemic approach* examining the role and performance of small parties with reference to three relationships: with the state, with the society and with other parties in the same political system.

It is worth summarizing these approaches in order to understand the general scope of this book.

A conceptional definitional approach
One of the most crucial questions in research is related to the political relevance of small parties. According to Sartori (1976: 123) a party qualifies for relevance 'whenever its existence or appearance affects the tactics of party competition and particularly when it alters the direction of the competition – by determining a switch from centripetal to centrifugal competition either leftward, rightward, or in both directions – of the governing oriented parties'. The conceptional definitional approach, developed by Smith (in this

volume), argues that the relevance of small parties is dependent upon the party system in which they operate.

Assessing the role of small parties requires first a classification of the number of parties that are involved in a competitive party system. In this context, Smith differentiates between one-party-dominant, two-party-balanced, two-and-a-half-party, multi-party-dominant and multi-party-undifferentiated party systems. In each of these five structural systems small parties play a slightly different role.

In a *one-party-dominant system* and in a *two-party system* with one dominant party, no party other than the ruling party has any significant impact on the party system because the need for coalition building is excluded. In a *two-and-a-half-party system* two larger parties and one third party are competing for a minimum winning coalition. It seems evident that in these party systems the blackmail and coalition potential of third parties can easily be eroded. A two-and-a-half system may then change into a two-bloc system in which several small parties might be involved in the process of coalition building (like the Greens in Austria and West Germany). In a *multi-party-dominance system*, the largest party does not normally hold the majority and is therefore dependent upon the support of one or even several smaller parties. In this category of party systems small parties exercise a significant impact (for example, in Italy and Denmark). In *undifferentiated multi-party systems*, no party has a majority and numerous kinds of governing alignments are feasible. In these party systems, small parties usually group around one of the larger parties and as such play a supporting role. A small party's influence may be less pronounced than in dominant multi-party systems (such as in the Netherlands and Belgium).

In sum, the conceptional and definitional approach suggests that small parties may have more or less political influence of some note in the different European party systems. Consequently, Smith has developed a classification that relates small parties directly to the main characteristic of all Western European party systems, which is the left–right dimension. Smith introduces three types of small parties. First there are the *marginal small parties*, which are located at the outer extremes of the mainstream left and right. These parties have only a limited coalition potential. A second group are called *hinge small parties*. They are located between larger established parties near the centre of the left–right dimension and have a fairly important coalition potential. A third type are the *detached small parties*, which cannot be classified on the left–right axis and are therefore out of competition. Regional and ethnic-based small parties belong to this group. Only occasionally, these small parties are included in coalitions.

The conceptual definitional approach helps with predicting the impact of small party types on coalition building. Furthermore, it provides some understanding of how Western European party systems function and change at a time when traditional party identification is decreasing and volatility among the voters is increasing. However, the approach does not systematically relate small parties to the different institutional characteristics of Western European societies.

A numerical and party family approach
In the traditional literature, the 'smallness' of a party has always been defined as a function of size. The numerical and party family approach, as introduced by Mair (in this volume), uses this definition only as a starting-point. It classifies parties according to the size of their electoral support over time and looks at how the small party vote breaks down among the different party families. As such the approach offers an inductive framework for analysis.

According to this approach, small parties are defined as enduring parties which have contested at least three (not necessarily successive) elections during the period from 1947 to 1987. Included are those parties which have polled between 1 and 15 percent of the national vote. In addition, once a party has been identified as small, it is always treated as a small party even if it receives more than 15 percent in a later election. Finally, for cross-national analysis, it is suggested that we calculate the vote for all small parties in a country as a block.

Given this definition and classification, Mair has differentiated between four party systems in which small parties operate with more or less political impact: *large party systems*, where small parties have no relevant impact (for example, in Austria, West Germany, Ireland and the UK); *small party systems*, with a vote turnout for a 'small parties block' of more than 50 percent (such as in Denmark and Sweden); *intermediate systems*, with an overall mean postwar vote for a 'small parties block' of 35 percent (Finland, Italy, Norway and the Netherlands); and *transitionary systems* that shifted from large party systems in 1947–66 to an intermediate or a small party system in 1967–87 or vice versa (Belgium, France and Switzerland).

As a further step, Mair relates the electoral success of small parties to the aforementioned different 'party families'. In doing so, he has found that the small party block is dominated by socialist, liberal and Christian parties. The Greens scored fairly low but this is simply due to the fact that they have not contested three elections yet (first criterion in the overall definition).

The numerical and party family approach offers several means for interpretation. First, it allows us to identify voter alignments and trends in terms of an increase or decrease of small parties or small party families. This kind of information is, for instance, clearly useful for analysing contemporary and up-coming coalition formation and maintenance. Secondly, the approach offers a framework for testing key assumptions about the impact of institutional and structural factors (for example, the electoral system, electoral participation and electoral volatility) on small parties' growth or decline in a comparative way.

The numerical and party family, as well as Smith's definitional and conceptional, approach focusses on the role of small parties in national party systems. Both approaches explicitly do not deal with the 'internal life' of small parties and their reason for success or failure.

A diachronic approach
This approach suggests that small parties are mortal organizations bounded by a lifespan (Pedersen 1982). The party lifespan can be described by means of four threshold concepts:

(a) the *threshold of declaration*, that is, when a group of people declares it will participate in elections;
(b) the *threshold of authorization*, that is, the legal regulations and requirements that have to be fulfilled by a party in order to participate in elections;
(c) the *threshold of representation*, that is, the electoral system which defines the 'ins' and 'outs' of small parties in the national party system (majority vs proportional system);
(d) the *threshold of relevance*, that is, the impact of small parties, for example, as coalition partners in national government.

In addition to these thresholds, Pedersen suggests that the 'ups' and 'downs' of small parties should be explained by four dimensions of 'lifespan curves':

(a) the modality dimension, in which small parties pass all four thresholds up-bound once or several times in their lifespan (uni-modal or multi-modal curve);
(b) the dispersion dimension, which informs whether small parties remain over decades or only last for one or two election periods;
(c) the flatness dimension, in which small parties have either an extended or a short lifespan;
(d) the skewness dimension, which describes the degree of symmetry of the lifespan curve. In a positively skewed lifespan

curve, small parties suddenly appear and gradually disappear. In a negatively skewed lifespan curve, small parties gradually appear and suddenly disappear. Some small parties have clear symmetrical lifespans.

Pedersen's 'diachronic approach' on party lifespan is a heuristic concept. It offers a framework for analysing the political and institutional conditions that lead to the 'survival' or the 'death' of small parties. It implicitly rejects the numerical approach and it also does not consider the party system as an independent factor for explaining the success of small parties, as indicated in the conceptional definitional approach. Rather, Pedersen's approach focusses on the dynamics of small parties' organization and their historical development. Thus, the diachronic approach clearly supplements the approaches of Smith and Mair.

A systemic approach

This approach, presented and developed by Pridham (in this volume), has broadly been utilized in other research in formulating new approaches to coalition behaviour in Western Europe (Pridham 1986) and in another collective project focussing on the role and importance of political parties in democratic consolidation (Pridham 1990). Its chief value is that it is thematically comprehensive; as such, it inevitably overlaps to some extent with some of the other approaches already presented, while at the same time offering new angles on the problem of small parties and including further concerns relating to the wider environment in which they operate. Thus, this approach is similar to Smith's conceptional definitional approach in agreeing that the significance of small parties must be assessed systematically, but its scope is broader in going beyond the structure of party systems to look at the context of political and social systems as a whole. Furthermore, though more specifically, there is some correspondence with Pedersen's approach of party life-cycles, especially concerning the relationship with the state and, more implicitly, with society.

These relationships, together with that between different parties in the same system, provide the basis of this systemic approach. Essentially, it follows the argument that the study of small parties needs, at least ultimately, to take into consideration such broader determinants for judging their strategies, possibilities for action and of course also the constraints which clearly must impinge on their performance.

Furthermore, by identifying a variety of key questions and themes under each relationship, the systemic approach allows for differentiation between the roles of small parties at different levels of the system, while acknowledging that there are obvious linkages between the three relationships. For instance, certain small parties might perform more effectively – indeed, enjoy greater opportunities – as institutional actors rather than as social forces (for example, Italy), or vice versa (such as the Greens in several countries). Finally, this approach must answer the basic difficulty that, given national cases, defining small parties proves to some extent illogical, as notably the example of Belgium shows (Deschouwer, in this volume).

Applying the approaches: towards a viable comparative framework
In the light of those four approaches, the country specialists in this book were asked to discuss more deeply the role and the function of small parties in Western Europe, drawing systematically upon the four approaches. The book begins with two comparative chapters dealing with problems of definition, classification and the electoral strength of small parties. It continues with six country studies in which the four approaches are applied as one framework. Hence, the national case studies start with identifying small parties, classifying them in 'party families' and relating them to the type of party system in which they operate. In a second step, the national studies focus on the life-cycle of small parties' development. In a last section, the country chapters examine the role and performance of small parties with reference to three relationships:

(a) with the state (for example, pro- or anti-system; role in government and/or opposition; electoral system; state finance for parties; representation in parliament; state resources and patronage/clientelism);
(b) with other parties (for example, political space and competition/polarization; relationship with large parties; party strategies and alliances/coalitional relationships);
(c) with society (for example, electoral strength; social bases and cleavages; organizational character and structure; links with interest groups, movements and the media).

It should be pointed out that some flexibility was allowed for national variation. For example, national case studies may place rather more emphasis on a certain approach over another. However, in some cases the various approaches were regarded as not incompatible and indeed as complementary.

For the purpose of this book, it was most important to develop a comparative framework which should be able to explain both the failure and the success of small parties in Western Europe. We have, therefore, chosen political systems in which small parties have been most successful and systems where small parties have had relatively less impact. In addition, we have considered four characteristics of political systems which seemed to be related to the failure and the success of small parties. One relevant factor is the size of a country. Our sample includes larger countries (Great Britain and Italy) as well as small countries (Belgium, the Netherlands, Denmark and Greece). A second important variable is the type of electoral system. Apart from Great Britain, all other countries under consideration have a proportional representation system which is most favourable to small parties. Thirdly, we included countries with high and low volatility in party systems. A high volatility is found in Denmark, Italy and Greece, whereas Belgium, Great Britain and the Netherlands are marked by a low volatility in the party system. Fourthly, we considered 'pluralism' in a society as a relevant variable. In our sample, we included non-plural societies (Denmark and Great Britain), semi-plural societies (Italy and Greece) and plural societies (Belgium and the Netherlands).

Concluding remarks

Bearing in mind the problems expressed about comparative studies of small parties (or the way small parties have been studied under comparative perspective), as noted above, it is most important to state that some of the difficulties are significantly reduced by applying the four approaches as one framework for analysis. This comparative framework clearly offers the advantage of greater scope for analysing small parties in different party systems, because it allows for flexibility in its application to country case studies. Thus, the framework is viable for studying small parties in all liberal democratic political systems.

The national case studies which follow in this book generally illustrate the fact that useful generalizations could be derived from our comparative framework. There are, for instance, similarities regarding the role and the function of small parties in Western Europe. In most countries, small parties mobilize those voters whose grievances have been ignored by the larger parties. Small parties give assurance to their voters that they are doing something on a local, regional or national parliamentary level about their causes of discontent. By making themselves the spokesmen of these voters, small parties affect political issues and the tone of political life.

Several small parties in Western Europe have brought controversial matters before the public. If the issues proved popular, they have often been adopted by one or more of the larger parties. As such, small parties have sometimes had an impact on national policy-making without necessarily being in government. In some countries, they also promote the process of change of party loyalties and prepare the way for increasing volatility. More generally, it is shown in this book that small parties clearly have a significant political and social function. They are likely to continue persisting and they play an important role in the dynamics of European political systems. They do not, however, tend to 'remould' the basic structure of the national party systems.

Appendix 1.1 Small parties by party family

Party family[1]	Nation	Party name	References
Communists	Austria	Kommunistische Partei Österreichs (KPÖ)	Steiner 1968; Fürnberg 1977; Gärtner 1978; 1979; Pelinka 1982; Spira 1984; Lichtblau and Winter 1986; Reinthaler 1985; Keller 1982
	Belgium	Parti Communist de Belgique (PCB/KPB)	Turf 1978
	Denmark	Danmarks Kommunistiki Parti (DKP)	Holmgaard 1966; Emanuel 1974; Kragh 1976; Rhode 1973
	Federal Republic Germany	Deutsche Kommunistische Partei (DKP)	Ebbinghausen and Kirchhoff 1973; Walter 1973; Heimann 1983
	Finland	Soumen Kansan Demokraattinen Liitto/ Soumen Kommunistinen Puolue (SKP/SKDL)	Hodgson 1967; 1979; Wagner 1971; Iivonen 1986; Matti 1966; Beyer 1984
	Ireland	Communist Party of Ireland (CPI)	Milotte 1984
	Netherlands	Communistische Partij Nederland (CPN)	Fennema 1988; Jonge 1972
	Norway	Norges Kommunistiske Parti (NKP)	Johansen 1966; Selle 1983; Gilberg 1973

Comparative perspective: the state of the art 15

Party family[1]	Nation	Party name	References
	Spain	Partido Communista de España (PCE)	Haubrich 1978; Hermet 1974; 1977
	Sweden	Vänsterpartiet Kömmunisterna (VDK)	Sparring 1973; Olsson 1986; Hermansson 1984; Hirdman 1974; Tarschys 1974
	Switzerland	Partei der Arbeit (PdA/PST)	Stettler 1980
	United Kingdom	Communist Party of Great Britain (CPGB)	Mair 1979; Hermann 1976; Pelling 1975; Kendall 1974
Small socialists	Denmark	Venstre Socialister (VS)	Schmiederer 1969; Lund 1982
	Finland	Työväen ja Pienviljelijäin Sosialdemokraattinen Liitto (TPSL)	
	France	Parti Socialiste Unifié (PSU)	Hauss 1978; Rocard 1969; Kergoat 1982; Criddle 1971; De Preux 1974; Fisera and Jenkins 1982; Nania 1966
	Ireland	Labour Party (LP)	Orridge 1977; Farrell 1970; Busteed and Mason 1970; Gallagher 1982
		Workers Party (WP)	Rooney 1984
	Italy	Portido Radicale (PR)	Aghina and Jaccarino 1977; Donolo 1980; Hanning 1981; Lucius and Metzner 1982
		Partido Socialista Italiano di Unità Proletaria (PSIUP)	Potter 1982
	Netherlands	Pasifistische-Socialistische Partij (PSP)	Platvoet 1985; Gerretsen and Linden 1982; Land 1962
	Norway	Socialistik Folkeparti (SF) Socialistisk Venstreparti (SV)	Lorenz 1982; Allden 1980

16 Small parties in Western Europe

Party family[1]	Nation	Party name	References
Liberals	Austria	Freiheitliche Partei Österreichs (FPÖ)	Frischenschlager 1974; 1981; Luther 1988; Perching 1983; Morass and Reischenböck 1988; Piringer 1982; Reiter 1982; Stirnemann 1986
	Denmark	Radikale Venstre (RV)	Rasmussen and Skovmand 1955; Larsen 1980
		Retsforbundet (RFB)	Kolding 1958
		Centrum Demokraterne (CD)	Thomas 1988
	Federal Republic Germany	Freie Demokratische Party (FDP)	Zülich 1973; Juling 1977; Kaack 1979; Dittberner 1987; Broughton and Kirchner 1984; 1986; Kirchner and Broughton 1988; Soe 1985
	Finland	Liberaalinen Kansanpuolue (LKP)	Arter 1988
	Greece	Union of the Democratic Centre (EDHIK)	Veremis 1981
	Italy	Partido Liberale Italiano (PLI)	Pridham 1988; Parisi and Varni 1985; Ullrich 1987
		Partito Repubblicano Italiano (PRI)	
	Netherlands	Demokraten '66 (D'66)	Daalder and Koole 1988; Godschalk 1969–70
	Norway	Venstre (VE)	Veivaag 1977; Naerbøvik and Grepstad 1984
		Det Nye Folkeparti (DNF)	Leiphart and Svasand 1988
	Sweden	Folkpartiet (FP)	Verney 1972; Lindström and Wörlund 1988; Gahrton 1970; 1972
	Switzerland	Liberale Partei der Schweiz (LPS)	Seiler 1988
		Landesring der Unabhängigen (LDU)	Ramseier 1973; Meynaud and Korff 1967

Comparative perspective: the state of the art 17

Party family[1]	Nation	Party name	References
	United Kingdom	Liberal Party (LIB)	Beith 1983; Bogdanor 1983; Cook 1976; Curtice 1988; Cyr 1977; Grimond 1963; Steed 1979; Rasmussen 1965; 1981
Christian	Belgium	Parti Social Chrétien (PSC) – Wallon	Daloze 1966; De Schryver 1946; Hallet 1958; Houben 1963; Irving 1979; Levie 1962; Van den Wijngaert 1976
	Denmark	Kristeligt Folkeparti (KrF)	Andersen 1975
	Finland	Suomen Kristillinen Liitto (SKL)	
	Netherlands	Anti-Revolutionaire Parti (ARP)	Irving 1979; Verbrught 1959–63; de Wilde and Smeenk 1949
		Christelijk-Historische Unie (CHU)	Beernink 1953
		Polititieke Partije Radikalen (PPR)	Jong and Verduyn-Lunel 1983; Jurgens 1971; van Ginneken 1976; Gaay-Fortmann 1983; Idenburg 1971
		Staatkundig Gereformeerde Partij (SGP)	Jongeling 1975
		Gereformeerd Politiek Verbond (GPV)	Jongeling 1975
	Norway	Kristeligt Folkeparti (KRF)	Lomeland 1971
	Sweden	Kristen Demokratisk Samling (KDS)	
	Switzerland	Evangelische Volkspartei	
Extreme right	Denmark	Fremdskridspartiet (FRP)	Wickmann 1977; Andersen 1977; Larsen 1978; Nielsen 1975; Olsen and Pedersen 1976; Thorndahl 1984
	Federal Republic Germany	Nationaldemokratische Partei (NPD)	Kühnl et al. 1969; Warnecke 1976; Nagle 1970; Dittmer 1969

18 Small parties in Western Europe

Party family[1]	Nation	Party name	References
	France	Parti de Forces Nouvelles (PFN)	Johnson 1980
		Front National (FN)	Schain 1987; Miltra 1988
	Greece	National Front (EP)	
	Italy	Movimento Sociale Italiano (MSI) Monarchists (M)	Rosenbaum 1975; Giovana 1972; Caciagli 1988
	Netherlands	Volks-Unie (VU)	Bouw et al. 1981; Bovenkerk et al. 1978
	Norway	Fremskrittspartiet (FRP)	Aarebrot 1988; Svasand 1987
	Spain	Fuerza Nueva (FN) Unión Nacional (UN)	
	Switzerland	Nationale Aktion für Volk und Heimat (NA) Schweizerische Republikanische Bewegung (SRB)	Gilg 1972; Sidjanski and Inglehart 1974
	United Kingdom	National Front (NF)	Walker 1977; Nugent and King 1977; Whiteley 1979; Edgar 1977; Harrop et al. 1980; Husbands 1979; Taylor 1979
Regionalists/ nationalists	Belgium	Volksunie (VU) Rassamblement Wallon (RW) Front Democratique des Francophones Bruxellors (FDF)	Schiltz 1977
	Denmark	Slesvigsk Parti (SP)	
	Finland	Svenska Folkpartiet (SFP)	Colliander 1926
	Ireland	Clann na Poblachta Sinn Fein (SF)	Garvin 1981; Pyne 1970
	Italy	Südtiroler Volkspartei (SVP) Union Valdôtaine (UV)	Weissenberger 1977
	Netherlands	Fryske Nasjonale Patij	Lucardie et al. 1987

Comparative perspective: the state of the art 19

Party family[1]	Nation	Party name	References
	Spain	Partido Nacionalista Vasco (PNV)	Payne 1974
		Enzkadiko Ezquerra (EE)	Letamendia 1977
		Herri Batasuna (HB)	Pérez Calvo 1977
		Convergenca i Unio (CiU)	
	United Kingdom	Scottish National Party (SNP)	Bochel and Denver 1972; Maclean 1970; Drucker 1979; Mansbach 1973; Mullin 1979; Sturm 1981
		Plaid Cymru (PC)	Balsom 1979; Steyer 1981
Agrarian/ rural	Denmark	Venstre (V)	Aagaard 1949; Monrad 1970; Bjorn 1977
	Finland	Keskustapuolue (KESK)	Sänkiaho 1971; Matheson and Sänkiaho 1975; Arter 1979
	Netherlands	Boerenpartij (BP)	Noöij 1969; Stam 1966
	Norway	Senterpartiet (SP)	Gabrielsen 1970; Greenhill 1962; Aasland 1977
	Sweden	Centerpartiet (CP)	Jonasson 1977; Larsson 1980
	Switzerland	Schweizerische Volkspartei (SVP)	Junker and Maurer 1968; Riesen 1972; Junker 1977
Greens	Austria	Vereinigte Grüne (VG) Alternative Liste (AL)	Haerpfer 1989; Christian 1982; Christian and Ulram 1988; Merli and Handstanger 1984; Nick 1986; Plasser and Sommer 1985; Dachs 1988; Gronner 1984; Gronner and Kitzmüller 1988
	Belgium	Ecologists (Ecolo) AGALEV	Deschouwer 1989 Stouthysen 1983
	Denmark	De Grønne	Andersen 1988; Schüttemeyer 1989

20 *Small parties in Western Europe*

Party family[1]	Nation	Party name	References
	Federal Republic Germany	Die Grünen	Kolinsky 1989; Langguth 1986; Mewes 1983; Müller-Rommel 1985; 1989; Papadakis 1984; Rothhacker 1984; Schmid 1987; Frankland 1989
	France	Les Verts (V)	Boy 1981; Bridgford 1978; Chafer 1984; Journés 1979; Nullmeier et al. 1983; Prendeville 1989
	Ireland	Green Alliance (GA)	Farrell 1989
	Sweden	Miljöpartiet de Gröna	Vedung 1989
	United Kingdom	Green Party (GP)	Rüdig and Lowe 1986; Byrne 1989

[1] Included are those small parties that gained between 1 and 10 percent of the national vote in postwar Western Europe. Small parties which do not belong to one of the eight 'party families' have not been included in the research survey.

Appendix 1.2 References on small-party families in cross-national research

Party family	References	Nations included
Small communist parties	Sparring 1966	Norway, Sweden, Denmark, Finland
	Upton 1973	Norway, Finland, Sweden, Denmark
	Cornell 1975	Scandinavian countries
	McInnes 1975	All European countries
	Kellmann 1988	All European countries including Turkey and Cyprus
	Waller and Fennema 1988	All European countries
Small socialist parties	Baumgarten 1982	Italy, Norway, Denmark, Portugal, Netherlands, France, Austria, West Germany
	Müller-Rommel 1985a	Netherlands, Denmark
Extreme right parties	Husbands 1981	All European countries
	von Beyme 1988	France, West Germany, Italy, Spain
	Falter and Schumann 1988	West Germany, France, Italy, Spain, United Kingdom, Benelux

Comparative perspective: the state of the art   21

Party family	References	Nations included
Agrarian/rural parties	Gollwitzer 1977 Elder and Gooderham 1978	Scandinavia, Eastern, Southern and Western Europe Norway, Sweden
Greens	Nullmeier et al. 1983 Kitschelt 1989 Müller-Rommel 1989	France, Sweden Belgium, West Germany Finland, Sweden, Denmark, West Germany, Ireland, United Kingdom, France, Belgium, Luxembourg, Italy, Switzerland, Austria

Appendix 1.3 References on several small parties in one country

Nation	References	Small parties included
Austria	Schaller 1988–9	Freiheitliche Partei (FPÖ) Kommunistische Partei (KPÖ) Grüne Parteien (VGÖ/ALÖ)
Denmark	Eysell 1979	Socialistisk Folkeparti (SF) Venstre Socialister (US) Kommunistiske Parti (DKP)
	Lund 1982	Socialistisk Folkeparti (SF) Venstre Socialister (US)
Federal Republic Germany	Rowold 1974	Deutsche Friedensunion (DFU) Deutsche Kommunistische Partei (DKP) Kommunistische Partei Deutschlands (KD) Deutsche Reichspartei (DRP) Nationaldemokratische Partei (NPD) Unabhängige Arbeiterpartei (UAP) Partei der Arbeit (PdA) Deutsche Gemeinschaft (DG) Deutsche Freiheitspartei (DFP) Aktionsgemeinschaft Unabhängiger Deutscher (AUD) Gesamtdeutsche Partei (BHE) Deutsche Union (DU)
	Fisher 1974	Non-extremist small parties (N = 16); extremist small parties of the left (N = 5); extremist small parties of the right (N = 10) (total N = 31 small parties)

Nation	References	Small parties included
	Gibowski 1987	Freie Demokratische Partei (FDP) Grüne
Ireland	Coakley 1983	Communists (CPI) Labour Party (LP) Workers Party (WP) Sinn Fein (SF)
Italy	Pridham 1988	Partito Liberale Italiano (PLI) Partito Repubblicano Italiano (PRI)
Norway	Svasand 1987	Conservative Party Christian Party Progressive Party
Netherlands	Jongeling 1975	Staatskundig Gereformeerde Partij (SGP) Geereformeerd Politiek Verbond (GPV)
United Kingdom	Drucker 1979	Scottish National Party (SNP) Plaid Cymru (PC) Marxist left National Front (NF)
	Fusaro 1979	Scottish National Party (SNP) Plaid Cymru (PC)
	McAllister 1981	Scottish National Party (SNP) Plaid Cymru (PC) Nationalist Party (NP)

2
In Search of Small Parties: Problems of Definition, Classification and Significance

Gordon Smith

The universe of small parties

One attraction in the study of small parties is that there is no shortage of available material. As long as our criteria are sufficiently generous, we can be confident of finding several examples in almost every party system – especially if those are included that get no further than the starting-gate and have no hope of gaining representation. Britain has the most restrictive electoral system in Western Europe, but the most permissive electoral laws: individuals can transform themselves into 'parties', collect a handful of signatures in support of their candidature and contest an election in the safe knowledge that failure only means the loss of a minimal financial deposit.

It is only sensible to exclude the plethora of also-rans from serious consideration. They are interesting mainly for their diversity: hopeful Utopians, hardened zealots, disgruntled rebels from established parties and those seeking simple self-advertisement. Yet one immediate conclusion can be drawn: the reservoir of potential small parties is inexhaustible, and in favourable conditions a party system may experience an 'explosion'. Such an eventuality alone provides a good reason for studying small parties.

Establishing a 'threshold of recognition' is a necessary step if discussion is to be at all manageable, but it should not be thought that analysis is thereby made much easier. There is no uniform 'small' party, and the wealth of descriptive terms – minor, micro, splinter, fringe and 'third' – indicates that the concept of 'smallness' has a variety of connotations as well as levels. A country analyst will naturally use the available terminology with an understanding of its applicability to the party system in question, and there is little risk of misunderstanding or ambiguity. No quibbles need arise about whether a party is small or not or whether a third party belongs in a distinctive category. Unformulated rules, intuition and knowledge of how the system works probably serve better than stringent tests or tight definitions.

Once we move to a comparative dimension, however, such confidence quickly evaporates. Trying to order the universe of small parties and to limit its extent inevitably means giving detailed attention to problems of definition and to finding satisfactory bases for classification. Both are essential if sensible generalizations are to follow – and ultimately they should lead to a better appreciation of the dynamics of the individual party systems. That, at least, is a desirable comparative strategy. Unless some such course is followed, there is the danger of just accumulating a vast amount of interesting data – the political scientist armed with a butterfly net chasing after elusive small-party specimens.

In the following account the question of definition is the central focus. But it soon becomes clear that the implications for the party system as a whole are an equally important consideration, even though there appears to be no entirely satisfactory means of relating small parties to general schemes of system classification. There are clearly limits to taking a purely theoretical approach, however, and the nature of small parties should be assessed by looking at their political relevance for Western European party systems. This procedure involves seeing how they fit into the total party spectrum, the roles they may play in government and opposition and the part they take in promoting change in a party system.

This twofold aim – to examine the conceptual basis and the political relevance of small parties – should help to clarify some questions that can be posed about the status of the small party. What *is* a small party, and is the concept a useful one? How do we judge its significance in the functioning of the party system? How, and how best, can small parties be differentiated from one another? Do present conditions in Western Europe – given the climate of electoral change – mean that an 'era of small parties' is a possible outcome?

Problems of definition

These questions are easier to ask than answer, and it is unfortunate that the matter of definition represents an initial stumbling-block. One solution is to ignore the problem – certain parties are 'indubitably small' – and to move on to isolate particular characteristics that are relevant to the inquiry in hand. A good example is the concept of a party's life-cycle – nascence, growth and decline – since being at some stage 'small' is an integral feature of the whole process (Pedersen 1982). This procedure is quite legitimate, but most classificatory schemes, for instance those on an ideological basis, may find homes for all kinds of small party. But they must fail essentially to distinguish small parties as a distinctive category. There are no obvious limits to the size of regional, extremist or protest parties; in all of these groups small parties are usually well represented.

A second solution is to be quite arbitrary. Peter Mair adopts this method elsewhere in this volume, and it has much to recommend it. The imposition of sharp upper and lower cut-off points has the virtue of simplicity, so that small parties can be located without difficulty once the limits have been set. The way is then open for the use of quantitative methods, and these lend themselves to a variety of direct comparisons, with the result that a number of generalizations can be made, as Mair shows for the Western European case.

Whilst there is little difficulty in fixing a minimum threshold of recognition – the criterion is usually the securing of parliamentary representation – it is another matter to set upper limits. Should we distinguish between small and very small parties? When does a small party become an intermediate one, and at what point do parties become large? Perhaps only a percentage point distinguishes two parties in different categories. Parties can also move from one group to another at successive elections, and whilst averaging a party's performance gives a more rounded impression, the average can itself be misleading if a party is subject to large fluctuations in support.

A quantitative approach of course cuts through the difficult knot of definition, but in so doing the intrinsic qualities of a small party are submerged in order to establish the basis of direct comparison. For example, we can classify systems according to the aggregate share of the vote taken by parties of varying size – small, medium and large – and we can then group countries according, say, to a preponderance or absence of small parties (Merkl 1980). But as useful as this overview is – not least in observing general trends – we are really no further in understanding what a small party is or what its particular characteristics are.

'Smallness' is, in fact, above all a *systemic* quality. In other words, the definition of a small party must not be divorced from considering the situation of one party in respect of all others in a particular party system. Smallness is a *relative* concept and therefore one that is *specific* to a party system. The emphasis on the relative size of parties in a system means that it becomes impossible to fix limits in advance: initially we have to look at the party system as a whole, and the result may be that a party labelled small in one context could have a quite different look in a different party constellation.

An approach through classification

Looking at whole party systems as a way of assessing small parties requires the use of a classification that brings out the relative size of the parties involved. It would be impossible to devise one that could take account of all possible permutations, and in practice any scheme that went beyond the isolation of one or two major features would be too unwieldy. In fact, few existing classifications are helpful in highlighting relative size as a principal variable. Thus, Sartori's massive 'framework' concentrates on the number of parties and the extent of party polarization (Sartori 1976). However, Blondel does focus on the question of relative size, although the rationale is implicit and we have to infer the balance of party strength at each stage (Blondel 1969). The five kinds of competitive party system he identifies lend themselves to an interpretation of the nature of small parties in a variety of contexts: one-party dominant; two-party balanced; two-and-a-half-party; multi-party dominant; multi-party undifferentiated.

At first sight it will appear that there is little indication of the role taken by small parties in this classification. Yet illustration from a number of Western European countries shows the extent to which the size and effect of a small party can vary just by taking the leading feature of the system in any of the five classes. This is a promising line of inquiry, but one difficulty is soon apparent: it is necessary to have some firm guidelines to judge the 'effect' a small party may have within the system – as a matter of record or in relation to its potential. This question is taken up by Sartori in discussing the 'relevance' of parties in a system, and it is useful to examine the criteria he sets out before examining the relative-size classification in detail.

Party significance: the rules for counting
Sartori formulated his 'rules for counting' the number of parties in a system with the aim of removing very minor parties from consideration (Sartori 1976: 121–5). This was a necessary step in order to put his analysis of party polarization on a firm footing (depending as it does on the number of parties); for it was important to exclude totally insignificant parties which had a negligible effect on the system.

Sartori devised two alternative tests to determine the relevance of a party. His first rule for counting – the coalition test – makes a party irrelevant if it 'is not needed or put to use for any feasible coalition majority'. The second test Sartori rather obscurely calls the 'blackmail potential' of a party. A party is relevant if it 'affects the tactics of party competition'. Its blackmail potential will become important if the party can have the effect of altering the direction of party competition, that is, from centripetal to centrifugal or vice versa. To be relevant a party must pass one of the tests, and Sartori sees a party scoring on one count or the other, but not both. Yet it is difficult to see the justification for this restriction: a party can be a feasible coalition partner and still exercise a competitive/blackmail power. This twin effect may relate to different parties, but there seems to be no reason why it should not apply to a single party as a 'double bind' – the promise combined with a threat.

The two tests seem straightforward, but application is less certain. There is the problem of the time span: a purely current judgement may find a party irrelevant, but over a longer term, judging by its record in coalition, the picture could be different. Again, determining whether a party is 'needed' for a coalition majority poses problems beyond that of making a numerical calculation, since there is always the possibility of an 'unholy alliance' being formed, and even though a party does not enter a coalition it may nevertheless come to the aid of the governing parties on occasion.

These qualifications do not lessen the value of the criteria, but they mean that any evaluation of the significance of a party has to be based on an informed judgement, and that applies with even more force to the question of a party being able to influence the behaviour of other parties. What should result is a useful discriminatory tool for assessing small parties within the classificatory scheme to which we can now return.

The one-party-dominant system

Taken in a literal sense, cases of absolute dominance in competitive party systems are a comparative rarity. The leading party is able to rule on its own account for a considerable period. Specifications of dominance can vary. One is the record of achievement at successive elections which gives a party an absolute majority on, say, at least three occasions. An alternative is to take a current position: the leading party is so far in advance of the others that it has not a remote chance of losing its majority from one election to another.

Such forms of dominance are clearly exceptional, but they raise an important point with regard to small parties: How are all the other parties in the system to be treated if one is really dominant? Take the case of two parties, one that regularly obtains 60 percent of the vote and the other just 40 percent. The latter has no coalition potential and apparently no competitive/blackmail potential or record either. It fares no better – in relation to the party system –

than a party a quarter of its size. The hypothetical example may appear to be exaggerated, but it underlines the essential aspect of relative size in defining a 'small' party besides showing how a party's significance has to be assessed.

In looking at examples in Western Europe, a distinction should be made between 'hard' and 'soft' forms of dominance, since this will affect judgements about other parties. 'Hard' dominance relies basically on structural features of society. Thus the situation in Northern Ireland prior to the imposition of direct rule in 1968, with an entrenched majority of Protestant voters giving unswerving support to the Ulster Unionists, exactly reproduced the conditions of the hypothetical 60/40 example. In contrast, 'soft' dominance permits more of a competitive outcome, although structural features may also be present. A contemporary example is present in West Germany, where the Christlich-Soziale Union (CSU) has enjoyed an absolute majority in Bavaria since the early 1960s and has even reached the level of 60 percent of the vote. Its major opponent, the SPD, trails far behind and is now below 30 percent of the total. Even though the era of CSU dominance may gradually be ending – and now appears to be 'soft' – for many years it seemed unlikely that the CSU would lose its overall majority. How, then, should the Bavarian SPD be labelled? Its share of the vote was far larger than that of other small parties in Bavaria, but were its attributes essentially different?

A number of parties have been dominant in the sense of winning majorities at three successive elections, but the majorities over the combined opposition parties are usually small, so that the feasibility of the opposition coming to power at any election has remained high. This 'soft' dominance was true in the case of the SPÖ in Austria throughout the 1970s, when the party was just able to attain an absolute majority of the vote, but subsequently it has had to rely on one of the other parties to maintain itself in government. Of course, in conditions of 'soft' dominance, the relative size of opposition parties is indeed important, and the largest of them has the chance of becoming the major governing party. At this point the scope for differentiating between groups of large and small parties becomes more apparent.

Small parties in a two-party system
Paradoxically, small parties are less relevant in a two-party system than when one party is dominant: the erosion of 'soft' dominance especially can reveal a variety of coalition possibilities, whereas the strict terms of a two-party system make all small parties irrelevant, since they have neither coalition nor blackmail potential. Governing

alternation between the two major parties, each at intervals being able to win a majority on its own account, precludes the need for coalitions.

Pure two-party systems – only two parties represented – are admittedly highly exceptional. Malta provides the sole Western European example, where even with a permissive electoral system (Single Transferable Vote) only the Maltese Labour Party and the National Party are in contention. Yet even in the looser sense of governing alternation between two major parties two-party systems are rare. Britain is the classic case thanks largely to the nature of the electoral system, which has arguably led to a form of 'suppressed multi-partism'. With one little hiccup of minority government, the Labour and Conservative parties have alternated in government since 1945. Despite the fact that neither party can win a majority of the popular vote, parliamentary majorities have been ensured through the operation of the electoral system. Throughout this whole period other parties have won representation without being able to affect the functioning of the system. Does this make them irrelevant as well as being small? The notable exception to majoritarian government in the UK during the postwar period occurred during Labour rule between 1976 and 1979 when, as a result of by-election losses, in 1977 the government was forced to rely on support from the small parties, especially by means of the Lib–Lab Pact, and when that support was withdrawn Labour faced inevitable defeat. Yet does this single case mean that at all other times the small parties did not count?

Sartori restricts his tests of relevance to the parliamentary arena, so that the electoral arena is neglected – for him, the 'tactics of party competition' refer to legislative and coalitional behaviour. But this procedure leads to the omission of the important electoral context, and it is particularly inappropriate when, as in Britain, the parliamentary representation of small parties need not at all reflect their electoral performance. The gross under-representation of the Liberal Party and later of the Liberal–SDP Alliance meant that the parliamentary tactics of the major parties were unaffected, but this was not so with regard to their electoral strategies: the battle for the centre ground of the electorate had the effect of altering the direction of party competition.

Concentration on the parliamentary party system also neglects the regional aspects of a country's politics. In fact, strong regional parties, with concentrated local support, are not penalized at all by a majoritarian electoral system, this being a significant qualification to Duverger's 'law' relating the majority vote to a two-party system. Regionalist pressures came to a peak in the 1970s, so much so that it was plausible to argue that Britain was on the point of acquiring a multi-party system. These pressures have abated (Levy 1988), but – to take just the case of Scotland – the Labour Party regards the Scottish National Party as its chief competitor, not the Conservatives, and this kind of competition draws attention to the need to include the sub-national as well as the national level of a party system, if the relevance of small parties is to be considered in all its aspects.

The problem of 'third parties'
Blondel's category of the 'two-and-a-half-party' system may appear to be a peculiar construction; yet it often occurs in practice – two large parties and a third one, lagging far behind the others, nevertheless having a considerable impact on the working of the party system. Are such third parties to be treated as small parties, or do they belong to a distinctive group of their own?

Just the fact of being 'third' is no particular recommendation, if a party is unable to affect the interplay of the two major parties. Nor is the size of the party necessarily a critical factor: a small third party may be much more influential than a larger one in another party system. The decisive element is the positioning of the third party in relation to the other two, that is, whether it lies between them (in respect of ideology and programme) and is thus an eligible coalition partner for both. This ability to act as a pivot in the party system gives a third party great coalition potential, if neither of the large parties is able to command a majority. Such a party also has competitive potential, since it imposes a centripetal bind on the larger parties: centrifugal behaviour forfeits the chance of forming a coalition. The power of a third party obviously diminishes if it is unable to occupy a central position; on the outer flanks it could become an appendage to one of the larger parties.

Given the specifications for a third party, it follows that there is only room for one of this type. The presence of two 'third' parties of comparable size robs both of power to act as *the* pivot. Although they may have coalition potential, the resulting pattern is likely to be that of a two-bloc system, and in that case they take their place as small parties.

All the characteristics of a bona-fide third party have been present in the West German party system. The Free Democrats (FDP) would, if size were the only consideration, without doubt be considered a small party since for many years they have hovered between 5 and 10 percent of the vote, with the Christian Democrats (CDU) and Social Democrats (SPD) together taking up to 90 percent of the vote. Yet the FDP has been in government longer than either of these two parties, and it is now over twenty years since the FDP was last in opposition. Until the 1960s the FDP favoured the CDU–CSU as partner, but it subsequently changed course and served in coalition with the SPD from 1969 until 1982 when it brought down the SPD-led government and returned to a coalition with the CDU–CSU. In exploiting its pivotal position, the FDP also forces both the CDU–CSU and the SPD to adopt moderate positions – the 'blackmail' effect has been evident.

Developments in the West German party system also show how a third party's status can be eroded. As long as only three parties were represented – with the preference for minimum-winning coalitions and without the CDU–CSU or the SPD being able to gain an absolute majority – the role of the FDP was guaranteed. But with the arrival of a fourth party, the Greens, the situation could change towards a two-bloc system, and the FDP would then revert to a small party (Smith 1987).

Positioning is all important for the emergence of a third party if it is to exploit its coalition potential, and parties that veer to the extremes also run the risk of becoming marginal. In Austria it once appeared that the small Freedom Party (FPÖ) could operate in a way similar to that of the FDP, since after modifying its right-wing and nationalist position it was able to serve in coalition with the Socialist Party after the 1983 election. Subsequently, however, under a new leader the FPÖ switched back to its former position, the coalition broke up, and the FPÖ became isolated: its right-wing stance made it unacceptable for the centre-right People's Party which, after the 1986 election, preferred to form an oversized coalition with the Socialists. The FPÖ is therefore now a small party not a third party.

Multi-party dominance
We here enter the realm of true multi-partism, but the number of variations possible within the multi-party format is considerable and not really containable within a few broad types. However, the multi-party-dominant form – one party particularly strong – is well represented: Italy and some of the Scandinavian countries are good examples. 'Dominance' in the sense used here is less pronounced than is the case of one-party predominance (as used by Sartori), and by the same token the other parties in the system have a greater relevance, since the largest party does not normally enjoy an overall majority and therefore has to rely on the support of one or even several smaller parties.

Two conditions usually apply to such a case. The first is that even though the dominant party falls short of a majority, its lead over the second party is usually substantial. The second condition is that the dominant party is indispensable for the formation of majority coalitions. Neither of these conditions is absolutely rigid – the lead over a second party need not always be substantial, and the dominant party can sometimes be excluded from government. These qualifications are exemplified by the nature of multi-party dominance in Italy and Denmark.

Italy has a flourishing multi-party system, with ten or more parties regularly represented, but the Christian Democrats (DC) have a looming presence: even though the party has only once had an absolute majority, it has been in every one of the nearly fifty governments since 1945. An important restriction on DC dominance is evident, precisely in the short average duration of coalitions. The fragility of the coalitions stems preponderantly from the intransigence of one or other of the junior coalition partners; since governments consist of up to five parties, there is always room for tension. Moreover, because of the need to include several parties in order to form a majority – and particularly the brevity of governments – breaking up a coalition does not necessarily mean that the party responsible will have to take an extended spell in opposition. It follows that a situation of multi-party dominance does not at all signify a weak position for small parties, and – just as Swift's Gulliver found himself pinioned helplessly by the efforts of smaller beings – so the DC for all its superior power finds itself subject to awkward and powerful constraints.

One condition is not met in the Italian case: the DC does not have a substantial lead over the second party, at least not in the more recent history of the Republic. At one time in the early 1980s the Communist Party (PCI) even seemed set to overhaul the DC. All the same, the DC has still to be counted as politically dominant, since the PCI because of its ideology and positioning in the system is effectively non-coalitionable. This exclusion, despite the fact that the PCI now appears an unlikely candidate as an anti-system party, means that in certain respects the party system is effectively truncated – the smaller parties really have no choice but to co-operate with the DC.

In some ways the Danish party system accords better with the idea of multi-party dominance, for the second party trails far behind the Social Democrats (Pedersen 1987a). At the 1979 election, for instance, the Social Democrats recorded 38.3 percent of the vote, with the second largest party having just 12.5 percent. Latterly, with the resurgence of the Conservatives, this gap has narrowed considerably, but since some nine parties are usually represented in the Folketing, the pattern is still recognizable. What distinguishes the Danish from the Italian party system is that, unlike the DC, the

Social Democrats do not have a firm and lasting hold on government, even though the party has often been content to form a minority administration. Instead, the smaller parties have been able to form alternative 'bourgeois' coalitions, thanks in part to the growth of the Conservative vote.

This development draws attention to an essential difference between the Italian DC and the Danish Social Democrats. Whilst the latter belong firmly to the left and therefore represent a polarity in the party system, albeit a moderate one, the DC, although perhaps not to be described as a 'centre' party, has the characteristic of being able to 'straddle' a large part of the system. The Danish pattern encourages the cohesion of several of the smaller parties on the right – five parties making up the coalition formed in 1988 – although it is also a fragile unity. Partly, the precarious nature of small-party government results from disunity among the coalition partners, but it also results from the competitive presence of the non-coalitionable, right-wing Progress Party. Despite the rather paradoxical outcome of small party prominence in a multi-party-dominant system, it is also perhaps a transient stage.

The 'undifferentiated' multi-party system

If no party has a large lead over any of the others and none is really essential for building a coalition majority, the party system will be relatively fluid with numerous kinds of governing alignment feasible. This category of party system is bound to include several different combinations of party size, and in this sense is a residual grouping. Typically, however, three or four may have between 15 and 25 percent of the vote, with as many again around the 5 to 10 percent mark. These specifications are not tight ones, and they apply broadly to countries such as Belgium, Finland, the Netherlands and Switzerland.

As the number of parties increases and differences in relative size diminish, the leverage or relevance of all parties declines, and the most affected are the smallest parties. In Switzerland, the 'irrelevance' of small parties is, so to speak, 'institutionalized': the four largest parties form a permanent governing cartel. The excluded parties have little more than a protest value, whatever their particular orientation, although the sub-national party system at cantonal level gives them a compensating weight.

In most multi-party systems the small parties are not free-floating, but tend to be attached to a group around one of the larger parties. There are thus a few well-recognized clusters which form the basis of alternative governing formations. A 'balanced cluster' – for instance, based on a left–right demarcation, as in Scandinavia – may make a particular small party an essential component for coalition building. But other patterns, especially one with a strong centre-based grouping, will reduce somewhat the importance of a small party. Thus, a centre grouping can be marginally adjusted in one direction or the other to give flexibility in the composition of a coalition.

These formulations inevitably ignore the complications that arise in practice, as becomes evident in looking at particular systems: they all tend to be atypical in one way or another. The Finnish party system fits the requirements of 'undifferentiated multi-partism', but coalition formation after the 1987 election resulted in an odd line-up. In that election, nine parties were successful in winning seats, three 'intermediate' parties shared two-thirds of the vote, and the other six parties were all below 10 percent. The three largest parties correspond to the three clusters of left, centre and right – with the small parties attached to them. For many years centre-left governments have been the norm based on the Centre Party and the Social Democrats, but also relying on smaller parties such as the Swedish People's Party (representing the small minority of Swedish-speakers in Finland) and the Communists. Yet after the 1987 election the era of 'centre domination' suddenly ended to be replaced by a left–right coalition: Conservatives and Social Democrats, together with two small parties, the Swedish People's and the Rural Party. This idiosyncratic coalition – non-adjacent as well as oversized – illustrates the problems of generalizing about multi-party systems. But it is also evident that the small parties are essentially appendages and useful coalition makeweights, and do not have any real power to determine the functioning of the system (Arter 1987).

A second example of the complications provided by a multi-party system is Belgium. The effect of the linguistic conflict has been to create a small-party system *par excellence*: the 1987 election gave eleven parties representation, six Flemish and five Francophone, and all of them below 20 percent. The three traditional parties – Social-Christians, Liberals and Socialists – all split on linguistic lines, but since they still have ideological affinities, the rupturing of the party system is not quite so acute as might at first seem. Essentially, some combination of the three traditional groupings – involving three or four of the six parties – provides the mainstay of coalition government. Nevertheless, the constraints of the linguistic issue do make for complications. First, it is essential to aim for a linguistic balance in the composition of governments. Secondly, economic issues intertwine with the linguistic problems, since the former are reflected within the language communities. Thirdly, the need to make progress in resolving outstanding constitutional problems relating to the linguistic issue means that oversized coalitions have to be sought, not only to broaden the consensus but specifically to secure the necessary two-thirds majorities required for constitutional changes (Dewachter 1987).

From all these points of view the small and specifically linguistic parties can play an important part, making it desirable to attract one or other of the two Flemish parties or the Brussels Francophone one. Although these three, now with a little over 10 percent of the vote between them, pose less of a threat to the traditional parties than previously, any sudden flare-up in tension between the language groups could quickly restore their fortunes. The coalition formed in May 1988 – which took more than five months to assemble – included four of the six 'traditional' groupings together with one of the Flemish parties and, with two-thirds of the total vote, was deliberately oversized. Small parties are now endemic to the Belgian party system, since the language division almost inevitably leads to party division as well. This feature is illustrated by the Greens, who – with a total vote of 7 percent – are split into two parties even though they have no real quarrels and are similar in programme and outlook (Deschouwer 1989).

Finally, we can look at the Dutch multi-party system which, unlike the more recent escalation in the number of parties in Belgium and Denmark, has for long had a large number of parties represented, due in part to the very permissive electoral system, but also because of the splintering effect of the religious cleavage superimposed on the socio-economic one. Despite the fairly large number of parties represented (nine in 1986), the party system in the Netherlands is by no means heavily influenced by the presence of small parties which only play a supporting role to the three largest ones – Christian Democrats, Labour and Liberals; together (1986) they controlled 85 percent of the vote. This supremacy is largely due to the Christian Democratic Appeal (CDA), which was the result of a successful merger of the three main religious parties in the 1970s. It is the size and, above all, the positioning of the CDA which make the party central to coalition formation, since it is able to side with the Liberals or with Labour to produce a governing majority.

The appendage of six small parties, the largest of them with only 6 percent of the vote, has little coalition or competitive relevance. That particularly applies to the tiny religious parties, but at one time the left-inclined radical parties, such as Democrats '66, did raise the possibility of a cohesive radical bloc emerging built around Labour. This potential was not realized, for the CDA sought to thwart such efforts since they represented a threat to the party's powerful straddling position (Daalder and Irwin 1989).

These various cases of undifferentiated multi-party systems support the view that small parties on the whole do not necessarily have a greater influence just because there are a large number of parties. Their impact may be less pronounced than in the 'multi-party-dominant' form. On occasion, they do exercise leverage and a power of veto, but in this connection it is important to examine the nature of the particular small parties in question, since it is a factor that can be more significant than their relative size. This raises the question of how small parties can best be distinguished from one another.

The distribution of small parties

Thus far the emphasis in this account has been on the role of small parties in structurally different types of party system, but a full evaluation of their significance depends on defining what kinds of party they are. That requires a classification relating them directly to the system itself. The general characteristic which unites almost all Western European systems is the concept of the left–right dimension, whatever the particular format of individual systems, so that the most economical classification of small parties will be one that shows their relationship to the left–right axis.

As a broad generalization, three distinct groupings can be determined:

First, the *marginal party*. Marginal small parties are situated at the outer extremes of the mainstream left and right. Even though their relative size may be significant, their coalition potential is limited since normally they can make overtures only to a single large party that has an affinity with them in some respects, and that party will usually not wish to estrange itself from its more moderate neighbours.

Secondly, the *'hinge' party*. Hinge parties are those operating near the centre of the left–right axis, and are thus located between two or even more larger parties. Their coalition potential is naturally greatest if they are acceptable partners on both left and right, and their power is enhanced to the extent that they are free to pursue a strategy of switching between the two.

Thirdly, the *'detached' party*. Detachment in this context refers to a party's displacement from the main left–right axis for a variety of particular reasons. To an extent, detached parties are 'out of competition', since their electoral appeal is usually to a special group; however, their detachment may occasionally be a recommendation for inclusion in coalitions – provided that their special claims are not so exacting as to make them non-coalitionable.

These minimal descriptions of three types of small party can best be amplified and qualified by reference to particular examples. Two good illustrations of right-wing marginal parties are the National Front in France (prior to the 1988 election) and the Danish Progress Party. Both are alike in having a low coalition potential, and both have been effectively treated as pariahs by other parties. Of the two, the Progress Party may prove to be the more durable force, since the party is now perceived to be adopting a more legitimate, if still radical, conservative course. The precarious nature of coalitions in Denmark – with governments often having to rely on shifting 'majorities for the occasion' – means that the Progress Party can effectively be allied with other bourgeois parties, whilst still being kept out of formal coalitions. None of these factors is operative for the French National Front which in a way prefers its marginal status and regards parliamentary politics as only one of its arenas of action, especially following its elimination from the National Assembly in 1988.

Marginality on the left as on the right is determined as much by the attitudes of other parties as by the nature of the party itself – which is probably true for the Italian Communists, although by no stretch of definition a small party. The secular decline into small parties is general for parties on the left of the Social Democrats, but coalition relevance is still a factor: in recent years the communist parties in Finland, France and Sweden have either participated in coalitions or else given legislative support to a minority government.

An important qualification has to be made to the view that hinge parties are in a strong position to make or break coalitions, since the presence of two small parties in the central area of competition lessens the influence of both over the direction of coalition formation. Much the same argument applies as shown earlier for the power of 'third parties' – that there can only be one of them. A proliferation of would-be hinge parties certainly makes governing more difficult, as has happened in Denmark: the style of government has adapted itself to the situation, and governments are prepared to accept support for individual measures rather than hope for a consistent majority.

Few parties are ever completely 'detached' from a party system to the extent that they are not in competition at all with other parties and entirely avoid taking sides on issues outside their orbit of interest. Regional/ethnic-based parties are relatively detached, because they have a predominant single claim involving a degree of autonomy and a well-defined electoral clientele. But other parties may compete with them, for instance by proposing measures of limited decentralization, as in Scotland where the Labour Party competes with the SNP (Scottish National Party). In the case of Belgium, the term 'detachment' is probably anyway a misnomer, since the linguistic dimension has become just as important as the left–right axis. Hence, the idea of detachment could equally be applied to parties that took no account at all of language differences. A distinction should also be made according to the extent of the regional claims. Outright separatism as voiced by the Basque nationalists leads to detachment, but parties such as the South Tyrol People's Party in Italy and the Swedish People's Party in Finland are well integrated in their party systems and have regularly participated in normal coalitions.

An entirely different kind of detachment is associated with the rise of the 'new politics' as a fresh dimension cutting right across the 'old politics' of left and right as characterized by the traditional party line-up. Green, alternative and ecological parties are now widely represented throughout Western Europe, and they all incorporate post-materialist values which underlie the new politics (Müller-Rommel 1989). Others can be added to the list such as the Radicals in Italy and the Feminist Alliance in Iceland. Whilst some – for example, 'pure' ecology parties – do represent a sharp break with the left–right dimension, many appear to gravitate towards a left-radical position, and in so moving they pose a direct challenge to existing left-wing parties both electorally and ideologically. This challenge is best seen in West Germany where the Greens can be regarded as being both a potential ally for the SPD as well as a new competitor.

Towards an era of small parties?

A discussion of the problems of definition and classification of small parties is a necessary stage before moving to consider the future role they may play, and it will have become evident that any generalizations have to take into account the fact that there is no inherent quality of being small, since that is a characteristic determined by looking at other parties in the system. Furthermore, it is also apparent that the positioning of a party – marginal, hinge or detached – will greatly affect the influence that a small party is able to exercise. Variations such as these tend to make blanket statements hazardous.

Yet there are some pointers. What is broadly true of Western Europe is that electorates are increasingly 'on the move', that is to say, voters are losing their strong identification with particular parties and are more inclined to use a discriminating choice. Former social cleavages have vanished or at least lost much of their political salience. This trend led Kirchheimer to argue that the future belonged to large, broadly based parties, and they would dominate at the expense of small, sectional parties (Kirchheimer 1966). Yet the apparent trend did not lead to any appreciable reduction in the number of parties; on the contrary, in several countries there has been a marked increase. Declining attachment to parties has brought a climate of electoral uncertainty: new parties can enter through 'windows of opportunity' that suddenly open in previously closed party systems. Their gains may be only transient, since there is no guarantee that initial attraction will lead to stable support: a high birth rate is balanced by a high death rate.

Yet in the currently more fluid electoral situation small parties, and particularly new ones, have one decided advantage over large, established parties: they are not saddled with the same burden of exercising governmental responsibility. With traditional electoral ties in decline, governing parties are subject to bouts of electoral dissatisfaction, because they are judged much more on performance; and this disenchantment can benefit parties that stand outside the governing arena, rather than just those governing parties that happen to be in opposition. The latter, precisely because they are unable to offer a distinctive alternative once they have jettisoned their old ideologies, have the problem of dealing effectively with the competition from their smaller rivals.

Rose and McAllister, in analysing the contemporary position in Britain, have described it as one of 'centripetal instability' (Rose and McAllister 1986), a description that is more generally applicable throughout Western Europe. The implication of 'centripetal' for smaller parties may be of importance, in the sense that if they embark on a deliberately centrifugal course, attempting to win support by means of polarizing party competition, they may be less successful than if they concentrate on the electoral middle ground and seek to find niches between the established parties, a strategy that favours 'hinge' rather than 'marginal' parties. Secure electoral havens, however, are difficult to defend in the face of the centripetal drive of the larger parties, so that it is the partially 'detached' party which may have the best chance of occupying a permanent place – related, for instance, to the dominant left–right dimension, but not completely caught up by the attentions of the major parties.

These qualifications make it appear unlikely that we can speak of 'an era of small parties' or that the 'undifferentiated' form of multi-party system would ever become the norm for Western Europe. Indeed, to concentrate exclusively on whether or not smaller parties are likely to become more plentiful could be an unproductive exercise. Instead, it is probably better to study the effects small parties can have on other parties and on the nature of the party system as a whole, especially in conditions of increasing electoral volatility.

A leading example concerns those small parties that in one way or another promote 'new politics' issues. They themselves may never achieve a decisive electoral breakthrough, and eventually they may even disappear (Bürklin 1987). Yet in their raising of new issues and mobilizing of public opinion they can have a permanent impact on the outlook of other parties. In so doing, they also modify the content of the predominant left–right lines of party competition.

The important point is that our search for small parties should not be primarily directed at isolating their particular features or assessing their individual life-chances, but rather at using them as a way of adding to our understanding of how party systems function and change. What is evident, as far as Western Europe is concerned, is the remarkable durability of the 'core' of three or four parties that characterize a system over a very long period (Smith 1989). This 'core persistence' is nevertheless modified by the impact of small parties: they create pressures to which the established parties have to respond and adapt.

3
The Electoral Universe of Small Parties in Postwar Western Europe

Peter Mair

Approaching the problem of smallness

Amidst the abundant literature which now portends a crisis of conventional politics in the Western European democracies, a special emphasis has been laid on the imputed challenge to the established and more traditional mass political parties. Traditional politics is itself now seen to be *passé*, and the large mass parties, which represent the clearest organizational embodiment of such politics, are now regarded – whether justly or unjustly – as increasingly inappropriate devices for the channelling of contemporary representation.

The vulnerability of traditional mass parties is seen to result from two distinct processes. In the first place, these parties are seen to be vulnerable in substantive ideological or policy terms, in that they reflect a set of concerns which no longer correspond to the diversity of contemporary interests. Secondly, they are seen to be vulnerable in organizational terms, in that a more educated, articulate and informed citizenry is seen to be no longer content with the passivity and/or anonymity by which participation in such parties is characterized, nor with the essentially oligarchic nature by which the control of such parties is thought to be exercised (Flanagan and Dalton 1984). Variously following both of these lines of argument, much of the contemporary literature consequently refers to the erosion of traditional parties, and suggests the potential for a realignment towards newer and smaller parties which are at once more sensitive to new issues and more amenable to new forms of participation. The emergence of ecology parties in most of the Western European democracies is often cited as the clearest reflection of the basis for such a realignment (Müller-Rommel 1990), but evidence can also be drawn from a wider group of parties ranging from the Radicals in Italy to D'66 in the Netherlands and to the Left Socialists in Denmark and Norway (Poguntke 1989).

At the same time, however, it is clear that each of these lines of argument involves quite different implications. To the extent that the first holds true, for example, then the key motor of change is the degree of *programmatic* dissatisfaction, and, should the traditional parties prove unable to adapt, the resultant realignment may be expected to favour support for *new* parties. To the extent that the second holds true, on the other hand, then the key change derives from *organizational* dissatisfaction, and one possible result might be a realignment which favours support for *small* parties.[1] Indeed, both processes can be conflated only to the extent that new parties tend also to be small parties, and vice versa, a point to which I shall return below.

The importance of distinguishing between new parties and small parties may also be underlined at the simple *definitional* level. Whereas the definition of what constitutes a 'new' party (as opposed to a 'new politics' party) would appear to pose no greater difficulty than that of affixing a date in time, the definition of what constitutes a 'small' party appears to be much more problematic. In this latter case, two principal options are available. First, one can define 'smallness' in terms of *relevance*, whether using the criteria devised by Sartori (1976: 121–5), or alternative criteria which may also be based on the systemic role of the party in question as Gordon Smith shows in this volume. Here, however, it is self-evident that one perhaps inevitably ends up by talking about relevant or irrelevant parties rather than about large or small parties *per se*. The second alternative is therefore more obvious, in that 'smallness' can be defined with respect to *size* – whether in terms of electoral support, parliamentary strength, organizational density or whatever. To be sure, small parties may also be irrelevant parties, and irrelevant parties may also be small parties; in the last analysis, however, as should be obvious, *smallness* as such must be a function of size rather than of role.

The intention of this particular chapter is to survey the electoral universe of small parties in postwar Western Europe. Over the course of the analysis I hope to show the extent to which the electoral fortunes of such parties have changed over time; to identify those countries and periods where such change has been most pronounced; and to identify which small parties in particular have been involved.

It should also be added that this is largely an inductive analysis: I will first specify a definition of what constitutes a small party, and then search for patterns and explanations of change in the aggregate electoral support for such parties. None the less, and almost wholly intuitively, one can hypothesize that the electoral support for small parties in Western Europe will have grown during the postwar years. The recent emergence of small ecology parties, for example, as well as the many analyses which suggest a decline in the traditional cleavages of class and religion and the concomitant crisis faced by those traditional and often large parties which mobilize along these cleavage lines, seems to imply that small parties may have become more important with time. Even then, however, one must be cautious about relating prognoses of change to a classification of parties which is devised in terms of size alone. As noted above, not all small parties are new parties, let alone new politics parties, and many mobilize along very traditional cleavage lines. The example of the Swedish People's Party in Finland is clearly pertinent here. Moreover, not all new parties are small parties, as, for instance, is evident in the electoral success of the new Christian Democratic Association in the Netherlands. Indeed, it is even questionable whether a categorization of parties simply in terms of size is of any theoretical relevance at all; but this is quite another question, and one to which I shall return at a later stage.

Despite these caveats, however, a largely non-critical reading of the contemporary literature would suggest that there has been an increase in the small party vote over time, and this is the overall hypothesis which I shall use to guide this analysis. In the following section I will attempt a classification of parties according to the size of their electoral support, and, on this basis, I will also attempt a classification of party systems according to the distribution of the different types of party. I will then go on to assess trends in the electoral support for small parties over time and offer some explanations for the variation in these patterns. Finally, I will look at how the small party vote breaks down among the different party families, and at the relative performance of the different subgroups of small parties, including 'new' small parties and 'old' small parties.

Classifying by party size

The first difficulty which is encountered in such an exercise is that of determining cut-off points in electoral support below which a party is small, and above which it is large. It is impossible to deny the essential arbitrariness of such an exercise – whatever the cut-off points might be – and it can only be hoped that those which are chosen will appear both reasonable and plausible.

First, not all postwar Western European parties can be considered for inclusion in the analysis. Since many parties contest just one or two elections, and disappear as abruptly as they once emerged, this analysis will be restricted to those which can be identified to be *enduring* parties, minimally defined as those which have contested at least *three* (not necessarily successive) elections during the period which I consider, that is, from 1 January 1947 (thus excluding the immediate and often deviating postwar elections) to 31 December 1987.

Secondly, not all enduring parties can be considered, in that some obtain such a minuscule proportion of votes that they cannot even be defined as small parties, but rather as *ephemeral* or *micro-parties*. Accordingly, I have considered only those parties which normally poll 1 percent or more of the national vote, retaining them in the analysis if they fail to reach this minimum on *no more* than three occasions.

Thirdly, within this latter group, *large* parties are defined – quite restrictively – as those which normally poll 15 percent or more of the national vote. More specifically, a party is defined as a large party if it falls below this 15 percent threshold on no more than three occasions.

Fourthly, and most important, the remaining parties are therefore defined – by exclusion – as *small* parties. These are parties which normally poll 1 percent or more, but which do not normally poll 15 percent or more.

It should also be noted that, for the purposes of this analysis, parties are defined as large or small *for once and for all* on the basis of their performance in all the elections which they have contested during the *overall period* which I consider. In other words, following the criteria outlined above, it is impossible for a small party to become a large party, or vice versa: once a party satisfies the criteria for smallness, for example, it is always treated as a small party, even if, as is sometimes the case, a certain run of elections taken in isolation would have led it to be defined as a large party. The People's Party in Sweden offers a case in point. On the basis of its performance across the period as a whole, the party is categorized as a small party, having fallen below 15 percent on six occasions. Had I taken the period from 1947 to 1973, on the other hand, then it would have been categorized as a large party, since during this period it fell below 15 percent on only two occasions. This approach is problematic, but it is also unavoidable: any attempt at a standardized quantitative definition (an alternative approach, for example, would be to measure a party's *average* vote over a given period rather than the *consistency* of its vote) will inevitably create what some readers may consider to be anomalies. The really important point to underline is that the classification of the parties is very much a function of the period chosen, and the adoption of a shorter or longer period would inevitably result in a modified distribution of the parties among the different classes.[2]

Finally, over the course of this analysis, I deal with the *block* of small parties and the overall small party vote in the individual countries, rather than with individual partics as such. *The small party vote at a given election is therefore the total vote won by all those parties which have been defined as small parties and which happen to have contested that particular election*, rather than being the total vote won by those parties which happen to be small at a particular election. As such, the results, either for a given election or for a given country or period, are not weighted by or controlled for the number of small parties which are actually in competition at that point.

The distribution of party types in Western Europe
On the basis of these criteria, Table 3.1 reports the breakdown of party types by country, indicating the total number of large, small and other parties, as well as their mean percentage vote across all elections in the period (see Appendix 3.1). As can be seen from the table, there is little variation in the number of large parties across the different countries, the values ranging from one (in Denmark and Sweden) to just four (in Belgium and France). In general, just 31 (15.5 percent) of the 200 parties for which data have been gathered may be classified as large parties. It must be emphasized, however, that these numbers refer to the total number of large parties which have contested elections during the period, and that the number contesting any given election may not be so high. In Belgium, for example, the linguistic divisions in the late 1960s and 1970s led to the disappearance of two large parties (the Social Christians and the Socialists) and to the emergence of two new large parties (the Flemish Christians and the Walloon Socialists), resulting in a total of four large parties in the Belgian case, not all of which concurrently contested any given election. In the Netherlands, the emergence of a new large party, the CDA, in 1977 also involved the disappearance of another large party, the Catholic People's Party. In any given Dutch election, however, the number of large parties has never been greater than two.

As is also clear from Table 3.1, however, there is quite a considerable variation in the numbers of small parties, ranging from just two (in Austria and the UK) to as many as eleven (in Denmark and the Netherlands) or twelve (in Belgium), not all of which were always in simultaneous competition. In general, 86 (43 percent) of the parties satisfy the criteria of smallness.

There is also quite a considerable variation in the mean total percentage vote per election won by both larger and smaller parties in the different countries. Across all countries, large parties tend to poll almost two-thirds of the total vote, as against less than one-

Table 3.1 *Numbers of parties and mean total percentage vote by type and by country*

	Large	Small	Other[1]
Austria[2]	2	2	3
% vote[3]	89.3	9.5	1.2
Belgium	4	12	1
% vote	57.5	40.7	1.8
Denmark	1	11	9
% vote	36.4	62.7	0.9
Finland	3	6	7
% vote	63.6	34.4	1.0
France	4	6	6
% vote	71.3	21.0	7.7
Ireland	2	5	7
% vote	77.4	16.4	6.2
Italy	2	8	16
% vote	65.4	31.1	3.5
Netherlands	3	11	6
% vote	57.9	39.5	2.7
Norway	2	6	2
% vote	65.4	33.5	1.2
Sweden	1	5	3
% vote	45.6	53.5	0.8
Switzerland	3	8	5
% vote	69.5	26.7	3.8
United Kingdom	2	2	5
% vote	84.7	12.8	2.5
West Germany	2	4	13
% vote	82.8	11.9	5.3
All countries	31	86	83
% vote	65.4	31.7	2.8

[1] The number of other parties refers to all those micro-, ephemeral or non-enduring parties identified by name in the various data sources, excluding those listed in these sources as 'others'. However, the actual number of such parties is likely to be substantially greater than that indicated here. The percentage of votes in this case includes those listed as 'others' in the various sources.
[2] The number of parties refers to the total number of parties which have ever contested elections between 1947 and 1987.
[3] The percentage of votes refers to the mean percentage of votes for each type of party across all elections.

third for the small parties, and just 2.8 percent for others. In some cases, however, notably Austria, the UK and West Germany, large parties are in an almost wholly dominant position, in each case polling an average of more than 80 percent of the national vote. At the other extreme, in Denmark and Sweden, small parties account for the majority of electoral preferences, while the other countries tend to spread out along intermediate positions.

Classifying party systems
This variation in the percentage of votes won by the different types of parties suggests that the countries themselves can be classified into what might be termed 'large party systems', 'small party systems' and intermediate systems, according to differences in the overall electoral balance. In order to effect a more sensitive classification, however, which will also take account of changes over time, I have divided the postwar period into two separate phases, from 1947 to 1966, and from 1967 to 1987, taking the mean percentage of votes for the different types of parties in each phase in each country as the basis for the analysis. The classification itself derives from a cluster analysis of the two key variables – the large party vote and the small party vote – which acts to group the country phases according to their proximity in squared Euclidean distance.

The results of the classification are reported in Table 3.2. In most cases, both phases in any given country were grouped within the same cluster, thus allowing an overall classification for the country as a whole. Both phases in Austria, Ireland, the UK and West Germany clearly emerge as cases of *large party systems*. Across all four systems, the mean postwar vote for large parties is 83.6 percent, as against just 12.7 percent for small parties. Both phases in Denmark and Sweden emerge as clear cases of *small party systems*. Across both systems, the mean postwar vote for the small parties is 58.1 percent, as against 41.0 percent for the large parties. Finland, Italy, the Netherlands and Norway emerge as *intermediate*

Table 3.2 *A classification of party systems*

Large party systems	Small party systems
Austria	Denmark
Ireland	Sweden
United Kingdom	
West Germany	
Intermediate systems	*Transitionary systems*
Finland	Belgium
Italy	France
Netherlands	Switzerland
Norway	

systems (in each phase), with an overall mean postwar vote 63.1 percent for large parties, and 34.6 percent for small parties. The remaining countries, Belgium, France and Switzerland, may be considered *transitionary systems*, in that the first phase in each of these countries is classified differently from the second phase. In the Belgian case, the linguistic fragmentation of the traditional parties results in a shift from a large party system in 1947–66 to a small party system in 1967–87. In France, on the other hand, the consolidation of a four-party system during the Fifth Republic involves a transition from an intermediate system to a large party system. Finally, in Switzerland, the gradual erosion of the large party vote across the postwar period as a whole results in a shift from a large party system in the first phase to an intermediate position in the second phase.

A note on the new democracies
While the new Western European democracies, Greece, Portugal and Spain, will normally be excluded from this analysis, in that the relative brevity of their periods of competitive party democracy makes it difficult to compare their experience with that of the other Western European systems, the recent elections in these countries can be analysed with a view to their incorporation in this particular classification. Table 3.3 reports a breakdown of the parties in these new democracies according to the same criteria adopted for the analysis as a whole. As can be seen from the table, the three countries evidence quite contrasting patterns, with Greece approximating to the large party systems, Portugal to the intermediate position and Spain, largely due to the presence of a host of regional parties, corresponding to the small party systems.

Table 3.3 *Party types in the new democracies*

	Large	Small	Other
Greece (1974–85)			
Number	2	3	4
% vote	76.5	11.6	12.0
Portugal (1975–87)			
Number	3	2	9
% vote	69.6	8.9	21.5
Spain (1977–86)			
Number	1	6	21
% vote	37.9	48.0	13.9

What is most striking about these data, however, is the relative importance of other parties – whether non-enduring parties, microparties or *ad hoc* alliances which persist for only one or two elections. Across all three systems, these groups account for an average of 15.8 percent of the vote, ranging from 12.0 percent in the case of Greece to a remarkably high 21.5 percent in the case of Portugal. By way of contrast, the mean vote for such parties in the thirteen established democracies is just 2.8 percent (see Table 3.1), with the highest figure being just 7.7 percent in the case of France.

This relatively high support for ephemeral parties or groups raises an interesting point, in that it is perhaps the clearest indication of the essentially *inchoate* character of these nascent party systems. Indeed, at a pinch, it may be plausible to interpret the aggregate vote for such parties, groups or individuals as a rather crude and inverse index of party-system structuration. To the extent that this is a plausible interpretation, then the contrasts between the three cases are revealing. Thus the Greek data show that the vote for 'others' has evidenced a sharp secular decline since 1974 – from 30.9 percent to 14.0 percent to 2.0 percent to 1.0 percent – and this may be indicative of a very effective and rapid structuration of the new party system. In Portugal, on the other hand, the vote for others is immensely erratic, and over the past three elections has moved from just 4.5 percent in 1983 to 20.7 percent in 1985 and to 10.0 percent in 1987. Finally, the vote for others in Spain actually reaches its peak of 21.9 percent in the most recent election in 1986, being just 10.8 percent and 10.1 percent in 1979 and 1982 respectively, which may well indicate that the Spanish system remains essentially unstructured.

Trends over time

The overall hypothesis which guides this analysis suggests that there has been a growth in small parties over time, and a corresponding decline in large parties. This can be tested in two simple ways: first, in terms of the numbers of parties (taking small parties alone, since the variation in the number of large parties is extremely limited); and secondly, in terms of the overall vote won by small parties and that won by large parties.[3]

As an initial test of this imputed trend, Figures 3.1, 3.2 and 3.3 report the mean values for all three measures over time, taking all countries together, as well as the trends in these data. The actual figures refer to three-year periods, in that a simple year-by-year trend would give undue weight to specific elections in those years in which the number of elections is extremely limited. Only one election occurs during 1980 (in West Germany) and during 1984 (in Denmark), for example, and only two elections in 1947, 1952, 1955, 1960 and 1978. The division of the postwar years into three-year periods, on the other hand, results in the number of elections per period ranging from a minimum of nine (in 1962–4) to a maximum of fourteen (in 1971–3 and in 1977–9), thus allowing more meaningful conclusions to be drawn.[4]

The results reported in Figures 3.1 to 3.3 are at once consistent with one another and offer some supportive evidence for the hypothesis. Despite evident erraticism, the number of small parties (Figure 3.1) shows a clear upward trend as we advance through the postwar period, peaking in the late 1970s, and thereafter registering quite a sharp decline. The overall vote for small parties (Figure 3.2) also evidences an upward trend, again despite an evidently erratic pattern, which in this case peaks in the early 1970s. As in the case of the number of small parties, however, the most recent years also evidence a decline. Finally, as can be seen from Figure 3.3, there is also a declining trend in the vote for large parties particularly through to the early 1970s, which, given the relative insignificance of the vote for others, reflects the virtual inverse of the small party vote.

In general, therefore, the hypothesis is confirmed, albeit not too

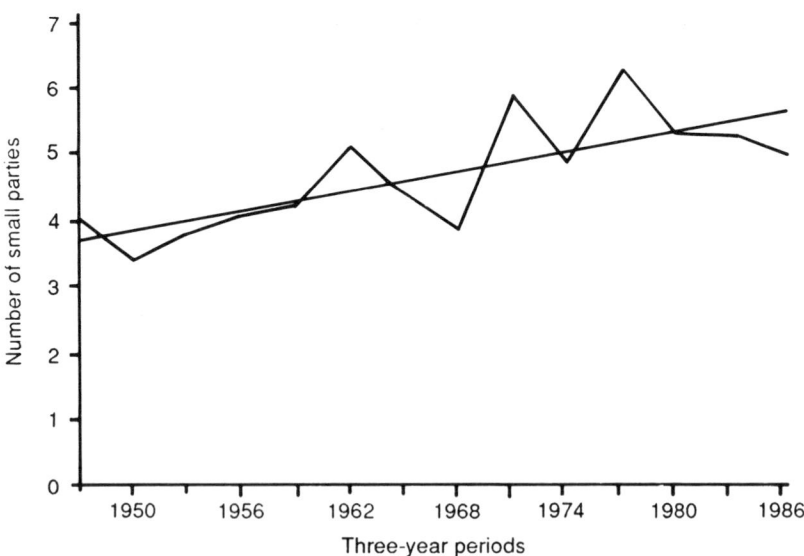

Figure 3.1 *Trend in overall number of small parties, by three-year period*

The electoral universe of small parties 51

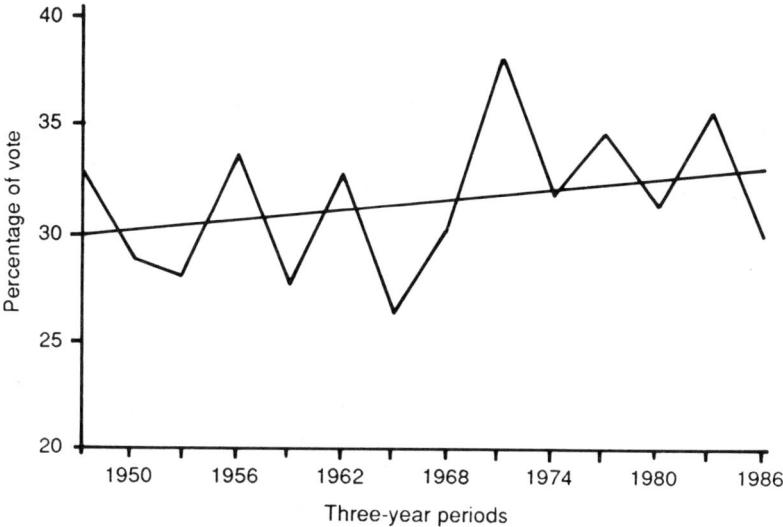

Figure 3.2 *Trend in overall vote for small parties, by three-year period*

emphatically: in both numerical and electoral terms, small parties have tended to become more important as the postwar period has developed. At the same time, however, it is clear that this growth is not so pronounced as some of the more apocalyptic literature on the crisis of party systems might have led us to expect. In the 1950s, for

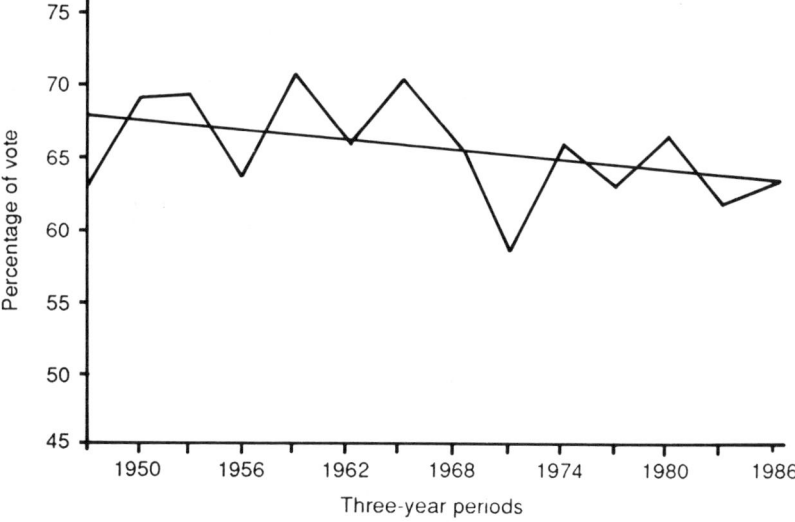

Figure 3.3 *Trend in overall vote for large parties, by three-year period*

example, large parties polled an average of 68.4 percent of the vote, declining to 63.1 percent in the 1970s before rising again to 63.9 percent in the 1980s. The small party vote also shows little evidence of substantial change, rising from 30.3 percent in the 1950s to 34.5 percent in the 1970s, and then falling again to 32.0 percent in the 1980s. In other words, the average vote for the large party block has fallen by less than 5 percent between the 1950s and the 1980s, while that of the small party block has risen by less than 2 percent. The trend is apparent, but it is not overly pronounced, and *in itself* certainly fails to offer any major support for the notion of a crisis of the large mass party.

As against this, however, it can be suggested that one obvious reason for this quite muted trend is simply the diversity of national patterns. Table 3.4 reports the coefficients derived from regressing the large party vote and the small party vote against time in each of the different countries,[5] and clearly identifies two quite opposing trends characterizing two distinct groups of countries. The first group of countries is constituted by Austria, France, Ireland, Italy, the Netherlands, Norway and West Germany, each of which is characterized by an upward trend in the vote for large parties and by a downward trend in the vote for small parties. The former trend is

Table 3.4 *National trends in large and small party vote*

Country	Regression equations (B)[1]		N
	Large party vote	Small party vote	
Austria	$79.25 + 0.149t$	$25.14 - 0.232t$	12
Belgium	$153.89 - 1.409t$	$52.33 + 1.360t$	14
Denmark	$55.35 - 0.281t$	$44.67 + 0.268t$	17
Finland	$96.59 - 0.492t$	$11.66 + 0.339t$	12
France	$-2.47 + 1.086t$	$99.71 - 1.158t$	10
Ireland	$56.18 + 0.311t$	$35.32 - 0.277t$	13
Italy	$64.43 + 0.145t$	$33.54 - 0.036t$	10
Netherlands	$53.10 + 0.071t$	$45.89 - 0.095t$	12
Norway	$60.37 + 0.074t$	$42.58 - 0.136t$	10
Sweden	$50.05 - 0.066t$	$52.01 + 0.023t$	13
Switzerland	$84.41 - 0.223t$	$26.52 + 0.003t$	11
United Kingdom	$130.56 - 0.677t$	$-26.70 + 0.584t$	12
West Germany	$49.76 + 0.484t$	$15.46 - 0.052t$	11
All countries	$76.17 - 0.115t$	$26.17 + 0.082t$	157

[1] The regression equations have been calculated by setting t to the actual election year.

particularly pronounced in France, where it exceeds 1.0, and is also quite substantial in Ireland and West Germany, where it exceeds 0.3. Of the remaining cases in this group, the positive trend exceeds 0.1, except in the cases of the Netherlands and Norway, where it only barely registers. The downward trend in the small party vote is also most pronounced in the French case, and again is quite pronounced in Austria and Ireland. In Italy, the Netherlands and West Germany, on the other hand, it remains very slight. The Dutch case should also be qualified to the extent that the emergence of the CDA in 1977 meant the concomitant disappearance of one large party (the KVP) and two small parties (the ARP and the CHU), and the appearance of a new large party (the CDA itself).

The second group of countries is constituted by those evidencing an upward trend in the small party vote and downward trend in the large party vote. In this instance the most striking case is that of Belgium, where both trends exceed 1.0, followed by the United Kingdom, Finland and Denmark. The trends in the Belgian case are of course exaggerated by the linguistic splits in the late 1960s and 1970s, which led to the disappearance of two large parties (the Social Christians and Socialists) and one small party (the Liberals), and which created four new small parties (the Walloon Christians, the Flemish Socialists and the Flemish and Walloon Liberals) and two new large parties (the Flemish Christians and the Walloon Socialists). In the two remaining cases, Sweden and Switzerland, the upward trend in the small party vote is muted, although there is quite a pronounced downward trend in the large party vote in the Swiss case.

In sum, the most evident cases of large party growth and small party decline are those of France, Ireland and Austria, while the most evident cases of large party decline and small party growth are those of Belgium, the United Kingdom, Finland and Denmark. It is the contrast between these two sets of cases which appears to mute the overall trend in Western Europe as a whole.

Accounting for small party success

The range of possible explanations for shifts in small party support in Western Europe is, of course, quite extensive, and any evidence of realignment could be attributed to new participatory demands, to new issue concerns, and so on. A systematic exploration of such factors is clearly beyond the scope of this brief survey.

An exploration of the *preconditions* of small party growth, on the other hand, would appear to offer a more viable line of inquiry, since such preconditions clearly involve a complex of institutional and structural factors which operate at the systemic level and which, therefore, are more readily measured and compared. To speak of the preconditions of small party growth in this sense is to speak of those factors which operate at the level of the institutional and structural context within which the parties compete, and which determine the sheer opportunity costs imposed by any given national system.[6] Three specific factors can be considered of particular relevance to this cross-national study: the *electoral system*; the level of *electoral participation*; and the level of *electoral volatility*.

Let us first look at the impact of the electoral system, which is the most obvious factor of relevance in any discussion of the preconditions of small party success. It goes almost without saying that, *ceteris paribus*, restrictive electoral systems which impose high thresholds and which offer major bonuses to large parties will be most unlikely to provide incentives for small party support. It can therefore be suggested that more proportional electoral systems will be more likely to favour small parties, and hence we can formally hypothesize that *the small party vote will be greater in more proportional electoral systems*.

In order to test this hypothesis, I have taken the mean values for the small party vote in each of the broad electoral phases (that is, 1947–66 and 1967–87) in each country, and related this to the corresponding mean value of the aggregate index of disproportionality. This latter index simply sums in absolute terms the differences between the parties' shares of the votes and their shares of the seats, dividing the resulting figure by two, and thus represents the simplest and most appropriate measure of the constraints imposed by the electoral system.[7]

Across all twenty-six cases, the relationship is indeed as expected, and confirms the hypothesis, with a correlation coefficient of –0.283. Thus, the greater the disproportionality of the electoral system in any given country phase, the lower will be the small party share of the vote. At the same time, however, and particularly given the crucial role of the electoral system, one might have assumed a stronger degree of association than that which actually emerges. Moreover, if one actually views a plot of the cases, the relationship also seems to be stronger than this correlation coefficient suggests.

This can be seen in Figure 3.4, where all the cases – with the exceptions of France and of the UK in 1967–87, in which the average value of the index of disproportionality is an exceptionally high 17.5 – are plotted according to their mean values on each of the measures. In fact, as is immediately clear from the figure, the low correlation can be seen to result from the quite deviant cases of

Austria and West Germany in the latter electoral phase. Excluding these cases increases the strength of the correlation to −0.423, and if the French and more recent UK cases are also excluded the correlation is further strengthened to −0.572. In sum, and across the large majority of cases, a large proportion of the variance in the electoral support for small parties can be explained by reference to the relative degree of constraint imposed by the electoral system.

The second potential explanation of small party success, and certainly of small party *growth*, concerns levels of electoral participation. To the extent that small parties are also less established parties, which lack the capacity for ongoing electoral mobilization, one can anticipate that their growth may partially be a function of increased electoral participation. Small parties may therefore be more likely to grow as new voters swell the active electorate.[8] This can also be linked to the third possible explanation, concerning the impact of electoral volatility. To the extent that small parties are less established parties, then they are also likely to be favoured by less committed electorates. In other words, a greater propensity for electoral change is also likely to be associated with small party growth.

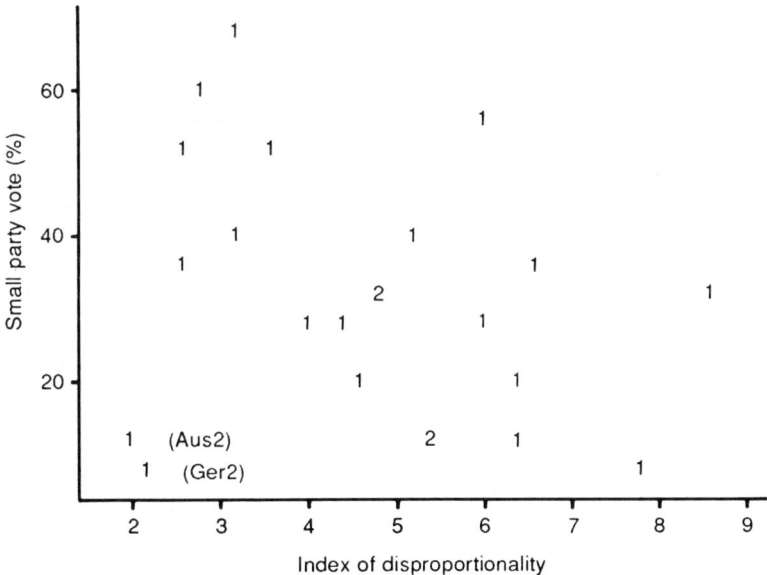

Figure 3.4 *Disproportionality and support for small parties*

The figure plots two values per country, representing the mean values of each index in 1947–66 and 1967–87, and excludes the case of France and that of the UK in 1967–87.

In short, two further hypotheses therefore suggest themselves: first, *the greater the electoral participation, the more likely it is that the small party vote will increase*; and secondly, *increased electoral volatility will result in a growth in support for small parties*. Both of these hypotheses can be tested quite easily. Data on electoral turnout are readily available, and in this case I have chosen to use an index which is based on turnout as a proportion of the adult population rather than of the enfranchised electorate *per se* (see Bartolini and Mair 1990). Data on electoral volatility are also readily available, and in this case I have simply taken the index developed by Pedersen (1983), which measures the aggregate gains of all winning parties (or, which is the same figure, the aggregate losses of all losing parties).

Both hypotheses suggest that a positive relationship can be anticipated between both the level of turnout and the level of volatility, on the one hand, and the small party vote, on the other, and this is confirmed by the correlation coefficients which can be derived by taking the individual elections as the relevant units of analysis: across all elections, the correlation coefficients between the small party vote, on the one hand, and turnout and volatility, on the other, are 0.114 and 0.246 respectively. To be sure, the level of association is not particularly pronounced, but the relationship is in the expected direction.

The explanatory capacity of both independent factors does emerge more clearly, however, when related to the distinction between the two sets of countries identified at the end of the previous section. It will be recalled that two 'extreme' sets of cases were then identified, the one – constituted by France, Ireland and Austria – characterized by a major decline in the small party vote and by a major increase in the large party vote, and the other – constituted by Belgium, the United Kingdom, Finland and Denmark – characterized by small party growth and large party decline.

If we then take this latter group and observe the trend in each of the two independent variables in relation to that of the small party vote, the results are quite striking. This extreme set of cases, which is marked by a substantial upward trend in the small party vote, is also clearly marked by a substantial upward trend in both turnout and volatility. The results are shown in Table 3.5, which reports the trends based on the standardized (Beta) regression coefficients, and the correspondence between the different factors is quite unmistakable.

A similar, if less striking or consistent, correspondence is also evident in the first group of cases, that is, those which are characterized by small party decline. In this instance, as expected,

Table 3.5 *Trends in turnout, volatility and the vote for small parties*

	Small party vote	Trend[1] in: Turnout	Volatility	(N)
Cases of small party growth (Bel, DK, Fin, UK)	0.361	0.348	0.180	(54)
Cases of small party decline (Aus, Fra, Irl)	−0.579	0.172	−0.308	(35)

[1] Beta coefficients.

volatility also registers quite a sharp *downward* trend, although turnout registers an upward trend. It is clear, however, that the upward trend in turnout, which characterizes Western European electoral participation as a whole,[9] is much less pronounced than is the case in those countries where the small party vote has increased substantially. These figures are also reported in Table 3.5.

In sum, while both turnout and volatility prove to be positively associated with the mean small party vote *per se*, they appear even more powerful predictors of the electoral *growth* of small parties. As systems become more volatile, small parties gain at the expense of large parties; as systems become less volatile, on the other hand, small parties lose support at the expense of large parties. Substantially increased turnout also benefits small parties, whereas small parties clearly tend to decline in a more stable participatory environment.

Distinguishing between small parties

Up to now, I have been treating small parties as a more or less uniform block which can be distinguished from large parties, on the one hand, and from micro- and ephemeral parties, on the other. I now wish to differentiate within that block of small parties, in order to assess the relative weights of the different ideological families, as well as those of 'old' and 'new' small parties, and in order to see which of these subgroups of small parties has tended to succeed electorally, and which has tended to decline.

Party families
Let us first turn to the relative weights of the different ideological

families. As can be seen from Table 3.6, the small party block is dominated by socialist, liberal and Christian parties, which together account for almost 48 percent of all small parties in Western Europe. The remaining parties are divided more or less evenly among the other party families, with agrarian and ecology parties constituting the smallest groups. It should be emphasized, however, that the low number of ecology parties is simply a function of the first criterion adopted in defining the overall universe of parties (see above), in that very few of these parties have proved to be enduring, in the sense that – as yet – they have not contested three elections.

Table 3.6 also reports the breakdown of large parties by party family, and the contrasts between the two types are quite marked. Despite the high number of liberal parties in Western Europe, for example, there is no case of a large liberal party, the closest approximations being the Liberals in Denmark and the People's Party in Sweden. The former have averaged 18.2 percent across the period as a whole, which is well in excess of the 15 percent threshold, but they have also fallen below this threshold on six occasions – in 1973, and in the five elections between 1977 and 1987. The People's Party in Sweden has polled an average vote of 15.8 percent, and has also fallen below the 15 percent threshold on six occasions – in 1968, and in the five elections between 1973 and 1985.

In general, the large party block is clearly dominated by socialist, Christian and conservative parties, which together account for more than 87 percent of all large parties. It is also interesting to note that

Table 3.6 *Small and large parties, by party family*

Party family	Small parties[1]		Large parties	
	N	%	N	%
Communist	7	8.1	3	9.7
Socialist	14	16.3	12	38.7
Christian	11	12.8	8	25.8
Liberal	16	18.6	0	0
Extreme right	7	8.1	0	0
Conservative and other right	6	7.0	7	22.6
Agrarian	5	5.8	1	3.2
Nationalist/regionalist	8	9.3	0	0
Ecologist	4	4.7	0	0
Other	8	9.3	0	0
All	86	100.0	31	100.0

[1] For a list of small parties by party family, see Appendix 3.2.

there is only one large agrarian party – the Finnish Centre Party – and that, while numerically weak, communist parties actually constitute a greater proportion of the large party block than of the small party block.

As can be seen from Table 3.7, which charts the electoral fortunes of the small party families by decade, the Communists are also the least successful of the small parties in electoral terms, with their share of the overall vote declining from 2.8 percent in the late 1940s and 1950s to just 0.8 percent in the 1980s, and with their share of the overall small party vote declining from 9.3 percent to 2.6 percent. Nor is this decline simply a function of declining rates of electoral intervention: across all four decades, the number of small communist parties contesting each election has remained remarkably constant. That said, however, it is also clear that the overall left small party vote has remained quite steady, with the decline in communist support being compensated by an increase in the support for small socialist parties, which have risen from just 2.7 percent of the overall vote in the late 1940s and 1950s to 5.8 percent in the 1980s, and from just 9 percent of the small party vote to more than 18 percent in the same period. There has also been a remarkable increase in the frequency of the electoral intervention of these parties between the 1950s and the 1980s. In the earlier decade, such parties contested fewer than one in three elections; by the 1980s, on the other hand, there is an average of at least one such party in each election. This new equilibrium within the left, which clearly mirrors the more familiar process which has occurred among the large parties in the French case, can be seen most evidently in Denmark and Norway, both countries being characterized by a decline in the communist vote, and by an increase in support for the new Socialist People's Party and Left Socialists.

In addition to the Socialists, the other relatively successful groups are the Ecologists, which first emerge in the late 1960s, the nationalist/regionalist parties, which reach their peak in the 1970s, and the extreme right, which also reaches its peak in the 1970s with the mobilization of the Danish and Norwegian progress parties.[10]

By way of contrast, both the Christian and liberal blocks have experienced an electoral erosion over time. This decline is more marked in the case of the Christian parties, whose share of the vote has fallen by roughly a third since the early postwar years. The Liberals, on the other hand, peaked in the 1960s and thereafter declined, despite an enormous increase in the frequency of their electoral intervention in the 1970s. None the less, even in the 1980s they continue to constitute the biggest electoral block among the small parties, accounting for more than 28 percent of the small party

60 Small parties in Western Europe

Table 3.7 *Electoral record of small parties, by party family*

Family	1947–59	1960–9	1970–9	1980–7	1947–87
Communist					
% overall vote (OV)	2.81	1.41	1.70	0.82	1.80
% small party vote (SPV)	9.30	4.66	4.94	2.55	5.68
N parties per election (NPE)	0.59	0.56	0.60	0.53	0.57
Socialist					
% OV	2.72	4.50	3.80	5.84	4.04
% SPV	9.02	14.84	11.04	18.23	12.70
NPE	0.31	0.74	0.84	1.00	0.68
Christian					
% OV	3.27	2.78	3.36	2.12	2.95
% SPV	10.85	9.16	9.75	6.62	9.31
NPE	0.55	0.56	0.76	0.59	0.62
Liberals					
% OV	9.90	10.58	10.46	8.98	10.01
% SPV	32.81	34.93	30.35	28.06	31.56
NPE	1.02	1.00	1.33	0.94	1.08
Extreme right					
% OV	0.80	0.41	2.12	1.39	1.19
% SPV	2.64	1.35	6.15	4.35	3.74
NPE	0.24	0.18	0.29	0.28	0.25
Conservatives and other right					
% OV	6.20	6.15	5.69	5.54	5.92
% SPV	20.56	20.28	16.48	17.31	18.64
NPE	0.41	0.50	0.47	0.35	0.43
Agrarian					
% OV	1.77	2.46	3.30	1.79	2.33
% SPV	5.88	8.13	9.56	5.58	7.35
NPE	0.24	0.32	0.31	0.19	0.27
Nationalist/regionalist					
% OV	1.30	1.34	2.38	1.73	1.68
% SPV	4.30	4.43	6.91	5.39	5.31
NPE	0.24	0.35	0.48	0.50	0.38
Ecologist					
% OV	0	0	0.22	1.15	0.29
% SPV	0	0	0.65	3.58	0.93
NPE	0	0	0.10	0.28	0.08
Others					
% OV	1.27	1.02	1.88	1.91	1.50
% SPV	4.20	3.36	5.45	5.96	4.76
NPE	0.31	0.38	0.48	0.50	0.41

vote, followed by the Socialists (with 18.2 percent) and the Conservatives and other right (with 17.3 percent).

Despite these changes, however, there is no really clear evidence of a general re-equilibrium either between left and right, with the decline of communist support being more than matched by the growth in socialist support, and with the increase in support for the extreme right being matched by a slight decline in support for more mainstream conservative parties.

New parties and old parties
On the face of it, these data would also appear to suggest that there is little evidence of a shift away from traditional politics, in that the decline of the Christian parties, for example, has been accompanied by a growth in both agrarian and nationalist/regionalist parties – at least through to the end of the 1970s. At the same time, however, much of the recent interest in small parties, and in the purported transformation of Western European party systems, derives precisely from the sense that new small parties are becoming electorally more important. How does this intuitive sense of change square with the lack of empirical evidence of any major re-equilibrium between the small party families?

The answer can be found in two ways. First, and most obviously, a number of the very new parties, and a number of ecology parties in particular, have been excluded from this analysis simply because they have yet to contest three elections. To be sure, such parties are likely to be here to stay; as yet, however, they have not satisfied the criterion for endurance which was specified at the beginning of this chapter. Secondly, and with reference to an earlier point, it must be emphasized that we need to distinguish 'new' parties, on the one hand, and 'new politics' parties, on the other, particularly since the former category is not really tapped by the earlier classification of party families. In other words, it may well be the case that 'new' parties are characterized by an 'old' politics.

In order therefore to test the extent to which new small parties may have proved more electorally successful than old small parties, I have divided the small parties themselves into two groups: those which first contested elections before 1950, which include those 'new' postwar parties which were simply reincarnations of previously established prewar parties; and those which first contested elections from 1950 onwards, which may properly be considered 'new' parties. It must be emphasized that this distinction bears no relevance at the ideological level; in this particular context, new parties are simply young parties.

Figure 3.5 charts the electoral fortunes of both groups, based on

62 *Small parties in Western Europe*

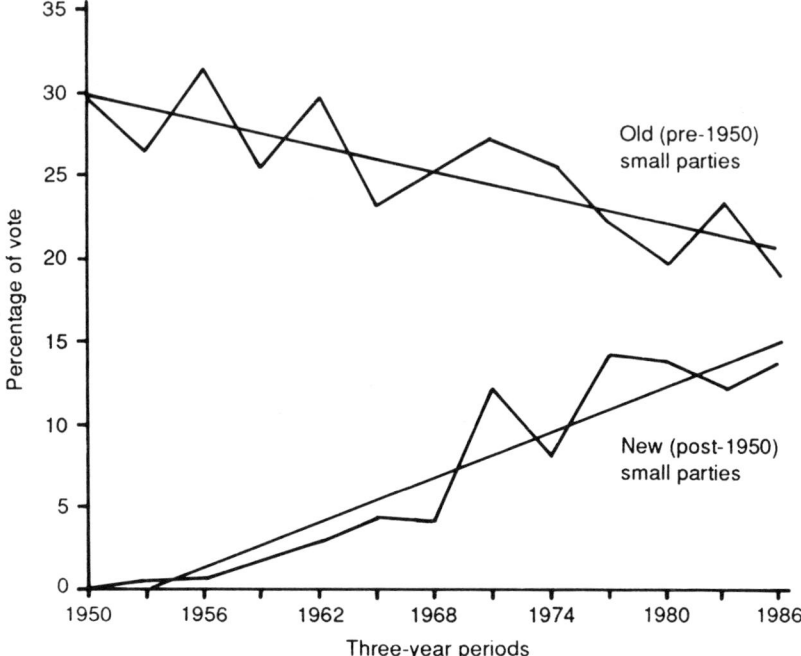

Figure 3.5 *Electoral performance of new small parties and old small parties (excluding France)*

the overall performance across all countries with the exception of France, where party mergers and splits are so commonplace that, in a sense, all parties may be considered new parties. The trends are readily apparent. Those small parties which were formed prior to 1950 evidence a clear secular decline in their overall electoral performance, while those formed since 1950 have registered a clear secular growth.[11] It is in this sense that we can speak of a genuine re-equilibrium: the successful small parties are the young small parties, whatever their ideological hue.

To be sure, the pattern is not uniform across the whole of Western Europe. New parties in Belgium now monopolize the small party vote (the only traditional survivor is the Communist Party), even if these parties are new in name only (see Deschouwer in this volume). In the Danish case, new parties have also proved quite successful, and now (that is, in the 1980s) command some 30 percent of the overall vote, and more than 40 percent of the small party vote (see Pedersen in this volume). New parties have also made a mark in Dutch politics, although they have now declined from a 1970s peak at which they commanded almost 16 percent of the total vote, and almost 35 percent of the small party vote (see Lucardie in this volume). Elsewhere, however, new parties are few in number and/or command just a minor, if often growing, proportion of both the overall vote and the small party vote.

Conclusion

Plus ça change, plus c'est la même chose. In general terms, it can be concluded that the electoral support for small parties has indeed grown in postwar Western Europe, but that it has not grown by any substantial amount. If there is one striking feature, it is that the relatively young small parties are those which are largely responsible for the overall growth in the small party vote, in that support for older small parties has actually declined over time.

That said, it must be emphasized that large parties remain popular with Western European electorates. While examples of substantial small party growth can be cited, as in Belgium, Denmark, Finland and the UK, examples of small party decline can also be cited, as in Austria, France and Ireland. Moreover, we can also conclude that if and when small parties do succeed, they are as likely to represent the right as the left. In short, small parties are like any other parties, and in these terms at least, size does not appear to be significant.

But this, in turn, begs the real question: what insights, if any, can be gained from a classification of parties which is based on size alone? If, for example, we find that there has been evidence of a realignment towards small parties, what does this tell us about the wider processes of political change in general, or of party-system change in particular? One conclusion might be that such a realignment poses potential difficulties in terms of the formation and maintenance of coalitions, in that it is more difficult for clear governing alternatives to emerge in more fragmented systems. As against this, however, it can be argued that any such conclusion requires certain key assumptions concerning the systemic role of such parties, rather than their size *per se*. In the Italian case, for example, a realignment from the large PCI towards the small centre parties would be likely to facilitate the process of government formation rather than making it more difficult.

Alternatively, and as intimated above, it might be argued that a growth in small parties implies a challenge to traditional politics. Again, however, this involves certain key assumptions about the nature and ideological role of small parties, rather than their size as such. As we have seen, the small party category actually embraces a diversity of political families and, in aggregate electoral terms at least, does not offer any evidence of a substantial ideological re-equilibrium.

In sum, while a classification of parties by size may be of some interest, size alone appears to offer a poor basis on which to understand the key differences which distinguish both the parties themselves and the wider systems of which they are part. To adapt Ernest Hemingway's remark about the rich, we may conclude that small parties are not really different; it's just that they win fewer votes.

Notes

I am very grateful to Hans Daalder for his many useful comments on successive drafts of this chapter; given his scepticism about the whole enterprise, however, I will gladly absolve him of any responsibility for its faults. I am also grateful to Stefano Bartolini and Paul Lucardie for their valuable comments. This chapter was completed while I held a Fellowship in the Netherlands Institute for Advanced Study, and I would also like to acknowledge the support offered by the Director and staff of that Institute.

1. For a discussion of the distinction between programmatic and organizational dissatisfaction, see Mair 1983: 405–29. It is also likely, of course, that wholesale organizational dissatisfaction may simply lead to a process of dealignment.

2. The data on which this analysis is based cover all elections (N = 157) held between 1 January 1947 and 31 December 1987. The data have been drawn from Mackie and Rose, 1982, as well as from the annual updates by Mackie and Rose in the *European Journal of Political Research*. Data on the elections of 1987 are drawn from *Keesings Contemporary Archives*. In some cases the Mackie–Rose data have been supplemented by more detailed country-specific sources. These include: for Belgium, Deschouwer 1987; Dewachter 1987; for Denmark, Bille 1989; Pedersen 1987a; for Greece, Papadopoulos in this volume; for Ireland, Mair 1987; for the Netherlands, Daalder 1987.

3. This and all subsequent analyses exclude the new democracies.

4. The very last period, 1986–7, involves just two years and eleven elections.

5. There is little point in regressing the number of small parties against time in the individual countries since, with few exceptions, there is only limited variation. Belgium and Denmark are the only cases in which the number of small parties has increased dramatically over time – from an average of less than three in the 1950s to an average of nine in the 1980s in the case of Belgium, and from an average of less than six in the 1950s to an average of ten in the 1980s in the case of Denmark. In Finland, the Netherlands and Norway, on the other hand, the number of small parties increases through to the late 1960s and early 1970s, and falls thereafter, while the number of small parties in the bulk of the remaining countries remains fairly constant over time.

6. For a discussion of the operation of some of these factors in the Danish case, see Pedersen in this volume.

7. For a recent discussion of the different indices of disproportionality, see Lijphart 1988.

8. The reverse, as Paul Lucardie has pointed out to me, is also of course true: the

The electoral universe of small parties   65

emergence of small parties may encourage the participation of formerly indifferent and non-participant electors.
  9. A Beta coefficient of 0.198 is derived when turnout is regressed against time across all countries.
  10. The French National Front is not included as it has not yet contested three elections.
  11. The pattern remains more or less the same even if we exclude the Belgian case, where the various linguistic splits have resulted in a party system which is almost entirely composed of 'new' parties.

Appendix 3.1   Types of party, by country

Country (period)	Large parties	Small parties	Others
Austria (1948–86)	Socialist Party People's Party	Communist Party Freedom Party	Democratic Progressive Party United Greens Alternative List
Belgium[1] (1949–87)	Social Christians Social Christians (F) Socialists Socialists (W)	Social Christians (W) Socialists (F) Liberals Liberals (F) Liberals (W) Communist Party Volksunie Rassemblement W Francophone DF Ecologists Vlaams Blok Brussels Liberals	RAD/UDRT
Denmark (1947–87)	Social Democrats	Communist Party Left Socialists Socialists People's Radicals Justice Party Liberals Centre Democrats Christian People's Party Conservatives Independents Progress Party	Schleswig Party Pensioners' Party Danish Union Liberal Centre Common Course Greens Humanity Party Communist Workers' Party Socialists Workers' Socialists Workers' Party
Federal Republic Germany (1949–87)	Christian Democrats (CDU/CSU) Social Democrats	Free Democrats German Party German Reich Party Greens	Communist Party Bavarian Party Centre Party Econ. Reconstruction

Country (period)	Large parties	Small parties	Others
			South Schleswig Voters
Refugee Party
All German People Party
Federal Union
German Peace Union
All German Party
NDP
Action for Democratic Progress
Women's Party
Finland (1948–87)	Social Democrats
Centre Party
Finnish PDL	Swedish People's Party
National Coalition
Liberal People's Party
Soc. Dem. League
Christian League
Finnish Rural Party	Small Farmers' Party
Liberal League
Constitutional People's Party
National Unity Party
Greens
DEVA
Pensioners' Party
France (1951–86)	Communist Party
Socialist Party
Gaullists
UDF	Radical Socialists
MRP
Conservatives
Unified Socialist Party
Independent Republicans
Ecologists	Poujadists
Union of Democratic Forces
Reformers' Movement Forces
Reformers' Movement
Democratic Centre
Centre Democracy and Progress
National Front
Greece (1974–85)	New Democracy
PASOK	Extreme Right
KKE
KKES	Neo-Liberals
Centre Union
United Left
Extreme Left
Ireland (1984–7)	Fianna Fail
Fine Gael	Labour
Clann na Poblachta
Clann na Talmhan
Sinn Fein
Workers' Party	National Labour
National Progressive Democrats
Aontacht Eireann
Democratic Socialist Party
Communist Party
Progressive Democrats
Greens

The electoral universe of small parties 67

Country (period)	Large parties	Small parties	Others
Italy (1948–87)	Communist Party Christian Democrats	Socialist Party Social Democrats Liberal Party Republican Party Monarchist MSI/DN Radical Party Proletarian Democracy	United Socialist Party Left Socialist Party Manifesto/Proletarian Unity Action Party Common Man Front Popular Monarchist Sardinian Action Party Sicilian Independence Movement South Tyrol People's Party Community Front Val D'Aosta Union Trieste List Pensioners' Party Venetian League Lombardy League Greens
Netherlands (1948–86)	Socialist Party Catholic People's Party Christian Democratic Appeal	Communist Party Pacifists Radicals D'66 DS'70 Liberal Party Peasants' Party Anti-Revolutionary Party Christian Historical Union Reformed Political League Reformed Political Party	Left-Wing Christians Retailers Centre Party National Catholics Roman Catholic Party Reformed Political Federation
Norway (1949–85)	Conservatives Labour	Liberal Party Centre Party Christian People's Party Communist Party Socialist People's Party Progress Party	Liberal People's Party Commonwealth Party

Country (period)	Large parties	Small parties	Others
Portugal (1975–87)	Social Democrats Communist Party Socialist Party	Centre Democrats Popular Democratic Union	Democratic Movement Popular Monarchist Party Union of Soc. and Dem. Left Movement of Socialist Left Popular Socialist Front Christian Democrats Revolutionary Socialist Party Socialist Unity Party Democratic Renewal Party
Spain (1977–86)	Socialist Party	Communist Party Union of Democratic Centre Popular Alliance (+ allies) Convergence and Unity Basque Nationalists Herri Batsuna	Christian Democrats Andalusian SP/Popular SP Spanish Labour Party Carlist Party National Alliance New Force National Union Falange 2 Catalan Republican Left Basque Left Galician National Popular Block Galician Party Galician Socialist Party Galician Workers' Party Aragonese Regionalist Party Canary People's Union Democratic and Social Centre United Left Communist Party (MUC) Galician Coalition Valencian Union
Sweden (1948–85)	Social Democrats	People's Party Moderate Unity Party Centre Party Communist Party Christian Democrats	Citizens' Coalition Middle Parties Greens

The electoral universe of small parties   69

Country (period)	Large parties	Small parties	Others
Switzerland (1947–87)	Christian Democrats Radical Democrats Social Democrats	Democrats Liberal Conservatives Swiss People's Party Evangelical People's Party Communist Party Independents' Party National Action Progressive Organizations	Free Market Party Republican Movement Autonomous Socialist Party Jura Entente Greens
United Kingdom (1950–87)	Conservative Party Labour Party	Liberals (and SDP) Ulster Unionists	Irish Nationalists Communist Party Scottish National Party Plaid Cymru National Front
N	37	97	117
%	14.7	38.6	46.6

[1] In Belgium, the linguistic splits in the traditional parties are treated as having created new parties which are then listed separately, the letter in brackets indicating whether the party is the Flemish (F) or the Walloon (W) wing.

Appendix 3.2 Small parties by party family (excluding Greece, Portugal and Spain)

Communist

Comm. P. (Aus)
KPB/PCB (Bel)
Comm. P. (DK)
Comm. P. (NL)
Comm. P. (Nor)
Comm. P. (Swe)
Comm. P. (Swz)

Socialist

Flemish Soc. (Bel)
Left Socialists (DK)
Socialist PP (DK)
Soc. Dem. League (Fin)
Radical Soc. (Fra)

Unified Soc. (Fra)
Labour (Irl)
Workers' P. (Irl)
Socialists (Ita)
Soc. Dem. (Ita)
Proletarian D. (Ita)
Pacifists (NL)
DS'70 (NL)
Soc. PP (Nor)

Christian

Walloon Chr. Soc. (Bel)
Christian PP (DK)
Christian L. (Fin)
MRP (Fra)
ARP (NL)

CHU (NL)
Ref. Pol. L. (NL)
Ref. Pol. P. (NL)
Christian PP (Nor)
Christian Dem. (Swe)
Evangelical PP (Swz)

Liberal

Freedom Party (Aus)
Liberals (Bel)
Flemish Libs (Bel)
Walloon Libs (Bel)
Brussels Libs (Bel)
Liberals (DK)
Radicals (DK)
Liberal PP (Fin)

Free Democrats (Ger)
Liberal Party (Ita)
Republican Party (Ita)
Liberal Party (NL)
Liberal Party (Nor)
People's Party (Swe)
Liberal Conservatives (Swz)
Liberal Party (UK)

Extreme right

Progress Party (DK)
German Party (Ger)
German Reich P. (Ger)
Monarchists (Ita)
MSI/DN (Ita)
Progress Party (Nor)
National Action (Swz)

Conservative and other right

Conservatives (DK)

Nat. Coalition (Fin)
Conservatives (Fra)
Ind. Republicans (Fra)
Moderate Unity (Swe)
People's Party (Swz)

Agrarian

Finnish Rural P. (Fin)
Clann na Talmhan (Irl)
Peasants' P. (NL)
Centre P. (Nor)
Centre P. (Swe)

Nationalist/regionalist

Volksunie (Bel)
Rassemblement W. (Bel)
Francophone DF (Bel)
Vlaams Blok (Bel)
Swedish People's P. (Fin)
Clann na Poblachta (Irl)

Sinn Fein (Irl)
U. Unionists (UK)

Ecologists

Ecologists (Bel)
Ecologists (Fra)
Greens (Ger)
Prog. Org. (Swz)

Others

Justice Party (DK)
Centre Democrats (DK)
Independents (DK)
Radical P. (Ita)
D'66 (NL)
Radicals (NL)
Democrats (Swz)
Independents (Swz)

4
Italian Small Parties in Comparative Perspective

Geoffrey Pridham

Three lessons for small party studies

> The study of small parties from the organizational point of view is, at least in Italy, largely neglected, as if the fact of being small automatically meant that they are also less interesting to analyse. In fact, it is not so. Exactly because they are smaller in dimension, these parties are more 'manageable' organizations, more sensitive to what happens outside them and therefore subject to more rapid change. Small parties offer excellent case studies, allowing us to identify within a relatively short temporal horizon both the responses of parties as organizations to certain challenges from the environment and the consequences, more or less unforeseen, that these responses can in their turn generate. Obviously, these processes of innovation and organizational change are also present in the large parties, but they are rather slower and less evident, and demand therefore a greater time to manifest themselves and for their evolution to be analysed. (Lanzalaco, 1985: 67)

This argument for the study of small parties, by an Italian political scientist, makes two initial points. Firstly, it acknowledges that this field has been as much neglected in Italy as elsewhere, despite its being a country frequently seen as a classic example of – among other things – small party politics. In general, small parties there have been researched in some historical work covering the period from the Risorgimento to Fascism, but their postwar development since 1945 has not been systematically studied save for some intermittent attention to their electoral support and discounting a few ephemeral publications on the earlier postwar years. Secondly, it represents one recent attempt to reverse this neglect and reflects a wider than just academic interest, obviously linked to the rising fortunes of some small parties in Italy during the 1980s.

The bibliographical note at the end of this chapter summarizes work done on Italian small parties.[1] In general, the possibilities for research on small parties in Italy exist because they are not as a rule 'closed' parties, that is, those operating in liberal democracies which for ideological or attitudinal reasons are not readily accessible to investigative research. One main hindrance is likely to be the poor organization of these parties, but their *centri studi* (study centres) often collect miscellaneous material, such as libraries or policy documents, and publish historical sources. Finally, it should be noted that the Italian press has regularly covered the small parties' activities in considerable detail.

There is nothing intrinsically wrong with the fact, nor is it really surprising, that new directions in party research should be prompted by recent political developments. In the case of Italy, the new interest in small parties has derived from their greater political visibility (in 1981 Spadolini, the PRI leader, became the first non-DC Prime Minister since 1945); also, more importantly, it has formed part of the ongoing debate about change in the Italian party system. From the late 1970s, the two large parties (the DC and the PCI) were declining, while small parties of different types (traditional, new-style and regionalist) were now on the upswing, but what did this mean? While Panebianco's explanation for the neglect of small party studies – 'in general, considered of little importance, they have been little studied' (Panebianco 1982: 341) – cannot really be true of Italy in view of their coalitional role since the war, they have in this case nevertheless been taken for granted. However, interpretive studies of the small parties should avoid the risks of time-bound assessments; for example, the 1987 national election in fact witnessed a reversal of the fortunes of some small parties. This problem recommends an historical dimension to small party studies – all the more so in the Italian case, where the most important small parties have long histories – and that must be the first lesson in any approach. The second lesson from looking at Italian small parties is classificatory. In particular, it revolves around the relative importance of different criteria for defining and thus selecting small parties in any such study.

The institutional criterion, that is, membership of the national parliament, is not a very strict one, as in Italy there is no required threshold for entry, with a system of proportional representation obviously favourable to small parties. If anything, the Italian case perhaps argues for distinguishing between parties continuously or regularly in the parliament and those which make only a temporary appearance. Moreover, in Italy the small parties with continuous parliamentary representation have included those regularly in government. In short, this particular case strongly favours an emphasis on broader political criteria in a cross-national definition of small parties, as distinct from third parties, on the one hand, and minor or fringe ones, on the other. Here, Sartori's definition is most helpful for Italy (on this definition, see the chapter by Gordon Smith in this volume). In classifying political parties, he preferred *relevance* to *size* on the grounds that 'the cumulative percentage method gives us no clue about whatever relevance any party might have' (Sartori 1976: 300, 304–5). As to their relevance, Sartori elaborated with respect to multi-party systems:

> A party qualifies for relevance whenever its existence, or appearance, affects the tactics of party competition and particularly when it alters the direction of the competition – by determining a switch from centripetal to centrifugal competition either leftward, rightward, or in both directions – of the governing-oriented parties. In summary, we can discount the parties that have neither (i) *coalition potential* nor (ii) *blackmail potential*. Conversely, we must count all the parties that have either a governmental relevance in the coalition-forming arena, or a competitive relevance in the oppositional arena. (Sartori 1976: 123)

Such a classification includes immediately those small centre parties, just mentioned as parties of government, under (i), and also under (ii) those parties not in government but whose presence or role has been significant – notably, the neo-Fascist MSI and the anti-establishment Radical Party, which for very different reasons have been described as 'anti-system'. While the former has been ostracized from coalition politics and the latter has excluded itself, they may both be said to have performed a 'blackmail' role – the one on the right, the other on the left.

Loosely treated political criteria can also complicate cross-national frameworks, since they may only highlight national-specific problems. This leads us to the third lesson: that it is essential to examine each national case of small parties both systemically and comparatively. Research on individual small parties is more likely than that on large parties to resort to descriptive approaches and, moreover, to lose sight of the overall dynamics of small parties' development given their usual strategic dependence on the larger parties. This problem is in fact evident in much work published on small parties in postwar Italy (see the bibliographical note). Adopting the broader approach offers, however, three advantages: it makes possible within-system comparison of different kinds of small parties; it is flexible in its treatment of small parties, considering some under one or other criterion only; and, finally, it makes cross-national analysis of small parties much more viable. Gordon Smith's arguments, presented earlier in this volume, therefore have considerable bearing on the Italian case.

Small parties and Italy's party system: patterns of continuity and change

If small parties are to be assessed systemically, we need to know what kind of party system they operate in, in order to establish: their political scope and whether this is more than peripheral; their legitimacy as actors, both institutionally and societally; and how rooted they are in the system and/or whether they are well placed or not to adapt to and benefit from the kind of change that Western European party systems have faced since the 1960s. Without entering too much into past and recent debate about Italy's party system, we should recall relevant party-system dimensions on the grounds that 'typologies of party system identify either relationships between the constituent parts of the system or properties of the parts of the system' (Lane and Ersson 1987: 157).

Italy's system is clearly multi-party if we count those party actors present in the parliament throughout the postwar period (see Table 4.1); and this is highlighted all the more by the practice of coalitions (apart from minority governments) including from three to five parties as in the *pentapartito* formula in the 1980s. The small centre parties have been significant in both respects. However, far from being a classic multi-party system, Italy's has been characterized by dominant elements when considering the relative strength of different actors. Galli, for instance, viewed this system in the 1960s and subsequently as a case of *bipartitismo imperfetto*, an 'imperfect two-party system', because of the electoral predominance of the DC and PCI as exponents of the Catholic and Marxist subcultures – 'imperfect' because of the lack of a homogeneous majority and of an opposition which could form an alternative government (Galli 1966). One may of course see the chance for small parties in this 'imperfection', all the more as ideologically they not only represent distinct political tendencies but are mainly located in the centre.

This point is emphasized by ideological distance, on which controversy has most focussed in defining Italy's party system. Sartori saw this as a case of 'polarized pluralism'; indeed, it was his archetype for this model, with many 'relevant' actors but also a high degree of ideological stretching (Sartori 1966). In such a case, competition was centrifugal, allowing therefore for scope in the centre for small parties, albeit in Italy conditioned by their dependence on a dominant party (the DC) and at some cost to system stability. However, a dilemma for the small parties arose from the 1976 election outcome, which marked a setback for their support and was followed by DC–PCI parliamentary convergence, a process which also alarmed the PSI. The situation since then, with a reversal of this process, has been theorized by Farneti as a case of 'centripetal pluralism', whereby:

> The social and political centre, as a continuous reference point for any governmental majority, is fed by the heterogeneity, the contradictions and the tensions of the two poles of the system, namely the right and the left. . . . The centre is not, as such, a highly homogeneous and cohesive

Table 4.1 *Political parties in Italy: parliamentary seats – Chamber of Deputies (percentage of vote in parentheses)*

Election	Total seats	Christian Democratic Party (DC)	Communist Party (PCI)	Socialist Party (PSI)	Social Democratic Party (PDSI)	Republican Party (PRI)	Liberal Party (PLI)	Neo-Fascists (MSI)	Radicals (PR)	Greens
1948	574	305 (48.5)	183 (with PSI) (31.0)	75 (12.8)	33 (7.1)	9 (2.5)	19 (3.8)	6 (2.0)		
1953	590	263 (40.1)	143 (22.6)	75 (12.8)	19 (4.5)	5 (1.6)	13 (3.0)	29 (5.8)		
1958	596	273 (42.4)	140 (22.7)	84 (14.2)	22 (4.5)	6 (1.4)	17 (3.5)	24 (4.8)		
1963	639	250 (38.3)	166 (25.3)	87 (13.8)	33 (6.1)	6 (1.4)	39 (7.0)	27 (5.1)		
1968	630	266 (39.1)	177 (26.9)	91 (with PDSI) (14.5)		9 (2.0)	31 (5.8)	24 (4.4)		
1972	630	267 (38.8)	179 (27.2)	61 (9.6)	29 (5.1)	15 (2.9)	20 (3.9)	56 (8.7)		
1976	630	263 (38.7)	227 (34.4)	57 (9.6)	15 (3.4)	14 (3.1)	5 (1.3)	35 (6.1)	4 (1.1)	
1979	629	262 (38.3)	201 (30.4)	62 (9.8)	20 (3.8)	16 (3.0)	9 (1.9)	30 (5.3)	18 (3.5)	
1983	630	225 (32.9)	198 (29.9)	73 (11.4)	23 (4.1)	29 (5.1)	16 (2.9)	42 (6.8)	11 (2.2)	
1987	630	234 (34.3)	177 (26.6)	94 (14.3)	17 (3.0)	21 (3.7)	11 (2.1)	35 (5.9)	13 (2.6)	13 (2.5)

area. It is usually internally divided into centre, left and right. It contains several social strata and above all several strata of collective mentalities, ideologies and forms of *Willensbildung*. . . . In other words, the basic idea of the model of centripetal pluralism is *not* the strength of the centre, but rather the weakness of the right and left poles of the political and ideological alignment which results from their heterogeneity. (Farneti 1985: 182–3)

'Centripetal pluralism' has, for our purposes, been significant as it has been marked by some convergence between the PSI and the small centre parties (the PSDI, PRI and PLI) as well as among the latter, a strategic option known as the 'lay-socialist pole'. In other words, the small parties have for the first time sought collectively to maximize their political scope in their common desire to exploit the DC's loss of dominance.

In doing so, they have overcome some past antagonism – notably, between the PSI and PLI – based in part on historical traditions, given that Italy's traditional small parties have long roots in the system dating back to the nineteenth century. On the other hand, those with shorter histories remind us of the problem of change in a party system and of the opportunities this may or may not present such parties. Whereas the PSDI is really an organizational and also an ideological variation of an old tendency (socialism), the Radical Party (PR) presents a more interesting case as a 'new' old small party. Originally founded in 1956, as a breakaway from the right-wing PLI (from the latter's progressive wing in protest at Malagodi's rightward strategy), it was for a decade ignored until it converted itself into a party of the 'new left'; while, more recently, it developed as the main exponent of environmentalism in Italy until the appearance of the Greens. Otherwise, new small parties have tended to appear on the radical or extreme left for two reasons – either because of a split in an established party (such as in the PSIUP in 1964 in protest at the PSI's centre-left alliance, just as the PSDI had been founded in reaction to the PSI's Popular Front alliance with the PCI in 1947) and/or associated with the vacation of political space by the PCI. Examples of the latter are the Party of Proletarian Unity (PdUP) and Proletarian Democracy (DP), established in 1974 and 1978 respectively. Then, very recently, the Greens have been formed, campaigning nationally for the first time in 1987.

Italy has therefore featured both new and old small parties, although such a distinction cannot always be a strict one. This is not merely because of the familiar difference between parties as organized entities and as political tendencies; it is also because of an amalgam between the old and the new in some cases, as with the

Radicals – 'old' organizationally, 'new' ideologically (for that matter, somewhat 'new' organizationally too in terms of structural style). We have, furthermore, cases of small parties which have remained dormant and found new prominence while not remodelling themselves, an instance being the Sardinian Action Party (PSdA), formed in the 1960s and acquiring greater popularity (in Sardinia) in the mid-1980s. Italian small parties therefore demonstrate different patterns of continuity and change, the (re-)emergence of regionalist parties being one further variation of growing small-party support in recent times. The South Tyrol People's Party (SVP), the Lombard League and the List for Trieste (popularly known as the 'Melon') are additional examples of this last category, although in their local contexts they may not – numerically, at least – be called small parties. In short, Italy therefore contains examples of Smith's broad groupings of 'detached' as well as 'marginal' and especially 'hinge' small parties.

Returning to the basic question of change in party systems, Italy has since the 1960s, especially since the mid-1970s, undergone changes comparable with those elsewhere in Western Europe. It suffices here to quote Pasquino's summary:

> In the 1970s Italian political parties and the party system underwent important and quickening changes. The determinants of these changes have been the alterations in electoral behaviour, both quantitatively in the distribution of votes among the different parties and qualitatively in the type of relationship existing between voters and parties. New relationships have appeared associated with the increasing fluidity of the Italian electorate as well as with a growth in the abstention rate. The emergence of an available pool of voters has influenced the strategies of the various parties and caused a revision of their organization and electoral appeals. (Pasquino 1983: 107)

This trend, which has continued to be true of the 1980s, has been most conspicuous for a decline in major-party support and growth in that for the small parties, also for the PSI, in the centre/centre-left of the spectrum. This has happened despite evidence of some challenge to parties *per se*, although some small parties have also suffered fluctuations of support in the last elections. More specifically, the small parties' growing prospects have been linked to the expansion of the 'opinion vote' as distinct from the two other types of voting behaviour in Italy – 'exchange voting' (based on state patronage) and the *voto di appartenenza* (based on subcultural dictates) – where the large parties enjoyed a monopoly. The success of the PRI in 1983, nearly doubling its vote from 3 percent to 5.1 percent (a significant shift by Italian standards), spotlighted this change. By contrast, in that same election the Radicals, having risen in support in 1979, now lost ground, although having more claim to be 'new' than the 'historical' PRI. Whether paradoxical or not, such recent patterns of change need to be put into context.

Small party persistence in the Italian system: six reasons

While the foregoing systemic context to small party development provides a broad answer to the question of life-cycles, this does need more specific attention, given the relative importance of small parties in Italy. As noted in the first section of this chapter, they have in most cases reached the threshold of relevance; but they have also shown a remarkable capacity for persistence, for the following reasons:

Historical
The Republicans (PRI) and Liberals (PLI) are clear cases of 'historical' parties, the former established in 1894 as Italy's second organized party (following the PSI in 1892), while the latter, albeit the dominant political force from the Risorgimento to Fascism, was not formally organized until 1922. The PSDI, the Social Democrats (in Italian, 'Democratic Socialists'), has an ambiguous identity unlike the other two parties. In Farneti's view, it 'can be considered as belonging to the tradition of Socialism, but to the practice of a centre-right party' (Farneti 1985: 86) in that it has continued to use Marxist-style symbolism while remaining pronouncedly anti-communist. In the formation of the postwar party system, the DC and PCI were the clear 'winners' because they could draw on the two main subcultures of Marxism and Catholicism and in the circumstances of Fascism's collapse, especially the Resistance, were able to crystallize and strengthen their mass base. The Liberals clearly suffered here from some association with the defeated regime, while the Republicans, despite the honourable Resistance record of some of their leaders, were unable to compete with the emerging strength of the two main parties. Of the other parties under consideration, the neo-Fascists (MSI) obviously suffered from their historical inheritance, while the Radicals are a curious case of a party largely abandoning its historical roots for a new identity. They have been successful in this respect because they have tapped new areas of political concern. By and large, however, the small parties have drawn strength from their histories in terms of prestige and profile, especially in the case of the PRI, the PLI and the PSDI.

Ideological
Following directly from this historical argument, the small parties

all represent recognized ideologies (in the MSI's case this is clearly not an advantage). That is, whatever their numerical inferiority to the three main parties (the DC, PCI and PSI), they usually have long-established positions in the ideological spectrum, although this is less true of the Radicals and not applicable to the Greens. The Republicans, while cross-nationally defined as 'liberal' and sometimes typed as 'social liberal' compared with the PLI as 'conservative liberal', all the same have their own tradition dating back to Mazzini and one injected with a policy profile over time (Pridham 1988). As Hanning has noted, the Radicals are difficult to place on the left–right spectrum for reasons already alluded to – the term 'new left' does not fully explain their identity (some have even called them 'poujadist'), just as post-materialism is awkward to classify in conventional left–right terms – but in effect they are most easily placed on the (radical) left (Hanning 1981: 272–3). In Italy, the question of ideology may be pursued further with respect to what Farneti has called 'continuity culture', reflecting on the stability and perhaps the depth of ideological affiliation. While none of these small parties has belonged to the predominant subcultures (the PSDI only somewhat tortuously), other subcultures have been recognized – for example, the liberal, sometimes called 'lay' (*laico*), which among other things is anti-clerical by tradition. According to Tarrow, 'there was always a small but influential "third force" that was never successfully colonized by either Marxism or Catholicism and served as a buffer between Left and Right' (Tarrow 1977: 197–8). The main difference between the two principal subcultures and the third, nevertheless, is that the former have been institutionalized through collateral networks linked to the PCI and the DC, while the lay subculture has by and large not (save for some localized version of this with the Republicans, especially in the region of Emilia-Romagna). Indicative of this looser infrastructure is the idea of the 'two souls' (*due anime*) of Italian liberalism, originating in the left and the right of the Risorgimento movement and represented today by the PRI and the PLI. If the Radicals have 'soul', it is literally in the 1960s sense of the word. Thus, while ideologically distinct, the Italian small parties have not enjoyed the cultural mechanisms for transmitting political values that have characterized the large parties.

Relationship with cleavages
This must be one of the most basic tests of small party persistence. Italy has been noted for several strong cleavages in its postwar politics, but the key point here is that the existence of overlapping cleavages has prevented the party system from crystallizing into two

cohesive blocs to the disadvantage of the small parties (Zariski 1972: 142). Taking Farneti's schema of different cleavages (Farneti 1985: 14–15), the PRI, PLI and PSDI appear on the same side as the DC on the economic, international and social cleavages in opposition to the PCI; while they are on the same side as the PCI on the church/state cleavage and have moved closer to the latter on the institutional cleavage – as more insistent on institutional reform, with the Communists becoming increasingly system-supportive. A variation on this theme of cleavages and parties is the argument in comparative literature about parties being 'structural' and 'non-structural', with the former based on particular cleavages such as ethnic, agrarian and religious, as well as class ones (Lane and Ersson 1987: 97). The most salient cleavage has been class, which explains the base of the two main parties as predominantly parties of the bourgeoisie and the working class – with, however, significant inter-class appeal. Notwithstanding this, the PRI has developed as a party of the 'enlightened bourgeoisie' and the PLI as high bourgeois, leaving the Radicals to become 'neo-bourgeois' (the young and highly educated) (Hanning 1981: 274). The religious cleavage (between strong or practising Catholics and others), while present, has been modified by the DC's ability to attract elements among the 'others', although those with an anti-clerical tradition are firmly included among supporters of the small lay and socialist parties. The agrarian cleavage does not apply, but the ethnic, even ethno-linguistic, cleavage clearly explains the strength of regionalist parties like the SVP (German speakers), the PSdA (Sardinian speakers) and the Union Valdotaine (UV; French speakers in the Val d'Aosta region). The post-materialist or environmentalist cleavage is rather new in Italy, with the Radicals initially benefiting from this, although it remains to be seen whether they succeed in containing the emerging Greens (Verdi) with the growth of environmentalist concerns.

Electoral system
Inevitably, this has helped to shape the party system, in particular in allowing small parties to cross the threshold of parliamentary representation and thus giving them institutional visibility. Italy's pure proportional representation system has clearly facilitated the survival of small parties, and also made possible the emergence of new ones – for instance, the Radicals made an impact in the 1976 parliament with only four deputies and 1.1 percent of the vote. There is a low threshold for parliamentary entry – small parties tending to benefit from the *imperiali* largest-remainder formula for distributing seats (Penniman 1977: 145–6) – although this has not

prevented some parties being only temporary actors on the parliamentary stage (see Table 4.2), the reasons for which have had more to do with their development as parties as such than with electoral failure. Thus, the electoral system is alone hardly sufficient as an explanation for small parties' survival, although it clearly helps those with their own resources for survival. One might also mention here the parliament's flexible rules for forming parliamentary groups, and also the existence of state finance, as further institutional facilities favouring them. Finally, this reason for small-party persistence should not pass without mention of the issue of electoral reform. Various proposals have been presented in recent years, all of them involving departures from, if not the abandonment of, pure PR as a system (Bartolini 1982: 213–16). It is clear that such change would threaten small party representation, and possibly even survival given other weaknesses.

Table 4.2 *Appearance and disappearance of small parties in Italy, 1946–79*

Party	Appears	Remains	Disappears	Reappears
Action Party (PdA)	1946		1948	
Sardinian Action Party (PSdA)	1946	1948	1953	
Dem. Republican Bloc (CDR)	1946		1948	
Socio-Christian Party (PCS)	1946		1948	
Agrarian Party	1946	1948	1953	
Labour Democracy (DL)	1946		1948	
National Dem. Bloc (BDN)	1946		1948	
National Bloc (BNL)	1946	1948	1953	
Muis	1946		1948	
Common Man Front (UQ)	1946		1948	
Popular Mon. Party (PMP)	1948	1953	1963	
PDIUM	1958		1972	
Comunita	1958		1963	
Union Valdotaine	1958	1963	1968	
PSIUP	1964	1968	1972	
PSU (PSI/PSDI)	1968		1972	
MSI–National Right (DN)	1972			
Proletarian Democracy (DP)	1976		1979	
Manifesto–PDUP	1979			
Radical Party (PR)	1958[1]		1963	1976

[1] With Republicans.

Source: Farneti 1985: 56

Participation in coalition government
Small parties with continuous parliamentary representation have enjoyed all the more political visibility because of their often regular role as coalition partners to the DC (see Table 4.3). This is due not only to the numerical requirements of majority building but also to the convention in Italian politics of opting for broad-consensus alliances, including a preference for inviting small parties into government even when not numerically necessary. This is particularly true of those small parties nearest the centre of the spectrum, notably the PRI and PSDI, which have been present in successive alliance formulas to a greater extent than the right-wing PLI. However, the *pentapartito* formula of the 1980s has seen a continuous presence in government of the latter party, following its previous shift towards a more centrist position. This combination of all the small centre parties in one coalition formula is of course a reflection of their enhanced role in Italian politics.

Prestige of individual leaders
The various small parties have at different times gained from the stature of certain leaders: notably, Saragat for the PSDI, Ugo La Malfa and Spadolini for the PRI, Malagodi for the PLI and Pannella for the Radicals. They may all be seen as charismatic leaders, who have in turn held high positions in the state – such as Saragat as Foreign Minister and subsequently President of the Republic (1964–71), and Spadolini as Prime Minister (1981–2). They often dominated their parties for a long time; for example, Malagodi was PLI secretary, 1954–72, and La Malfa was the effective leader of the PRI for two decades, although not formally party secretary all the time. It followed that they determined if not monopolized party strategy and were crucial in attempts to reform their parties (in the case of Malagodi in the 1950s, La Malfa in the late 1960s), so that their parties came to be closely identified with them. Equally, the lack at other times of such leaders of stature has reduced the political visibility and strategic impact of small parties – one thinks of some PLI secretaries since Malagodi and those like Tanassi and Pietro Longo who followed Saragat as PSDI leader. As a whole, the comment of Zanone (PLI secretary, 1976–85) that 'for the small parties, the identification of image with the secretary is almost inevitable, above all because of the effect of television' is only too true. The increased political role of the mass media has played an important part in small party appeal, given too that since the 1960s the Italian press has to some extent favoured the small centre parties, reflecting its general preference for the liberal outlook (Sassoon 1986: 155). At the same time, political visibility is not

automatically or easily transmitted into electoral support. The minimal effect of charisma on Italian parties' electoral strength underlines the fact that, from this viewpoint, the role of small party leaders is at best a secondary consideration. This may of course change somewhat with the continued growth in 'opinion voting', for the 'Spadolini effect' in the 1983 election was a major reason for the PRI's marked rise in votes then. This election took place half a year after Spadolini's premiership, and the PRI strongly exploited his record in office during the campaign. However, at the 1987 election, when Spadolini was less salient, the PRI suffered a reversal in support.

Taken together, these six reasons for the persistence of small parties in Italy help us to answer the first two of the questions listed at the start of the second section. That is, the first three reasons are crucial to these parties' maintenance of their individual political space in a system that has been highly polarized in the postwar period. The fifth and sixth reasons are relevant to the legitimacy of these parties, specifically those of the centre, for the ideological reason also distinguishes them in this respect from the neo-Fascists. The electoral system is really an intermediary reason, both reflecting proportionately their political space and also guaranteeing their role in the state. In short, these reasons explain why parties which have normally won low single-figure percentage support have enjoyed a political presence of some significance.

Italian small parties: three relationships in the Italian system

Relationship with the state

The main concern here is what advantages small parties have derived from their main role in the state and whether these have helped or hindered them in their adaptation to change. An immediate distinction has to be drawn between those which have tended to be in government and those which have remained in opposition.

As to the first category, the composition of governments since the Second World War is detailed in Table 4.3. This shows that all these parties are included in the grand coalitions immediately after the war and also, with some variation, in the centrist governments that followed up to the mid-1950s. After a period of alliance uncertainty, the centre-left formula was adopted in the earlier 1960s, leading to a divergence between the PRI and PSDI (pro-centre-left) and the PLI

84 Small parties in Western Europe

Table 4.3 *Composition of Italian cabinets, 1945–90*

Period of office (number of months)	Prime Minister	Parties in the cabinet
1 6–12/1945 (5)	Parri	Action Party, DC, PCI, PLI, PSI, PDL (Democratic Labour)
2 12/'45–7/'46 (6)	De Gasperi I	DC, PCI, PSI, Action Party, PDL, PLI
3 7/'46–2/'47 (6)	De Gasperi II	DC, PCI, PSI, PLI, PRI
4 2–5/'47 (3)	De Gasperi III	DC, PCI, PSI
5 5/'47–5/'48 (11)	De Gasperi IV	DC, PSDI, PLI, PRI
6 5/'48–1/'50 (20)	De Gasperi V	DC, PSDI, PRI, PLI
7 1/'50–7/'51 (17)	De Gasperi VI	DC, PSDI, PRI
8 7/'51–6/'53 (23)	De Gasperi VII	DC, PRI (abstention of PSDI and PLI)
9 7/'53 (½)	De Gasperi VIII	DC (external support of PRI)
10 8/'53–1/'54 (5)	Pella	DC (external support of PRI, PLI and Monarchists; abstention of PSDI)
11 1/'54 (½)	Fanfani I	DC
12 2/'54–7/'55 (16)	Scelba	DC, PSDI, PLI (external support of PRI)
13 7/'55–5/'57 (22)	Segni I	DC, PSDI, PLI (external support of PRI; abstention of Monarchists)
14 5/'57–7/'58 (13)	Zoli	DC (external support of Monarchists and MSI)
15 7/'58–2/'59 (7)	Fanfani II	DC, PSDI (external support of PRI)
16 2/'59–3/'60 (13)	Segni II	DC (external support of PLI, MSI and Monarchists)
17 3–7/'60 (4)	Tambroni	DC (external support of MSI)
18 7/'60–2/'62 (18)	Fanfani III	DC (external support of PSDI, PRI and PLI)
19 2/'62–6/'63 (16)	Fanfani IV	DC, PSDI, PRI (abstention of PSI)
20 6–12/'63 (5)	Leone I	DC (abstention of PSI, PSDI and PRI)
21 12/'63–7/'64 (7)	Moro I	DC, PSI, PSDI, PRI
22 7/'64–2/'66 (19)	Moro II	DC, PSI, PSDI, PRI
23 2/'66–6/'68 (27)	Moro III	DC, PSI, PSDI, PRI
24 6–12/'68 (5)	Leone II	DC (abstention of PSU and PRI)
25 12/'68–8/'69 (7)	Rumor I	DC, PSI, PRI
26 8/'69–3/'70 (7)	Rumor II	DC (external support of PSI and PSDI; abstention of PRI)
27 3–8/'70 (4)	Rumor III	DC, PSI, PSDI, PRI
28 8/'70–2/'72 (18)	Colombo	DC, PSI, PSDI, PRI
29 2–6/'72 (4)	Andreotti I	DC (external support of PRI, PSDI and PLI)
30 6/'72–7/'73 (12)	Andreotti II	DC, PSDI, PLI (external support of PRI)
31 7/'73–3/'74 (8)	Rumor IV	DC, PSI, PSDI, PRI
32 3–11/'74 (8)	Rumor V	DC, PSI, PSDI (external support of PRI)
33 11/'74–2/'76 (15)	Moro IV	DC, PRI (external support of PSI and PSDI; abstention of PLI)
34 2–7/'76 (5)	Moro V	DC (external support of PSDI; abstention of PSI, PRI and PLI)

Period of office (number of months)	Prime Minister	Parties in the cabinet
35 7/'76–3/'78 (19)	Andreotti III	DC (abstention of PCI, PSI, PSDI, PRI and PLI – they moved to external support 1977)
36 3/'78–3/'79 (12)	Andreotti IV	DC (external support of PCI, PSI, PSDI and PRI)
37 3–8/'79 (4)	Andreotti V	DC, PSDI, PRI
38 8/'79–4/'80 (8)	Cossiga I	DC, PSDI, PLI (abstention of PSI and PRI)
39 4–10/'80 (6)	Cossiga II	DC, PSI, PRI
40 10/'80–6/'81 (8)	Forlani	DC, PSI, PSDI, PRI
41 6/'81–8/'82 (13)	Spadolini I	PRI, DC, PSI, PSDI, PLI
42 8–12/'82 (3)	Spadolini II	PRI, DC, PSI, PSDI, PLI
43 12/'82–8/'83 (8)	Fanfani V	DC, PSI, PSDI, PLI (abstention of PRI)
44 8/'83–8/'86 (36)	Craxi I	PSI, DC, PRI, PSDI, PLI
45 8/'86–3/'87 (7)	Craxi II	PSI, DC, PRI, PSDI, PLI
46 3/'87–7/'87 (4)	Fanfani VI	DC, PSI, PRI, PSDI, PLI
47 7/'87–4/'88 (9)	Goria	DC, PSI, PRI, PSDI, PLI
48 4/'88–8/'89 (15)	De Mita	DC, PSI, PRI, PSDI, PLI
49 8/'89–	Andreotti VI	DC, PSI, PRI, PSDI, PLI

The party of the Prime Minister is given first among the list of cabinet participants. The tenure of each government lasts until the inauguration of the subsequent one.

Source: Pridham 1988: 52–3

which opposed this formula and stayed in opposition. The subsequent 'national solidarity' formula, involving co-operation with the PCI from the mid-1970s, included all these parties at first, but the PLI withdrew when this co-operation became closer as a legislative coalition. The most recent alliance, the five-party formula or *pentapartito*, has included all these parties (PRI, PLI and PSDI) in government from the early 1980s with some slight variation.

Comparing the three parties, the PRI has been the most regular party of government and the PLI the least regular (their totals for the first 40 postwar years were 256 months, or more than 21 years, in the case of the PRI and 158 months, or more than 13 years, in the case of the PLI). This excludes periods of external or parliamentary support by these parties for individual governments. Without entering into particulars on local and regional coalitions, it can be said that these parties have also played a regular part here, though much more so in the case of the PRI and PSDI than the PLI, again underlining the former parties' advantage in being closer to the centre (Pridham 1988: 47–8). This is partly because sub-national coalitions have often conformed to national-level formulas, although by no means rigidly. In fact, the mid-1970s saw an important departure with the formation of many more coalitions in cities of the broad left, where the PRI and PSDI were willing to join with the PCI but not with the PLI.

This role in government has not always meant that, on grounds of numerical inferiority, these parties have necessarily held only minor positions. One can think of prominent examples like the Republicans' Sforza (Foreign Minister under De Gasperi) and La Malfa (various economic portfolios during the centre-left coalitions), not to mention Spadolini as Prime Minister as well as later Defence Minister, and Liberals like Einaudi (Finance and Treasury ministries after the war, also briefly the Foreign Ministry) and Malagodi (briefly Treasury Minister under Andreotti, 1972-3). For the Social Democrats, most prominent was Saragat, who among other things held the Foreign Ministry in the 1960s. On occasions, some small-party leaders have also been given the status of Deputy Prime Minister (for example, Saragat and La Malfa), clearly here their individual prestige playing a part as well as 'coalition reason'. Furthermore, small parties have sometimes benefited from divisions among the larger parties or when the DC has been particularly vulnerable to pressure, hence their success in acquiring major portfolios. It was of course demonstrated only too well by Spadolini's appointment as Prime Minister in 1981. This followed the DC's loss of credibility with involvement in major scandals, combined with the new collective weight of the small parties and the PSI because of their strategic convergence. Another historical example of this phenomenon was the circumstances of Saragat's election as President in 1964. Not only were the three lay parties of the then coalition (the PSI, PSDI and PRI) agreed on Saragat's candidacy, but they were able to exploit factional differences within the DC over rival DC candidates (Kogan 1983: 194-5).

The most obvious advantage that these small centre parties have derived from their role in government is 'institutional presence', which has generally helped to compensate for their weaknesses in other respects (notably, organizational). This is less true of the PLI, which was absent from the cabinet from 1957 right through to 1972, and again from 1973 to 1979. The PLI's long absence eventually undermined that party's development, producing a strategic change under Zanone in the later 1970s. More specifically, the advantages of government have been twofold: policy influence and patronage. The former is difficult to establish in view of the brevity of so many Italian governments, but where such parties have held certain major portfolios through successive coalitions such influence is understood, for example La Malfa's role in economic affairs in the centre-left alliance. His record here was salient, partly because of his own national reputation but also since he diverged from government policy in later centre-left coalitions by advocating greater austerity. The PRI's programmatic commitment has been prominent and consistent over time. However, the PRI has tended to be wary of exploiting state patronage for simply party reasons, usually differing here from other parties regularly in government. While this practice for a long time gave advantages to such parties, in terms of consolidating certain sectors of support, more recently public controversy over scandals (the 'moral question') has worked to the advantage of the PRI, as in the case of its slogan in the 1983 campaign: 'Giovanni Spadolini: an Italian politician who does not resemble Italian politicians'. By contrast, the PSDI has suffered from a poor image over the involvement of its leaders, Tanassi and Pietro Longo, in respectively the Lockheed and P2 scandals.

Turning to small parties remaining in opposition, the MSI is a straightforward case of 'anti-system' politics. Its attitude to the state has over time been nevertheless somewhat ambiguous, both because of internal divisions between radicals and outright reactionaries and as its line has varied – from a 'moderate' one during the 1950s and 1960s to an intransigent one in the 1970s including some links with political violence (Spotts and Wieser 1986: 96–9). In general, it has lacked legitimacy, not being regarded as system-supportive, for which reason it has been excluded from government. There was some discreet co-operation with it on the part of the DC in local government during the 1950s, but the case of the Tambroni government of 1960 which enjoyed the parliamentary support of the MSI caused outrage leading to the fall of that government within a few months. The Radicals are really different, for the label 'anti-system' sometimes attached to them is little more than polemical. They are essentially a protest party (in many ways, more a protest *movement*), using their parliamentary membership to gain publicity for their issues through skilful use of obstruction and amendments and to embarrass the governing parties (as well as playing a 'blackmail' role *vis-à-vis* the PCI with respect to the electorate of the left) (Teodori et al. 1977: chap. VII). As such, they have been highly successful by their own standards, notably in utilizing the constitutional provision for referendums from the divorce issue onwards.

This examination of the small parties' relationship with the state therefore shows a more differentiated picture than previously assumed. While these two categories may be typed as respectively cases of 'coalition potential' and 'blackmail potential', to use

Sartori's definition, significant differences between parties are evident as to their effectiveness in converting that potential into success. This includes their ability to respond to change, the PRI expressing demands for a new approach to government and the Radicals advocating civil liberties. Admittedly, their institutional roles do not fully explain their success, just as the MSI's intermittent 'blackmail' role *vis-à-vis* the DC owed more to its extra-parliamentary exploitation of right-wing protest. Furthermore, the small parties' institutional activity and performance cannot guarantee their consistency and stability in that respect. For that, we have to consider the other two relationships.

Inter-party relationships
The principal concern here is with small parties utilizing their political space for strategic purposes, and in particular how this has or has not enhanced their own development in Italy's multi-party system. Not being static, political space is therefore, among other things, subject to strategic choice as a determinant. As Sjoblom has noted in *Party Strategies in a Multiparty System*, 'the relations between the parties in a specific party system can be highly varied and can sometimes change rapidly – however, they usually follow definite patterns' (Sjoblom 1968: 158). This is because 'the behaviour of a political party is largely conditioned by the qualities of a political system wherein the party acts', although individual parties may pursue different strategic goals (Sjoblom 1968: 17, 78ff).

It is thus appropriate to begin with strategic constraints before assessing strategic choice or movement. In general, the major constraint on the small parties must be the numerical and political predominance of the large parties. For instance, Allum applied the Namierite model from eighteenth-century England to the Italian system, identifying a permanent 'court' party (the DC) and a permanent 'out' party (the PCI), each allied with minor parties (Allum 1973: 63–6). He also concluded regarding the small parties that 'their highest aspiration, both individually and collectively, could only be the conditioning of the Christian Democrats towards either conservative or reformist policies' (Allum 1973: 63). In other words, those allied to the 'court' party were essentially dependent on it – they either coalesced with the DC or remained outside government. There was restricted scope for their influence and at best they were acting as a 'corrective'. The latter was made possible, though not assured, on the DC side, since its motive among others in seeking broad-based coalitions was to enlarge the social consensus by such measures as including the small parties. In this sense, the small parties have been called 'intermediary parties' as distinct from exercising a pivotal role for which numerically they have not been competent.

We have also to consider further the problem of political location in comparing the various small parties and their strategies, since the left–right spectrum has been predominant in postwar Italy. As noted earlier, the PRI's placement in the centre (some say on the centre–left) has given it a special advantage compared certainly with the PLI. The latter's location on the centre-right, if not further right, has effectively restricted its options, since any 'opening to the right' has been weakened by the MSI's lack of legitimacy and the anti-Fascist consensus. Its one bold attempt to activate a rightist strategy, by Malagodi in mobilizing opposition to the new centre-left alliance formula, proved initially successful in the 1963 campaign (the PLI's vote rose from 3.5 percent to 7 percent), but ultimately it failed to consolidate this new advantage. In effect, the PLI's room for movement had to be leftwards, all the more as the axis of Italian politics shifted in that direction in the 1970s. Under Zanone, the PLI did move also in that same direction from 1976, but by that time it found the centre crowded (Craxi's PSI was meanwhile also moving towards the centre).

The PRI, by contrast, has always been better placed to operate as a 'corrective', being traditionally the DC's 'most loyal ally'. For example, its reformist line in the centre-left alliance illustrated that role. Its centrist position also allowed the PRI some scope for strategic initiative, although one might say that this was also due to the strategic choice (indeed to the imagination) of La Malfa. This was evident on two occasions: his advocacy of the centre-left alliance and a decade later his attempted 'opening' to the PCI. Both occasions also showed that, in doing so, his party was very dependent on strategic movement by the larger parties. These two 'openings' were of course constrained by problems at the time of the political left's legitimacy, which in the PSI's case were more easily overcome. As the prospects for the centre-left strengthened, it was however convergence between the two main actors – the DC and PSI – which mattered most, although the PRI was seen as helping to play a 'bridging' role in terms of 'connectedness' in the ideological continuum. La Malfa's famous initiative late in 1977 for closer involvement of the PCI in the national government (it was not perfectly clear whether he was advocating its entry to the cabinet) was very much his idea. While a few months later the PCI did 'enter the majority' (that is, join a legislative coalition), his move provoked some concern among the other political parties.

The two most recent strategic developments among the small

parties have been the rise of the Radicals, followed much later by the emergence of the Greens, and the convergence among those in the centre known as the 'lay-socialist pole'. In the first case, the Radicals succeeded in opening up a new area of political space, with a confrontational strategy towards the parties of government, whose own strategies were of course co-operative. This basic difference lay behind the fact that the Radicals' strategy was not translated into alliance options in the conventional sense of coalition choice, the party also choosing to remain outside coalitions in local government. This 'purist' approach is linked to the Radicals' identity, so that their strategy may be described as issue-linked. The *polo laico-socialista* is, on the other hand, very much linked to the pursuit of power, indeed to a greater share of it in its challenge to the hegemony of the DC. This represents an attempt by the small parties (in conjunction with the PSI) to acquire for the first time a pivot role, first made possible numerically by the 1979 election with the PCI's loss of support and return to opposition. But the effectiveness of this 'pole' is very conditional on harmony among its component members, and this has not always existed. In particular, rivalry between the PSI and PRI has surfaced since they are electorally more in competition in appealing to the same reservoir of centrist 'opinion voters'. In this process, the two other parties of this 'pole' have so far gained less advantage. The PSDI has felt keenly the stronger competition from the now more centrist PSI among those voters inclined to the socialist sector of this 'pole', while the PLI's abrupt shift to the centre in the later 1970s failed to carry full conviction, especially since it was internally contested.

Relationship with society
This deals most directly with the question of small parties and political change, attention focussing on their electoral appeal and support. But first it is necessary to consider briefly their organization as an indicator of their stability as social actors.

By definition, being 'small' parties, their memberships have inevitably been low. For instance, the PSDI's total has usually ranged between 200,000 and 300,000; that of the PRI and PLI is somewhat lower, around 100,000 to 150,000 (although the PLI has recently undergone considerable decline, while the PRI total has risen as a by-product of its new voting appeal); the Radicals have a membership of little more than 3,000, but then they are not essentially a membership party like the others. Cross-nationally, these figures compare reasonably well with small parties in other Western European countries, but this reflects the general tendency for active partisan affiliation in postwar Italian politics. Their membership is, however, well behind that of the large parties, with the DC and PCI both having close to two million members each, although some of the small parties have also articulated collateral organizations: for example, the trade union links of the PRI and PSDI with the UIL, and even the neo-Fascists have their own trade-union collateral in the CISNAL. The PLI has been most noted for its links with business and industry, and has been close to the employers' federation Confindustria. More recently, there has been some *rapprochement* between industry and the PRI, notably by Agnelli of FIAT. The Radicals predictably have not formed any special link with established interest groups, although they have been known for their association with various collective movements, such as of the feminist and anti-militarist variety. The new peace movement in Italy (born in 1981) has not involved supporters of the small centre parties to any great extent, simply because of their firm Atlanticist position on defence. The other form of movement worth mentioning is that of terrorism, which in Italy enjoys a certain mass base. There have been party links in two opposite directions. The MSI's upswing in electoral support in the early 1970s was accompanied by some semi-covert contact with 'black terrorism'. The MSI chose to deny such links, mainly individual ones among the party's radical wing. This denial was not generally believed, and such links with political violence helped to undercut the party's new support. In recent times, there have also been individual links with some 'left' terrorists on the part of the Radicals. The Radicals have chosen to display such links, as part of their provocative line towards the establishment, for which particular reason they have been identified as 'anti-system'.

Looking briefly at the small parties' structures, these are easily typed as top-heavy – no surprise in view of the emphasis so far on the role of their leaders. The parliamentary wings of these parties have dominated over their extra-parliamentary organizations. In the case of the small centre parties, the personnel of their parliamentary groups and their executive organs have overlapped considerably. As a whole, membership participation has been low since activism among their small totals has been inhibited by territorial spread, and in any case is completely dependent on voluntarism. The PLI in particular has long operated as a party of notables, while generally these parties have strictly been unprofessional – the PRI was habitually known for its 'artisan' style of organization, at least until La Malfa began to modernize it, a process that was resumed under Spadolini. In short, these small parties have not enjoyed the kind of *apparato* that would give backbone to their links with supporters and act as a mechanism for converting new ones. Of the three parties in question (the Radicals being excluded as lacking conventional electoralism), the PRI has shown the most healthy organization in recent times. No doubt this relates to its greater public success than the others, and it seems to be a question of electoral momentum stimulating organizational revival rather than vice versa, judging by the situation after the 1983 election. Nor is there any strong likelihood the small parties will break out of the vicious circle of restricted albeit identifiable political space and minimal organization. The organizational superiority of the major parties is still very much one of their advantages, despite declining subcultures. One obvious alternative link with society is of course via the mass media, which the PRI has been the most successful in exploiting (Spadolini, among other things, is an ex-editor of *Corriere della Sera*, 1968–72). This brings us to these parties' electoral appeal, especially among 'opinion voters'.

Although the small parties have drawn some strength from territorial traditions of support – local strongholds, such as the PRI has enjoyed in parts of Romagna, Sicily and the Marches – the majority of their support has recently been found among voters with loose attachments, that is, 'opinion voters'. This is precisely why their political visibility (through parliamentary and governmental membership) has been important. In the past, the electoral bases of these parties have been narrowly defined – for example, the Liberals were traditionally favoured by the high bourgeoisie, especially in fashionable residential districts, as well as by big industrialists and landowners (in the South) – but recent electoral dealignment in Italy has allowed them to spread their support more widely, although without necessarily increasing it. For instance, the Liberals have made some inroads among white-collar workers (Barbagli et al. 1979: 140–1). The PRI has similarly seen a rise in support among this sector and among the professional middle class as a whole, notably in 1983 as part of an 'urbanization' of its electoral base (Corbetta and Parisi 1984: 25–9). Significantly, only a third of the PRI's supporters in that election had voted for it in the immediate past, according to one survey (Corbetta and Parisi 1984: 55). With the greater reliance on 'opinion voters', therefore, these parties have become more 'national' in their electoral bases, although working-class support for them has remained minimal over time (the PSDI electorate is also largely a bourgeois one). Studies of the Radicals' supporters have also shown that they are largely an 'opinion party' at the electoral level (Hanning 1981: 274–6).

In short, the various small parties have been beneficiaries of dealignment trends in Italy to differing extents. For this reason and in the light of examining their overall relationship with society, it seems that the small parties are unlikely to consolidate their new support by way of any realignment. All this creates uncertainty about their future, or rather it makes this especially dependent on the course of political events, whatever the interest that has been occasioned in small parties in Italy in recent years.

Conclusion: theorizing from the Italian case?

This cautionary conclusion may be largely a question of new opportunities entailing risks. It might well reflect habitual scepticism in Italy about the prospects for change in a system which, judging by postwar patterns, has shown remarkable continuity. But it does nevertheless derive from one evident feature of small party development – that as a whole the cases in question have been rather more prominent as institutional actors than as social forces, whatever the historical reasons for their persistence. Of the two different scenarios, the small parties are more likely to continue 'persisting' than to achieve any 'remoulding' of the Italian party system. So far, it is the dynamics of that system which have changed rather than its structure, if we accept the model of 'centripetal pluralism'. The 'newest' of these small parties – apart from the Greens – is in fact historically not so new, and in any case doubts have been cast on the Radicals' capacity for persistence (there have been talks about merging with the PSI). Perhaps more likely is an intermediate scenario: some form of merger, or at least closer alliance, *between* the various small parties. Recently, some of them have shown serious signs of decline – the PSDI, and to some extent the PLI. Their survival might eventually become linked to a more institutionalized 'lay-socialist pole', although the question of its leadership could well be contentious. That scenario would be made probable in the event of electoral reform.

It is the electoral system, as the 'intermediary' reason for small party persistence, together with the practice of broad-consensus coalitions, that most distinguishes the Italian case from other Western European examples. Proportional representation is common to many of the latter, but their versions of this often include qualifications (3 percent or 5 percent exclusion clauses) which would damage the political chances of the Italian small parties. The other four reasons, and particularly the first three, are highly applicable to other countries as indicators of small-party persistence. However, the most important lesson from the Italian case is not over particular variables but the argument that the study of small parties is only really viable by taking a systemic approach.

Note

1. Political parties and the party system in Italy have long been a major field of work on that country among political scientists in Italy and abroad. For work in Italy, see Fondazione Feltrinelli, *La Scienza Politica in Italia: Materiali per un Bilancio* (1984), especially the report on empirical research. Electoral behaviour has, as elsewhere, been the principal growth area in that field, and here small parties have been given some attention. For a more detailed report on party research in Italy, see Mario Caciagli, 'Partiti e sistema partitico in Italia: un trend report', paper to the conference of the ECPR standing group on Southern Europe, Barcelona, 1982. This emphasizes the enormous amount of research on the major parties, above all the PCI, while the literature is 'almost non-existent on the smaller parties'. Apart from R. Leonardi's chapters on small parties in the volumes on the 1976, 1979 and 1983 elections edited by H.R. Penniman (in the series of the American Enterprise Institute), it mentions some ephemeral publications like those of A. Ciani on the PLI (1968) and of G. Averardi on the PSDI (1977). On the other hand, there have been several fairly recent publications on the Radicals, especially that by M. Teodori, P. Ignazi and A. Panebianco *I Nuovi Radicali* (1977). The period between the Risorgimento and Fascism is covered well, including M. Di Lalla, *Storia del Liberalismo Italiano dal Risorgimento al Fascismo* (1976), G. Conti, *Il Partito Repubblicano dalle Origini al Momento Attuale* (1947) and some works by the PRI leader G. Spadolini, who is a professional historian, e.g. his *I Repubblicani dopo l'Unità* (1960). These are all substantial historical works. The major exception to the neglect of these parties by political scientists is the three recent volumes published by the Cattaneo Institute: P. Corbetta and A. Parisi, *Il Voto Repubblicano alle Origini del 26 giugno* (1984); A. Parisi and A. Varni (eds), *Organizzazione e Politica nel PRI 1946–1984* (1985); and A. Parisi (ed.), *La Dirigenza Repubblicana* (1987); on respectively the electorate and the organizational and leadership development of the PRI. These clearly reflect the interest in the enhanced prospects of that party. Of course, the various publications on the Radicals (mentioned above) reflected that same contemporary interest when they made an impact in the late 1970s.

5
The Birth, Life and Death of Small Parties in Danish Politics

Mogens N. Pedersen

'Smallness', 'relevance' and the systemic approach

Small parties have always been an endemic part of Danish politics. Even during the formative years of the Danish party system as well as during the period that lasted until 1920, when there was a plurality electoral system, there were always more than two parties, and some of these were quite small.[1] The operation of several parties in a party system may go hand in hand with various patterns of electoral strength. The Danish party-system format has to be characterized as a multi-party system with one fairly large, and for long periods even slightly dominant, party (the Social Democrats) which, however, never attained the position of a predominant party (Sartori 1976: 128ff, 192–201). The important fact to be stressed is that throughout this century the Danish party system has always contained a number of quite small parties, a number of medium-sized parties and only one relatively big party.

Considering only the period after 1920, the overall patterns of the parliamentary party-system format are shown in Table 5.1.

Irrespective of the definition of the concept of 'small party', Table

Table 5.1 *Approximate number of parties in parliament (the Folketing) in various groups of strength by decade*

| Decade | Percentage of seats | | | | |
	Less than 10%	10–20%	20–30%	30–40%	More than 40%
1920s	1	2	1	1	—
1930s	4	1	1	1	1
1940s	4	1	1	1	—
1950s	3	1	1	1	—
1960s	3	1	1	1	—
1970s	7	3	—	1	—
1980s	5	3	—	1	—

5.1 indicates that Denmark has had its full share of small parties. If to the small parties in parliament are added the even smaller parties which did not gain representation, the number of such parties operating in Danish politics must be among the highest in Europe – the Dutch and the Swiss party systems are the only serious contenders in this respect.

The second important observation to be made from Table 5.1 is the absence of a really large party. One has to go back to the heyday of the Agrarian Liberal Party at the beginning of this century to find an instance of a party polling more than 50 percent of the vote. Even at the height of the Social Democratic period in Danish politics, this party never commanded more than 46 percent.

In order to explain the terminology that will be used in the following chapter, this first look at the format of the party system in Denmark has to be accompanied by a few methodological remarks.

Given the peculiar distribution of party strength in Denmark, it does not make sense to develop the concept of 'smallness' at great length, especially when excluding some parties from examination on the grounds they are too small to warrant inclusion. In particular, there is little point in arbitrary distinctions, that is, numerical 'cut-off points' without strong justification. Only two quantitative distinctions make some theoretical and empirical sense in the Danish case.

The first one is the distinction between parties that polled less and parties that polled more than 2 percent at any given election. This is simply the distinction between represented and unrepresented parties. Since it is the intention of this chapter to follow – in analytical terms – the small party from its very beginning to its eventual end, however, it would not make sense to concentrate only on those lucky parties that have gained representation.[2] The second, less important, distinction is that between, on the one hand, parties that are strong enough to elect members to the committees of the parliament and, on the other, parties which have to stay outside the committees. As these committees typically consist of 17 members, and the total size of the Folketing is 179 members, this suggests a second distinction around 6 percent. But since small parties often create *ad hoc* coalitions in order to muster enough strength in the elections (by proportional representation) of the committees, this is really a weak secondary distinction between various degrees of 'smallness'. Its relevance, however limited, will be discussed at the appropriate place in this chapter.

The same is true about the celebrated Sartorian distinction between 'relevant' and 'irrelevant' parties (Sartori 1976: 119–25). Although criteria of 'relevance' are difficult to operationalize, the very notion makes theoretical sense, as amply demonstrated by Sartori. It does also make a lot of practical sense: leaders of very small as well as somewhat larger parties understand perfectly well when and in what way their party belongs among the relevant, and when they are just relegated to political impotence. But since it is one of the aims of this chapter to study the passage from 'irrelevance' to 'relevance', it would not make sense to use the distinction for the purpose of excluding any parties from inspection.

Instead of pursuing a conceptual discussion, it may be more useful to follow the usage of the Danish political language. Most Danes would tend to agree that most of their parties are 'small'. Actually, only the Social Democrats, the Agrarian Liberals and the Conservatives have qualified in political parlance as 'major' parties; in recent times, however, the Socialist People's Party has been mentioned together with these parties. The remaining parties have all been dubbed 'small', even if at one point in time – after the 1973 election – the vocabulary became very confused.[3] The reader should bear this simple meaning of 'smallness' in mind in the following discussion.

In this chapter, the analytical perspective is derived from a theoretical approach that will be summarized in a moment. In order to apply this approach in a thorough way, one has to give less priority to other relevant approaches mentioned by Müller-Rommel elsewhere in this volume. Thus, it was deemed impossible – for stylistic reasons and scarcity of space – to pursue fully at the same time both the 'lifespan' approach and the 'systemic' approach that guides many other chapters in this volume.

This does not mean, however, that systemic relationships are considered irrelevant, nor are they excluded from the following pages. It just means that the relationships between the small parties and 'society' are all dealt with in the appropriate places, according to the logic of the lifespan model. The reader will have to look at the systemic relationships in the light of this model, which is particularly suitable to the Danish case.

The lifespan model

The following pages contain a description and an analysis of the role played by small parties in Danish politics, based on a conceptual framework developed by the author some years ago.[4] The basic idea is that of a lifespan which a party will pass through from its inception till its disappearance, the underlying hypothesis thus being that parties are mortal organizations. They are, as it were, born; they pass through infancy, youth, adulthood and old age; and each of these passages can be scrutinized.

That parties are mortal organizations is well documented in comparative literature (Janda 1980: 162–9). Other scholars have pursued the related idea that political instability and the occurrence of new – and hence small – parties are related (for example, Borre 1980; Mayer 1980; Pedersen 1983; Smith 1978; Wolinetz 1979). In general organization theory these ideas are commonplace: survival of the organization is often considered the paramount goal, which at times will take precedence over other goals (Gouldner 1959: 405); but not all organizations will survive; large firms are better survivors than small firms (Dill 1965: 1092ff); even large organizations may not survive infinitely, and they definitely undergo ageing processes (Downs 1967: 5–23).[5]

The lifespan of parties can be divided into a number of discrete phases, marked by successive thresholds which the party passes in its early years (upwards) and again (downwards) when after a number of years, or decades, it eventually[6] begins to lose support. The thresholds to be considered are:

(a) the threshold of declaration;
(b) the threshold of authorization;
(c) the threshold of representation; and
(d) the threshold of relevance.

According to the number of thresholds passed – and to the various descriptive, eventually statistical, characteristics of the lifespan curve – not only may one classify any given party, but it is also possible to discuss the probable success and failure of parties in these conceptual terms. The necessary definitions of the thresholds will be provided as they are discussed.[7]

Crossing the threshold of declaration
The line of demarcation between political parties and other social organizations is somewhat blurred. Definitions of the concept of party vary somewhat between authors, and these differences tend to get reflected in the way scholars enumerate parties at any given moment in any given political system. Fortunately, most electoral systems are more practically oriented than political scientists – they normally set up at least some formal requirements that an organization will have to fulfil in order to qualify *de jure* as a political party. For that reason, it is not necessary to enter the old scholastic discussion on the topic of the essence of party.

This fuzzy line of demarcation is, however, also to some extent a fact of political life, reflecting its very complexity. It is simply often difficult to identify precisely the moment when a new party comes

The birth, life and death of parties: Denmark   99

into existence. When does a faction in a parliamentary party group turn into a new (splinter) party? When does a small organization or a social movement outside parliament become a 'real' party? It is often hard to tell, since passing the *threshold of declaration* does not necessarily entail a manifest declaration. However, in practice, the very fact of a declaration to the public about the formation of a new party usually provides the party leaders *in spe* with a good opportunity to make news and put the new party 'on the map'. In some cases, on the other hand, efforts to register as a new party start in relative obscurity, known only to rather small circles of devotees. Should one, in such cases, totally neglect treating the new group as a party or as a proto-party?

If one therefore asks how many parties exist in the Danish party system, one should not restrict oneself to the eight parties represented after, or the ten parties represented before, the latest election in 1988. Nor to the roughly fifteen parties that have qualified *de jure* for participation in recent elections. It is not a wild guess to say that a handful of other organizations or small groups exist which consider themselves national parties – and which one may wish to classify as *proto-parties*: groups that work with the aim of some day qualifying as parties that present candidates for public office at Folketing elections. These groups range from a minute neo-Nazi group to equally small groups on the far left of the group of socialist parties. A number of the latter have as a matter of fact passed the *threshold of declaration* in recent years, and some of them have even passed the threshold of authorization; but as their poor showing in elections has demonstrated (see Table 5.2 below), they have in some cases been so small that – in terms of popular support – they do not differ much from a number of other esoteric political groups.

A special type of party which can be said to belong to this category of proto-parties is the party created by one or more members of a parliamentary party, who break away to form their own group, but without at the same time starting to organize an electoral party. Until 1965 a simple declaration by one or several members of the Folketing would not only constitute a declaration of intent but also be an adequate basis for authorization as a party by the president of the parliament. This way of bringing a party into existence was not unusual: between 1920 and 1965, for instance, fifteen parties were registered by means of this procedural device. Of these attempts to start a new party, one-third failed at once, since the parties did not even nominate candidates for the next election; another third participated in the next election without luck, and only the last third succeeded.

In 1965 this procedure for simultaneous declaration and authorization was cancelled by the Folketing majority. The immediate reason for this change was the declaration by two former members of the Agrarian Liberal Party that they wanted to form a new party, Liberal Centrum. Since that year, individual members of factions that break away from the 'mother party' have had to proceed as all other groups and organizations which declare themselves a new party.

Crossing the threshold of authorization
In order to become a party in the legal sense, that is, a group which is allowed to present candidates for office at national elections, it is mandatory in Denmark to become registered. Such registration requires that the organization or group collects a certain number of certified signatures from voters who are willing to support such registration. If the number of valid signatures surpasses a specified number, the Minister of the Interior declares the party authorized to participate in the next election. The requirements set down in the electoral law have always been modest: between 1915 and 1965, 10,000 signatures were required; since 1965, the requirement has been a total of signatures amounting to at least 1/175 of all registered voters, at the moment about 19,000 signatures.

Larsen (1975) has analysed all attempts to register new parties during the period 1915–75. It is necessary here to refer to some of his findings about successes and failures of these new parties, especially the frequencies of authorization. Larsen found forty-three cases of attempts to register by using the procedure just described. Of these only three were turned down by the Ministry of the Interior, and two of these were able to supplement their application with additional signatures well in time before the next election. Thus, only one attempt was a failure.

It is hence fairly easy to register as a new party. Apparently Danes are often willing to give new parties a try, *vide* the discrepancy between the 19,000 signatures provided by new parties and the very poor election results of some of the new parties, such as 2,000 votes for one of the small socialist parties in the 1984 election. The very process of registering does – at least in the era of television – provide the new party with a number of excellent opportunities to command a platform from which to reach the electorate, for example when the party declares itself, when signatures are delivered in the ministry and when approval is given.

Approval as party is therefore an important event, because it automatically creates new opportunities for the new parties. The most important opportunity is free access to the electoral campaign broadcasts of state-controlled radio and television. With (until recently) only one television channel in Denmark, access to these broadcasts is essential. The rules have been clear: every registered party has equal rights during the televised campaign; as soon as the date for the election has been decided, special conditions are set in motion with regard to political newscasting. 'Political curfew' is the term often used for these conditions, and for good reasons: all parties are given exactly the same amount of time for their presentation; they all receive the same amount of financial and editorial support for the preparation of their presentation programmes; they also command exactly the same time during the televised discussions of the party leaders immediately before the election. Thus, the leader of an obscure party that may poll 0.1 percent in the election has the same right to speak and to participate as have the Prime Minister and the (unofficial) leader of the opposition. Fairness and many-sidedness have become understood in Denmark as 'equal time'.

Crossing the threshold of representation
When proportional representation was introduced in 1915–20, it was made clear from the very beginning that, at the same time as proportionality was aimed at, this should not prevent setting the threshold of representation somewhat higher than strict proportionality would dictate. Since proportionality is primarily obtained by means of a very complicated distribution of so-called 'supplementary seats', the threshold is defined in terms of the conditions that a party will have to satisfy in order to qualify for the distribution of the pool of these seats.[8] The conditions set in the electoral law have varied over time, becoming more demanding after the Second World War, and then being slightly relaxed in 1961, when the present regulations were established. In order to qualify for supplementary seats a party must either have won one 'constituency seat'; or, within at least two of the three regions into which the country is divided, it must have obtained a total of as many votes as on average were cast per constituency seat; or it must have obtained, in the whole country, at least 2 percent of the valid votes cast.

These complex threshold conditions have always been contested, even to the extent that one may say that the debate in Denmark on the electoral system equates with the debate on the so-called *spaerreregler* ('threshold clauses'). Not surprisingly, the small parties have always been opponents, while the three larger 'old' parties (the Social Democrats, Agrarian Liberals and Conservatives) have been in favour of some restrictions. Elections since 1973 have, however, resulted in a balance between large and small parties which effectively blocks any attempt to change the rules in a more restrictive direction. Apparently this old conflict is for the time being no longer a serious political issue, even if discussions go on from time to time.

Conditions of breakthrough
It would be very useful if students of parties and party systems could predict the fate of a new party approaching the threshold of representation. What are, for instance, the chances that a new party will break through in its first electoral contest? Is it possible to pinpoint special factors that account for the sudden rise to the rank of parliamentary party, or even to the rank of an influential and relevant party? Are there institutional conditions that support such growth? Do the historical conditions of the party itself – that is, its organizational characteristics and the conditions around its very appearance as a party – contain any clues to its success or lack of success? These questions will now be discussed.

The discussion will start with a mapping of the fate of all first-time contenders since the introduction of PR in 1920. Table 5.2 provides four items of information: first, the name of the new party (in Danish); secondly, the year of the first appearance as electoral contender; thirdly, the percentage of the vote obtained at this first election; and fourthly, a rough classificatory description of the party's degree of success: that is, if it crossed the threshold of representation, and if it also gained enough seats to enable it to elect members to the parliamentary committees.

The first observation to be made is that the chances of considerable electoral success immediately are slim indeed. Of twenty-five parties that tried, only three immediately gained not only representation, but also enough seats in parliament to obtain immediate access to the committee system. At the other extreme, half of the new parties did not even reach the 1 percent mark at their first try. And only eight parties out of the twenty-five made their way into the parliament. But one should then also add that at least some of the new small parties had better luck at the next election. Not forgetting that the Communists (DKP) entered the Folketing twelve years and five elections after their first attempt, five other parties made it on their second try (Danmarks Retsforbund, DNSAP, Frie Folkeparti, Dansk Samling and Kristeligt Folkeparti). Of twenty-five attempts made, only eight were success stories, and out of these six happened in recent times, that is, after the Second World War. An interesting observation is that the level of support obtained by the first-time contenders apparently tends to be higher after 1945 than before.

Is it possible to find some kind of pattern in these twenty-five

Table 5.2 *New parties in Danish politics, 1920–88, and their results at the first electoral contest*

Party	Election	Percentage of vote	Success
Erhvervspartiet	1920 (Apr.)	2.9	medium
Centrum	1920 (Apr.)	0.9	poor
Frie Socialdemokrati	1920 (Apr.)	0.7	poor
Danmarks Venstresocialistiske Parti (DKP)	1920 (Sept.)	0.4	poor
Danmarks Retsforbund	1924	1.0	poor
Landmandspartiet	1924	0.9	poor
DNSAP	1932	0.1	poor
Frie Folkeparti	1935	3.2	medium
Dansk Samling	1939	0.5	poor
Nationalt Samvirke	1939	1.0	poor
De Uafhængige	1953 (Sept.)	2.7	poor
Socialistisk Fp. (SF)	1960	6.1	high
Fredspolitisk Fp.	1964	0.4	poor
Liberalt Centrum	1966	2.5	medium
Venstresocialisterne	1968	2.0	medium
Kristeligt Folkeparti	1971	1.9	poor
Fremskridtspartiet	1973	15.9	high
Centrumsdemokraterne	1973	7.8	high
Pensionistpartiet	1977	0.9	poor
Arbejderpartiet (KAP)	1979	0.4	poor
Int. Soc. Arb. Parti	1981	0.1	poor
Marx.–Lenin. Parti	1984	0.0	poor
De Grønne	1987	1.3	poor
Humanistisk Parti	1987	0.2	poor
Fælleskurs	1987	2.2	medium

Source: *Folketingets Håndbog* 1977 and 1987

historically discrete phenomena? Since there does not exist much, if any, guidance in the political science literature, let us just suggest a number of possible factors that may 'explain' success:

Particular political profile characteristics of the new party Does the new party present itself primarily in terms of class interests, or does it appeal to the voters in other general or special terms? Does the new party present itself as a revolutionary or, in one way or another, an 'anti-system' party, or does it base its activities on less far-reaching claims?

Particular 'situational' conditions with respect to the appearance of the new party Is the new party an offspring of existing parties, or is it a creation *de novo*? Is the new party supported by influential organized interests, or is it unaffiliated to interest organizations? Does the new party come into existence as a result of dramatic events, exposed from the very beginning in the media, or does it 'just' come into existence as another electoral option? Is the leadership of the new party comprised of well-known media personalities, maybe even charismatic figures, or do their faces not ring a bell?

Meticulous research on the older Danish cases (Christensen 1977) suggests answers to these questions, even if such answers are admittedly based upon shaky ground. It is appropriate to start by repeating that the data base consists of twenty-five cases, of which only a third can be considered 'success stories'. There is no room left for fancy statistical methodology here.

First observation: it does not make sense to look for answers in connection with the period 1920–45. There is simply no discernible pattern in the data. Second observation: when the six post-1945 'success stories' are compared with the nine cases of not-so-successful electoral performance, a certain pattern appears. There is no relationship observable between electoral success and political profile characteristics: thus, for example, some extreme left-wing parties did well, while others failed miserably. Looking for factors where successful parties score high values, one ends up with two, both of them related to the 'situational' characteristics of the new parties.

In seven of the fifteen cases, the first appearance of the new party was characterized by considerable drama (such as a sudden party split, a cabinet crisis or a vote of no confidence). In five of these seven cases the new party was successful. And in six out of seven cases in which the party's leader(ship) was highly visible and spectacular, if not outright charismatic, the new party was successful. It is noteworthy that out of the six 'success stories' (the SF, LC, VS, CD, FRP and Faelleskurs), the first four also shared the important characteristic of originating as a kind of splinter party from an existing party. On the other hand, this characteristic is not as interesting, since another four parties with the same background did not fare at all well in their first electoral contest.

Even if such findings are not conclusive, they do at least suggest a working hypothesis: that the chances of a new party crossing the threshold of representation are to a high degree related to the 'situational' characteristics of the first electoral campaign. The combination of a highly visible leadership and a dramatic situation involving conflict between an older party and the new offspring party has tended to be a winning one.

The small party in parliament

The workload

Passing the threshold of representation constitutes a great step in the life of the small party. Being a parliamentary party means easier access to the press, and it provides the party with a daily platform in the Folketing. It also adds to the party's resources substantial financial support, thus making it possible to procure secretarial assistance and expert advice. The new Danish scheme for public support of political parties provides each party with a fixed amount per vote received in Folketing, county and municipal elections, thus making this support proportional to the electoral strength of the parties.[9]

Being represented does, however, impose duties on the small party. First and foremost, it requires from the party a consistent stand on numerous political issues. Thus, the small party is, at a minimum, supposed to present its view during the readings of all bills. This imposes a considerable burden upon each of the members of the small party group, whereas the corresponding workload for larger parties is much lighter.[10]

In a parliamentary party group other activities have to be performed as well. Thus, even small parties are most of the time able to elect members to the seventeen-member standing committees of the Folketing. The elections to these committees are carried out according to a proportional representation method. This normally means that a party is only able to elect committee members if it has obtained ten seats (corresponding to approximately 6 percent of the vote). But even smaller parties are able to break through this barrier by forming coalitions with other parties. In 1986–7 two 'proto-groups' or 'non-partisan' coalitions were formed for this occasion.[11] Even if such *ad hoc* coalitions do not give the small party access to all standing committees, and in particular do not make it possible for the party to become represented on the central and most influential ones, it will, however, provide the party and its members with important information.[12]

It only requires a little arithmetic to see that such influence is paid for in terms of an increased workload for the members. It has been calculated that in the largest party the average member will 'follow' half a standing committee, while the members of the smallest groups are each involved with four standing committees. A corollary is that the possibility of specialization is proportional to the size of the party group, *ceteris paribus*. The smallest parties never command more than one member per committee, and this member will on top of everything have to cover a share of the total span of issues that is approximately eight times as great as the share that a member of the largest party group is entitled to. (Damgaard 1982: 67)[13]

The high rate of activity and the disproportionate workload of members of small parties, however, relate not only to the legislative process proper. All kinds of activities in parliament are included, and especially those, like parliamentary questions, that are based primarily upon individual motivation and ambition.[14] Why is it that members of the smallest parties carry a much higher workload than members of the bigger parties? At least three factors account for this phenomenon.

First, sheer necessity. The procedural rules of the parliament are based upon a principle of equity. Each party is basically entitled to the same rights, irrespective of size and strength, and such rights apparently are usually also considered duties. It is against parliamentary norms not to participate in the handling of bills and other tasks. It is thus not at all easy for a small party to 'specialize' by concentrating on some issues at the expense of others.

Secondly, the member of the small party is much more visible and exposed than is the average member of parliament. He/she is not to the same extent allowed to think of him-/herself as representing partly the party and partly the constituency.[15] He/she is certainly not allowed to act that way. The small party will typically have built up a small but highly active national organization, whose members are often militant and very keen to see that the overall mission of the party is fulfilled. The hyperactivity of members of parliament is partly a result of this pressure, not only in the small left-wing parties in which the national organization commands supremacy, but also in other small parties. It also has a lot to do with the simple fact that competition among candidates is intense. Only few, if any, can afford the luxury of issue-specialization that the member of a larger group may indulge in.[16]

A third, and probably the most important, reason why representatives of small parties have to work harder is that not only the individual member, but also the small party itself, is placed in a situation characterized by fierce competition. Such competition calls for extraordinary activity. This particular aspect will be discussed in the next paragraphs.

The systemic position of small parties in Danish politics
The mixture of small and medium-sized parties – and the absence of

a dominant party – provides the basic scenario for Danish policy-making. Since the beginning of the twentieth century, no party has been able to form a majority government. Two so-called 'blocs' have for decades been competing for government position: on the one hand, the Social Democratic Party, forming the nucleus of a 'socialist' bloc; on the other, mostly two parties, the Conservatives and the Agrarian Liberals, forming or leading a 'bourgeois' bloc. Neither of these two nuclear groups commands a majority. Thus, both of the blocs have to vie for the support and participation of a number of smaller parties, which are located on the left and the right side of the political spectrum, as well as in the very centre. Figure 5.1 will serve as a summarizing,[17] unidimensional[18] illustration[19] of the peculiar setting of Danish politics.

It is clear that three groups of smaller parties surround the two nuclear groupings. First, there have been a diachronically varying number of left-wing socialist parties, all of which in recent times have paid at least lip-service to democratic values, and most of which have been basically pro-system parties in terms of behaviour.[20] These parties will either support a left-wing coalition or at least usually not obstruct a governing coalition in which the Social

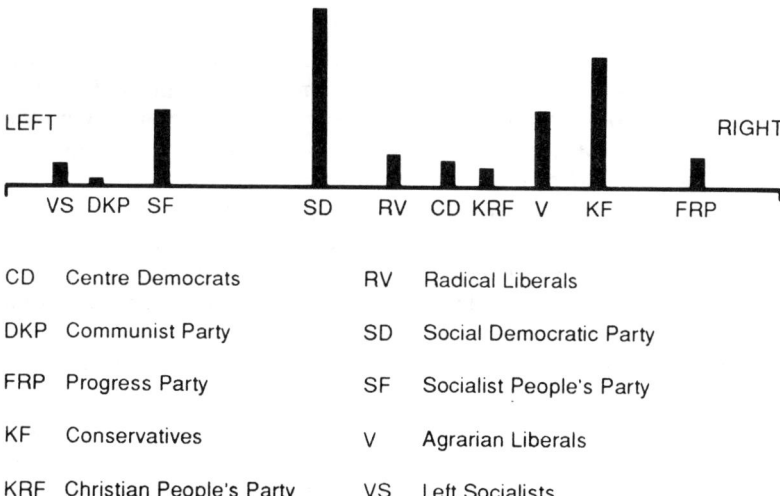

Figure 5.1 *A unidimensional representation of the Danish party system in the mid-1980s*

The height of columns indicates relative electoral strength at the election of 1984. The Justice Party and two very small left-fringe (socialist) parties participated in the election of 1984, but have been omitted from the figure.

Democrats take part. They have not yet participated in a government coalition, partly because they have not yet been invited, and partly because the opportunity to form such a coalition has not presented itself in recent years. Secondly, there is a party to the very right, the Progress Party, whose behaviour has proven to be less reliable in terms of *Koalitionsfähigkeit*. In its early years, the rhetoric of this peculiar party had an anti-system ring that made it look like a threat. It still does not always count itself among parties that will support a bourgeois government. It has never been in government, and it is very doubtful that it will ever become a member of a government. But its presence is as influential as that of the left-wing opposition for the functioning of the major bourgeois parties as well as of the party system as such.[21] Thirdly, some small parties, among which the old Radical Liberal Party is archetypal and also the most influential, are located in between the two nuclear groupings, serving as potential participants in coalition governments.[22]

Given the very delicate balance between the two major contending blocs, even small parties at the centre of the political spectrum may be called upon to serve in minority coalition governments or to give institutional or more casual support to a cabinet. But also the small parties on the fringes often have to consider lending support to a minority government and thus ponder their bargaining positions. Even members from Greenland – of which there are two – are sometimes allowed a chance to provide crucial support for governments.[23]

In a political arena structured in this way coalition formation becomes the predominant occupation of politicians. Not only do they have to forge a coalition from time to time that will sustain a government (and elections are on the average called every second year), but they also have to build up legislative coalitions on a day-to-day basis, using the building bricks provided in the form of (mostly cohesive) parties. And, while this perpetual bargaining goes on, the party leaders regularly have to consider the probability of an election being called at short notice.

The small party in the political arena: the threshold of relevance equals the threshold of representation
In this bargaining game the small parties play a pivotal, but for themselves dangerous, role. With unstable minority situations as the most typical outcome of government formation, the small parties always have to prepare for the next merciless electoral fight. In the brief intervals between elections they have, first, to make the crucial decision whether to support or fight the incumbent government – or whether to try to achieve a brokerage position, eventually joining the government if such opportunities present themselves.

Secondly, they have to develop a political and ideological platform that is visible, unique and easy to defend and exploit, and this is no easy task in a political arena which is crowded with parties, all trying to exploit new, developing cleavages and issues in order to survive. Most of the small parties lack the linkages to major interest organizations that characterize the three major parties. This makes it easier for the small parties to manoeuvre and to exploit the issues of the day. On the other hand, they also lack the financial as well as the mobilization support that is provided by this linkage.[24]

We may sum up this picture by stating the proposition that virtually all Denmark's small parties are for most of their lifetime 'relevant' in the Sartorian sense, if not because they have 'coalition potential' then because they possess 'blackmail potential'. This holds true of course for the small centrist parties, which either have been in government or have participated in most of the legislative coalitions formed after 1973. By putting constant pressure on the Social Democratic Party as well as upon each other, the small left-wing parties clearly possessed blackmail potential during the first decade after 1973. After the formation of the 'bourgeois' government in 1982, the fast-growing Socialist People's Party – no longer a small party in the ordinary sense – was drawn into the opposition's attempt to create an 'alternative majority'. But it can also be argued that the Progress Party throughout its lifetime has had blackmail potential in the sense that its existence 'affects the tactics of party competition and . . . alters the direction of the competition – by determining a switch from the centrifugal competition either leftward, rightward, or in both directions – of the governing-oriented parties' (Sartori 1976: 123).[25]

Thus, the threshold of relevance after the expansion of the party system in 1973 has tended to become identical with the threshold of representation.

The painful part: going down
The constant headache for the leaders of Denmark's minor parties is how to keep the party above the 2 percent of the vote that constitutes the threshold of representation. Several of the small parties poll between 2 and 4 percent most of the time. Between elections it quite often happens that one or another of these parties drops below the threshold percentage in the opinion polls. Small parties, however, often seem to survive, because they are able to regain strength during the electoral campaigns.[26]

The high degree of aggregate volatility of the small party vote reflects very fluid electoral support for most of these parties. Although the Communist vote as well as the vote for other older minor parties may be somewhat more stable, the voters who support the newer minor parties apparently are relatively unfaithful. The small parties have to be agile, always looking out for new issues and niches. The centrist parties in particular compete in a tight market; they often try to mobilize new categories of voters. Apparently therefore the voters at the centre of the political spectrum are very unstable.

The comments made here are brief, but they are easily substantiated. Thus, it has been found that party identification tends to be less for the (small) centre parties than at the fringes of the party system (Borre et al. 1983: 86ff). Evidence from opinion polls as well as 'academic' surveys indicates that individual volatility in small parties is greater than in the major parties (for example Borre et al. 1976), and recent ecological analyses corroborate this view.[27]

Considering the modest size of many Danish parties, and the high volatility in these parties in particular, it is no wonder that they fear dropping below the threshold of representation. Nor should it be surprising that they fight the very notion of a specific threshold clause in the electoral law. Any attempt to increase the threshold to 4 or 5 percent, for instance, has been met with resistance from an array of minor Danish parties. A look at the distribution in Table 5.1 (above) suggests the potential strength of this opposition.

Table 5.3 forms the basis for the discussion of the final parts of the lifespan *problématique*.

An inspection of Table 5.3 raises a number of questions that relate to the 'downhill slope' of the lifespan curve. For example, what is the actual probability of a minor party being ousted from the

Table 5.3 *Position in the life-cycle in about 1988 of parties active during the period 1945–88*

Stage in the life-cycle	Number of parties
1 'Old' parties continuously represented throughout period 1945–88	4
2 Parties formed after 1945 and still represented after 1988 election	4
3 Parties formerly represented, still campaigning in the election(s) of 1987 and/or 1988	4
4 Parties formerly represented, no longer active/in existence	4
5 Parties formed after 1945, never represented, but still campaigning 1987–8	4
6 Parties formed after 1945, never represented, no longer active/in existence	2
7 All parties operating during period 1945–88	22

Folketing? What tends to happen to those unfortunate parties that pass the threshold of representation in a downward direction? Are they able to recuperate, or are they condemned to oblivion? How and why do parties tend to disappear from existence? This kind of question is as important and pertinent as those that relate to the creation and breakthrough of new parties.

In his worldwide survey of political parties, Kenneth Janda registered a considerable mortality rate among political parties. Of all parties in fifty-three countries, no less than 39 percent of those parties which were active in the 1950s had ceased to exist in 1979 (Janda 1980: 162–9). Even in the relatively stable democracies of Western Europe, 15–20 percent of incumbent parties disappeared over a period of thirty years. The data presented in Table 5.3 indicate that the Danish multi-party system is fairly typical in terms of mortality rates. Of twenty-two parties operating in Danish politics between 1945 and 1988, about a quarter are no longer active in electoral campaigns. If one only considers parties which at one point in time have been represented, the proportion is the same. If the period under inspection is narrowed down to the one covered by Janda, the fit with the European average becomes even better. A few remarks will qualify this quantitative observation.

In Denmark small political parties tend to live on for quite some time, even if they do not succeed in getting represented (see Table 5.2). After a number of unsuccessful campaigns, however, it becomes increasingly difficult to keep up the spirits of the faithful. But only in a few cases has a party decided to dissolve itself. The 'typical' fate of any disappearing party consists in slowly fading away, as members and sympathizers seek an outlet for their zeal, ambitions and idealism in other, sometimes new parties, as happened in 1973 with the rise of the Progress Party.

The same gradual disintegration awaits those parties which after a period of representation drop out of the Folketing. The struggle for life is, however, often quite protracted. The prayers for a political comeback may be heard by the voters, even if such comebacks are in many respects comparable to first entrances in terms of the difficulties imposed. Nevertheless, three small parties stand out in the history of the Danish party system as notable for their comeback after having been ousted from parliament. The Left Socialists after one election period fell below the threshold of representation in 1971, but they returned to parliament in 1975. More interesting was the almost parallel revival of two of the older minor parties in Danish politics. The Danish Communist Party and the Justice Party had gained representation before the Second World War. In 1960 they were both severely defeated. The Communists were punished for their stand on the Stalinist issue, and many of their former supporters turned to a new small party, the Socialist People's Party. The Justice Party was severely punished for its participation in a three-party cabinet coalition that ruled between 1957 and 1960. In the dramatic election of 1973 these two surviving party organizations had another lease on life. On that occasion, one had the rare opportunity to see some of the very senior Communist politicians return to the Folketing after twenty or twenty-five years in the political wilderness.

In all these three cases the revival took place during the period of turbulence in Danish politics in the 1970s, and in the two latter cases it can be argued that it was the electoral upheaval in combination with a drastic change in the platform of these parties – a heavy stress on opposition to Danish EEC membership – that made a short-lived recuperation possible. Such exceptions should, however, not lead the reader to believe that parties are immortal organizations.[28]

Conclusion

This chapter has studied the small parties in Denmark from a developmental perspective. It has been argued that throughout this century several parties have qualified as 'small', irrespective of the definition of 'smallness'. Small parties tend to come and go. The Danish politicians have not put up substantial barriers for participation and representation of new political groups, but have on the contrary emphasized fair and equal treatment of all parties, however small. The threshold of representation, therefore, is quite low.

The small party in parliament – and especially its individual members – has to carry a heavy burden in terms of legislative and other parliament-related work. This is so partly because the small party in parliament faces tough competition. Since 1973 the small parties have been competing within the confines of three rather narrow ideological 'spaces': the left and the right fringe, and the very centre of the party spectrum. They have to be very active, and even then their existence is unsafe. Their voters tend to be much more volatile than are the voters of the larger parties. On the other hand, the small parties also tend to be influential or relevant most of the time: they possess coalition potential and/or blackmail potential. In such a crowded party system the threshold of relevance tends to become identical with the threshold of representation. But the life of the small party is always at risk: there is no guarantee that relevance and representation will last for ever. It may even happen that a small party plunges from a position in a government coalition to the not-so-glorious status of being a formerly represented party.

Notes

1. Maurice Duverger (1959: 222–3) had to devote considerable space to this aberration from his theory. His answer was wrong (Elklit 1986; Rasmussen 1972), but his questions were pertinent.
2. Some methodological problems concerning the proper definition of the concept of (small) parties are discussed in Pedersen 1982.
3. The special conditions before, during and after the election in December 1973 have been analysed at length in Pedersen 1988.
4. Cf. Pedersen 1982. The author is only aware of one attempt to utilize this framework in empirical research (Herzog 1987).
5. For an up-to-date summary of the literature on organizational change and the ageing of organizations, see Heffron 1989: chap. 5.
6. The lifespan model does not imply that all parties are bound to disappear after a certain, shorter or longer period. It only postulates that many parties will do so. Parties are still relatively new phenomena.
7. The reader should be aware from the outset that the author does not reserve the lifespan notion to small parties. They do, however, have a higher mortality rate, and the concept will therefore be more useful.
8. The most up-to-date description in English of the complicated Danish electoral system is Johansen 1982.
9. This scheme of support was introduced in 1986; cf. *Folketingstidende – Årbog og Registre 1986–87* (1988). Even parties that only poll 1,000 votes in a Folketing election are entitled to financial support.
10. Thus Pia Kjærsgaard (MF, Progress Party) had to speak on 39 bills in 1986–7, while Hans Hækkerup (MF, Social Democratic Party) only spoke on 8 bills. Both members were young and in their first term.
11. One consisted of three left-wing parties (57, 23 and 3 members), the other of the remaining parties and groups of the right and centre (43, 24, 8, 5, 4 and 1 members). Essential information about the activities of the parties in parliament can be found in *Folketingstidende – Årbog og Registre* (formerly *Folketingsårbogen*).
12. About the working conditions for small parties before 1973, see Pedersen 1987a: 8–9. After 1973 small parties have become more numerous and therefore, as a collective force, also more powerful.
13. Specialization and division of labour in parliamentary party groups are extensively discussed in Damgaard 1977; 1982; and Damgaard et al. 1979.
14. Thus in 1986–7 eleven members posed 50 percent of 1,690 questions. Only one of them belonged to the largest party. The four most industrious members asked almost 500 questions. They all emanated from the two smallest parties.
15. See Damgaard 1982: 16 for some inconclusive evidence in this respect.
16. These considerations are not based upon systematic empirical research. For a few glimpses by 'insiders', see Møller 1974; and Thorndahl 1984.
17. For more extended discussion, see e.g. Damgaard 1974; and Pedersen 1967; and most recently 1987a.
18. There is fair agreement among Danish political scientists that most of the time

the party system fits a unilinear model quite well. Recent discussions can be found in Nannestad 1986; and Pedersen 1987a.

19. The graphic presentation is almost identical to one proposed by Castles and Mair (1984). It was based upon a left–right placement of parties made by five Danish experts in the early 1980s.

20. The Communist Party (DKP) was represented 1945–60 and again 1973–9; the Left Socialist Party (VS), 1968–71 and 1975–87. Only the Socialist People's Party (SF) has been continuously represented from 1959.

21. For discussion of the Progress Party, see e.g. Pedersen 1987a; 1988.

22. These patterns are discussed at length in Pedersen 1987a. For a discussion of the traditional role of the Radical Liberal Party, see Pedersen 1967.

23. During the periods 1960–4 and 1971–3 a representative of Greenland even served as a member of the cabinet in the capacity of Minister for Greenland Affairs.

24. The Radical Liberal Party traditionally received some support from the Smallholders' Union. This linkage is no longer as important as it was during the first half of this century.

25. For a thorough discussion of party-system change 'the Sartorian way', see Bille 1989, whose conclusions are followed here.

26. The conditions of small parties during electoral campaigns are discussed at greater length in Pedersen 1987a: 28–9; cf. also Pedersen 1982.

27. Thus the findings of Thomsen (1987) indicate that only 15 percent of the voters for major parties switched party between elections, against 50 percent in the small parties, cf. Pedersen 1987b: 340.

28. In mid-1988 it also looks as if the Justice Party is about to stop campaigning. Even the Danish Communist Party has opened up discussions with other (unrepresented) parties about an eventual merger.

6
Fragments from the Pillars: Small Parties in the Netherlands

Paul Lucardie

In a sense, all Dutch parties are small; but some are smaller than others. Pillarization or segmentation of society and politics has resulted in a multi-party system that allows small parties considerable room. Within every pillar dissidents of some sort have at one time or another broken away from the major party to found a small party, because the major party betrayed or compromised its principles; or because the major party refused to renew and adapt itself to modern times. In ecclesiastical terms (typical of Dutch culture) the former dissidents are called *integralists*, the latter modernists or *ecumenicals* (Daalder 1965–6).

Usually, the major parties have tried to ignore these smaller parties and to exclude them from consociational decision-making processes. Thus, the small parties have been practically outside the pillarized system, even if they remained oriented towards their pillar of origin in an ideological sense. They reacted by trying either to reconquer this pillar of origin (usually the *integralist* response) or to break through the pillars (the *ecumenical* strategy). In the 1960s and 1970s, the pillars themselves began to crumble and small parties proliferated. Some of them have managed to consolidate their electorate by building micro-pillars themselves. Others seem to be desperately looking for 'new politics' that might mobilize new (middle-class) voters. However, in the 1980s the three major parties have begun to devour the fragments they left in the two preceding decades.

The numerical definition

If we apply Peter Mair's criterion to all Dutch parties that have existed since 1945, two or three should be classified as large – the Dutch Labour Party (PvdA) and the Catholic People's Party, which merged with two other parties into the Christian Democratic Appeal (CDA) in 1980 – and eight parties would be considered 'small' (see Mair in this volume). However, in the 1980s three of these 'small' parties ceased to exist, whereas one, the Liberal Party (VVD), has won more than 15 percent at every election from 1972 to 1989. At least eight parties would be defined as 'micro-parties' because they fell below 1 percent of the vote on more than three occasions. Nevertheless, two of these parties have also reached peaks of 5 percent and played an important role in the realignment of the Dutch party system (see Table 6.1).

Hence, in the Dutch case, Mair's numerical criterion leads to rather heterogeneous categories; therefore, another, more qualitative definition of 'small' will be used here.

A systemic definition

Dutch political scientists tend to define small or minor parties in a more qualitative or systemic sense: parties that do not belong to the traditional *zuilen* (pillars) which dominated the Dutch political system (Daalder 1965–6: 172; Niezing 1963: 264).[1] The terms 'marginal' or 'micro-parties' are rarely used; they might refer to parties that fail to win any seats in parliament (Lucardie 1986: 72). Thus the category of small parties includes D'66, which won 11 percent of the vote in 1981, as well as the Centre Party which has never gained more than 0.8 percent. Though this double-Dutch conception of small parties may offend the analytical mind of an Anglo-Saxon reader, it seems theoretically more fruitful than a strictly quantitative definition.

The parties outside the pillar system have rarely taken part in government and they have had little impact on the political agenda. Occasionally they might mobilize discontent and encroach on the electorate of the larger parties; but most of the time they attract together no more than 10 or 15 percent of the electorate.

In the 1960s and 1970s the Dutch pillars began to crumble; but even then the Christian Democrats, the Liberals and the Labour Party dominated the political scene. From 1963 to 1972 their share of the popular vote fell from 88 percent to 73 percent; but since then it increased again to 85 percent in 1986. However, as the pillars have ceased to be impenetrable monoliths, the major parties have had to compete more than before with each other as well as with old or new small parties. Hence small parties might develop some competitive or blackmail potential (Sartori 1976: 123). In fact, most of them do try to 'blackmail' one of the large parties by emphasizing their commitment to ideological principles 'betrayed' by the large party.

Thus the Christian Democratic Appeal (CDA) has to compete with three small *integralist* Christian (Protestant) parties; the

Fragments from the pillars: the Netherlands 117

Table 6.1 *Dutch election results, 1946–86*

Party[1]	Percentages of the popular vote at parliamentary elections[2]												
	1946	1948	1952	1956	1959	1963	1967	1971	1972	1977	1981	1982	1986	1989
ARP	12.9	13.2	11.3	9.9	9.4	8.7	9.9	8.6	8.8	merged into CDA				
CHU	7.9	9.2	8.9	8.4	8.1	8.6	8.1	6.3	4.8					
KVP	30.8	31.0	28.7	31.7	31.6	31.9	26.5	21.9	17.7					
CDA										31.9	30.8	29.4	34.6	35.3
PvdA	28.3	25.6	29.0	32.7	30.3	28.0	23.5	24.7	27.3	33.8	28.3	30.4	33.3	31.9
VVD	6.4	8.0	8.8	8.8	12.2	10.3	10.7	10.4	14.4	17.9	17.3	23.1	17.4	14.6
Total large parties	86.3	87.0	86.7	91.5	91.6	87.5	78.7	71.9	73.0	83.6	76.4	82.9	85.3	81.8
D'66										5.4	11.1	4.3	6.1	7.9
CPN	10.6	7.7	6.2	4.8	2.4	2.8	3.6	6.8	4.2	1.7	2.1	1.8	(0.6)	
PSP					1.8	3.0	2.9	3.9	4.5	0.9	2.1	2.3	1.2	4.1
PPR								1.4	1.5	1.7	2.0	1.7	1.3	
SGP	2.1	2.4	2.4	2.3	2.2	2.3	2.0	1.8	4.8	2.1	2.0	1.9	1.8	1.9
GPV			(0.7)	(0.6)	(0.7)	0.8	0.9	2.3	2.2	1.0	0.8	0.8	1.0	1.2
RPF								1.6	1.8		1.2	1.5	0.9	1.0
RKPN										(0.6)	(0.2)	(0.2)		
EVP									0.9	(0.4)	(0.5)	0.7	(0.2)	
DS'70								5.3	4.1	0.7	(0.6)	(0.4)		
KNP		1.3	2.7				4.7							
BP/RVP					(0.7)	2.1		1.1	1.9	0.8	(0.2)	(0.3)	(0.4)	0.9
CP/CD										(0.0)	(0.1)	0.8		
NMP								1.5						
Other parties (which never won seats)	(1.0)	(1.6)	(1.3)	(0.8)	(0.6)	(1.5)	(2.7)	(2.4)	(0.7)	(0.9)	(1.1)	(0.6)	(1.1)	(1.2)
Total small parties (excl. D'66)	13.7	13.0	13.3	8.5	8.4	12.5	16.8	21.3	22.8	11.0	12.5	12.9	8.6	10.3
Total	100	100	100	100	100	100	100	100	100	100	100	100	100	100

[1] Abbreviations are explained in Appendix 6.1.   [2] Percentages in brackets = without seats in parliament.

Labour Party (PvdA) also faces small and radical competitors; and the Liberals have been attacked from both the right and the left, by the *ecumenical* Democrats '66 (D'66) and by the hybrid Farmers' Party. In the terminology of Gordon Smith, most smaller Dutch parties should be regarded as 'marginal' or extremist; only D'66 and Democratic Socialists '70, perhaps briefly the Political Party of Radicals, can be called 'hinge parties', whereas the short-lived ethnocentric Centre Party might be seen as a 'detached' party (see Smith in this volume).

As a whole, therefore, the systemic approach seems particularly applicable to the Dutch case.

Small-party families

Almost all families are represented by small parties in the Netherlands:

1 *Liberal* The Democrats '66 are usually seen as a left-wing or radical liberal party, even if they defined themselves as 'pragmatic' and opposed to all ideologies in 1966. Since the late 1970s, however, their leaders have not shunned away from the label 'liberal' (Terlouw 1976; Van Mierlo 1988).

2 *Agrarian* A Farmers' Party (Boerenpartij) was founded in 1958 to represent the interests of farmers who objected to state intervention; but in the 1960s this vaguely Christian, conservative populist party attracted many voters in poor urban areas; in 1981 it changed its name into Rightwing People's Party, but failed to win any seats in parliament; it could be classified as 'extreme right' as well.

3 *Extreme left* This family consists of the Communist Party of the Netherlands (CPN), the Pacifist Socialist Party (PSP) and to some extent the Political Party of Radicals (PPR), which was founded in 1968 by radical Catholics, but secularized during the 1970s; yet it will be classified here as a 'new politics' or 'new left' party. To a lesser extent, the CPN and PSP have moved also in that direction.

4 *Extreme right* The Boerenpartij of the 1960s and 1970s could be regarded as a case here; probably also the ephemeral Centre Party, which won one parliamentary seat in 1982; as well as its offshoot, the Centre Democrats, which entered parliament in 1989.

5 *Ecologist/new politics* The PPR in the 1970s and 1980s; attempts to establish a Green Party have not been very successful during the 1980s. The PSP, CPN and D'66 have also

adopted ecologist or green issues and a 'new politics' style, to some extent. In 1989 the CPN, PSP and PPR joined the Green Left alliance.
6 *Regionalist/nationalist* The Frisian National Party, represented only in the provincial parliament of Frisia; the Centre Party could be called nationalist, in a different, ethnocentric sense.
7 *Socialist* The Democratic Socialists '70, resulting from a right-wing split from the Labour Party in 1970, renamed Democratic Social Party in 1982 and disbanded in 1983; their socialism was always in doubt, but the party failed to develop a new ideology – like the PSDI in Italy, the Centre Democrats in Denmark and the Social Democrats in Britain.
8 *Religious* The right-wing fundamentalist Reformed Political Association (Gereformeerd Politiek Verbond, GPV), Reformed Political Federation (RPF) and Reformed Political Party (Staatkundig Gereformeerde Partij, SGP); more ephemeral proved the Roman Catholic Party of the Netherlands (RKPN), which held a seat in parliament from 1972 to 1977; and the left-wing Evangelical People's Party, which held one parliamentary seat from 1982 to 1986. This category seems typical of the Netherlands.

Because of the religious factor, the Dutch party system cannot be considered completely one-dimensional. Even so, voters place all parties fairly consistently on a left–right scale (see Figure 6.1).

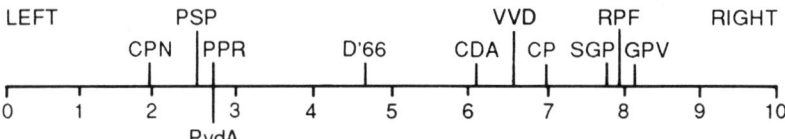

CDA	Christian Democratic Appeal	PSP	Pacifist Socialist Party
CP	Centre Party	PvdA	Labour Party
CPN	Communist Party (Neths)	RPF	Reformed Political Federation
D'66	Democrats '66	SGP	Political Reformed Party
GPV	Reformed Political Association	VVD	People's Party for Freedom and Democracy
PPR	Political Party of Radicals		

Figure 6.1 *Position of small and large parties on the left–right dimension in the Netherlands, 1986 (van Holsteyn et al. 1987)*

Life-cycles

The number and variety of small parties in the Netherlands make interesting material for Pedersen's typology of party lifespans (Pedersen 1982 and in this volume).

A remarkable difference can be observed here between secular and religious parties: the former tend to lead shorter lives, with one or two electoral peaks, whereas the latter seem to enjoy eternal life, with hardly any ups or downs. The SGP, for example, founded in 1918, has never attracted more than 2.5 percent or less than 1.8 percent of the popular vote. These stable and loyal voters are also highly organized – 13 percent of them carried a membership card in 1986 – and pillarized: they belong to particular Calvinist churches, they read a particular newspaper, they send their children to a particular Calvinist school and to Calvinist youth organizations, and so forth (Janse 1985).

Secular right-wing parties such as the Centre Party and Democratic Socialists '70 are very different: both peaked one or two years after they were founded, but fell below the threshold of representation within a decade. The populist and vaguely Christian, semi-secular Boerenpartij experienced two electoral peaks and lasted about twenty years.

Secular left-wing parties may lead a longer, but not a quieter, life. The Communist Party fell from 10.6 percent of the vote in 1946 to 2.4 in 1959, climbed again to 4.5 in 1972 and fell to 0.6 (below the electoral threshold) in 1986. Democrats '66 also had several electoral peaks.

From Figure 6.2 it can be inferred that the 1960s and early 1970s were peak years for small parties. They could benefit from the 'winds of change' – weakening religious and class ties and social and cultural unrest, resulting in electoral dealignment (Andeweg 1982; Irwin and Dittrich 1984). In the 1970s four new parties entered parliament; together with existing small parties the new parties won 37 out of 150 seats in 1971 as well as in 1972. At the same time, however, twenty other parties took part in the elections without winning any seats. Since 1972 the number of marginal parties (parties without seats) has gone up and down rather erratically, while the number of small parties and their share of seats in parliament have declined. Though the threshold of representation is not very high in the Netherlands – 0.67 percent of the number of valid votes (nationwide) suffices to win a seat in parliament – it proves too high for most new parties. In the 1980s only three new parties entered parliament; by 1989 only one of them, the Reformed Political Federation, was still there.

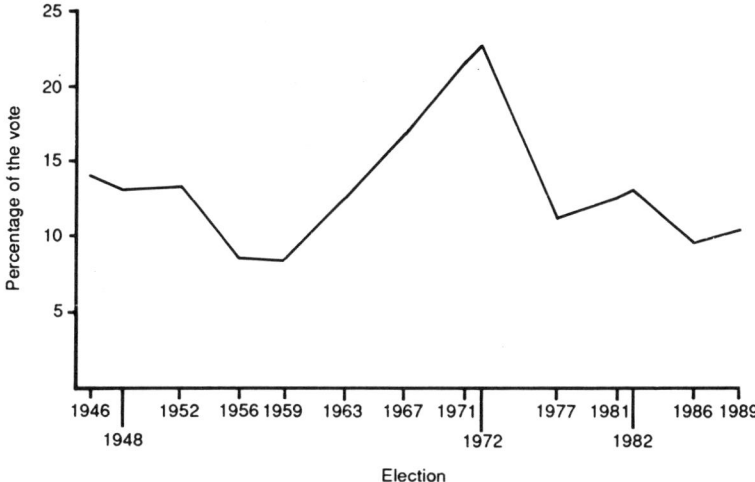

Figure 6.2 *Small parties' share of the popular vote at parliamentary elections, 1946–89*

New parties were set up before every election; the thresholds of declaration and authorization were not very high either: one had to register at the National Board of Elections (Kiesraad) the name of the party or list, then collect twenty-five signatures of electors and deposit 1,000 Dutch guilders for each one of the nineteen voting districts in which one can present a list of candidates.[2] Yet some parties remain stuck between registration and participation at elections: in 1989, for example, 64 parties were registered, of which only 9 obtained one or more seats at the parliamentary elections, 16 presented unsuccessful candidates, but 39 did not take part at all – either because they had tried their luck before and were leading a dormant existence, or because they were waiting for a better occasion, or for other reasons (Lucardie 1990: 127).

Whilst many parties pass the thresholds of declaration and authorization and a few the threshold of representation, very few small parties have crossed the threshold of relevance since 1946. Democrats '70, established in 1970, rose to relevance as early as 1971 when they won eight seats and joined a coalition government; but in 1972 the party bolted the coalition and lost votes as well as relevance. A new coalition was formed which included two other small parties, Democrats '66 and the Political Party of Radicals; this lasted until 1977. The PPR became irrelevant in terms of coalition potential when it shifted to the left and lost more than half of its electorate in the 1970s; but D'66 was back in the government benches from 1981 to 1982 and was still regarded as a potential coalition partner by the major parties in the late 1980s.

Relationship with the state

In the Dutch pillarized and consociational political system, small parties are almost by definition excluded from government. The exceptions have already been mentioned above. In a period of rapid change, dealignment or depillarization, fast-growing small parties were allowed to join government coalitions: DS'70 in 1971, D'66 and the PPR in 1972. All three could be classified as 'hinge' parties at the time – even if the PPR was already shifting towards the (extreme) left in 1972. By 1989 the PPR was generally seen as a permanent opposition party, not unlike the Communist Party or the Pacifist Socialist Party.

Thus, most small parties in the Netherlands are permanently in opposition to the state, at least at the national level. Many of them do take part in local government, however. Together they can boast aldermen (*wethouders*) in about 10 percent of all municipalities. Moreover, 4 percent of all burgomasters – appointed by the national government, more or less in proportion to their party's share of the electorate – carry membership cards of small parties (Vulperhorst 1986: 37). There are exceptions here: the PSP has always refused on principle to have its members appointed burgomaster; Boerenpartij members were not appointed either. Both might be considered anti-system parties, ideologically opposed to the state – condemned as a stronghold of capitalism, militarism and patriarchy by the former, and as a bureaucratic Leviathan by the latter. Members of both parties have been elected aldermen in a few cases, nevertheless, but not without difficulties or conflicts. Since 1982 the Communist Party can claim a burgomaster, in the north-eastern town of Beerta, where the party won 53 percent of the vote at municipal elections in the same year.

Officially, the state apparatus should not discriminate against members of small parties who apply for a position. A ban on Communists in the civil service was lifted in 1969. However, even in 1979 an engineer was refused a position as inspector at the state-owned Post, Telephone and Telegraph Company when a security check by the Dutch Intelligence Agency revealed that he had been a member of the CPN for two years. Parliament disapproved of the Postmaster's decision, however. Even anti-system parties are allowed free time on radio and television in the Netherlands and are entitled to state subsidies for political education, youth programmes and scientific research. For example, in 1986 each small party could claim between 84,000 and 123,000 Dutch guilders for scientific research (depending on the size of the party) and between 41,000 and 94,000 for political education and training (Koole 1986: A1100/107). With Marcuse (1969) one might interpret this as repressive tolerance. Yet there are limits to Dutch tolerance: members of the ethnocentric Centre Party in municipal councils are often ignored or boycotted by their colleagues. The marginal Netherlands People's Union (Nederlandse Volksunie) was declared illegal in 1978 because it promoted racial discrimination and hatred (Bouw et al. 1981: 101). The People's Union had never won any seats anywhere, but its militant youth squads exercised some influence in the streets of major cities. Less marginal leftist parties have acquired some influence by mobilizing people in actions against nuclear missiles, nuclear energy and, around 1970, United States intervention in Vietnam. The Boerenpartij started as a movement of farmers, which organized boycotts and demonstrations against the corporatist Board of Agriculture (Landbouwschap).

Thus one might agree with Herzog (1987) that even small parties without coalition or competitive potential may have some impact on the political system by expressing discontent outside the conventional arena, testing the rules of the game. Perhaps one should define this as mobilization potential, rather than blackmail potential. Small or marginal parties with mobilization potential attract attention from the media (as well as from other parties) which may help them to win seats in parliament.

Once elected to parliament, representatives from small parties have basically three options: (a) total opposition to 'the system', presenting radical alternatives or Utopian models; (b) limited opposition, often focussed on one particular (governmental) party, reminding this party of its principles, acting as its (external) conscience; (c) articulation of marginal or diffuse interests, representing weakly organized minorities which are neglected by larger parties.

Extremist anti-system parties might prefer the first option; their ideology justifies an outright rejection of the political system, including its rules of the game. Instead of parliamentary democracy they advocate either a more authoritarian system (theocracy, corporatism, fascist dictatorship) or a more direct democracy (workers' councils, soviets, communes). This kind of radical opposition has become rare in the Dutch case. The Pacifist Socialists still favour a direct democracy based on workers' councils, and very orthodox Calvinists still cherish theocracy deep in their bosoms, but practically all of them respect the rules of parliamentary democracy. In parliament they devote most attention to one 'reference party', often the party they once broke away from. Confronting its day-to-day policies full of compromises with its lofty principles, they hope either to correct the practice of the reference party or to rob it of its voters. The second function of small parliamentary parties can be combined with the third one. Thus Calvinist members of parliament may defend the interests of small municipalities and of fishermen, whereas Pacifist Socialist, Communist and Radical MPs often speak up for students, conscientious objectors, ethnic minorities or gay people. For this purpose they table motions and file questions in large numbers; parliamentarians of the PSP, PPR and D'66 have especially distinguished themselves in these activities (Visscher 1988).

Relationship between parties

As long as the Dutch party system remains partly pillarized or segmented, competition is not open but more or less structured (Irwin and van Holsteyn 1988). While the small left-wing parties CPN, PPR and PSP compete mostly with the Labour Party, the small Protestant parties GPV, RPF and SGP compete with the Christian Democratic Appeal for Protestant voters. In both cases the small parties try to outdo their reference parties in their commitment to progressive or Christian ideals. The major parties are accused of betraying or compromising their principles and deluding their loyal voters. In a way, the small parties act as the external conscience of the major parties.

The major party often tries to silence its external conscience by crushing the small parties. In recent years, the Labour Party has nearly succeeded in eliminating its left-wing rivals from parliament. But the price was high: the PvdA was seen as extremely leftist by the electorate, hence it might have deterred centrist voters (van der Eijk 1987). The radicalization and renewal of the PvdA in the late 1960s, polarization against Christian democratic parties of the centre in the 1970s and vague suggestions of a 'united left' coalition government in the early 1980s – which proved rather unrealistic – contributed to this leftist image. Since 1982, however, the Labour Party has tried to regain the centre and aims for a coalition with either the CDA or the VVD and possibly also D'66, but not with the PPR, PSP or CPN. At the 1986 elections, it even refused a tactical electoral alliance – linking party lists in order to maximize the number of seats for all parties – with the small left-wing parties. Abandoned by the PvdA, the small leftist parties have begun to cooperate more with each other. At the elections for the European Parliament in 1984 they presented a common list, which managed to win two seats; in 1989 this form of co-operation was continued. Within each party groups or factions emerged that pressed for a closer alliance or a merger, whereas more orthodox or *integralist* wings opposed this. At the 1986 parliamentary election the three parties linked their lists but refused a closer alliance, let alone a merger. At the 1989 parliamentary elections the three parties agreed to present a common list – including also the marginal Evangelical People's Party and independent candidates – under the label 'Green Left'. It is very likely that they will merge within a few years.

The Christian Democratic Appeal proved less effective in crushing its small competitors than the Labour Party did. On the contrary, it seems to aim more for secular right-of-centre voters than for fundamentalist Christians (Irwin and van Holsteyn 1988). As the small Protestant parties appeal only to voters that belong to orthodox churches or church groups, their potential electorate is limited anyhow: about 12 percent – half of the maximum potential of the leftist parties (Niemöller and van der Eijk 1984). Before the 1986 elections there was some talk about co-operation between the CDA, GPV, RPF and/or SGP – named 'the Staphorst coalition' after the village of Staphorst, one of the main strongholds of orthodox Calvinism in the Netherlands. Yet this option seems as unlikely as a 'united left' coalition. Like the small left-wing parties, the Protestant parties began to co-operate in the 1980s, both at the local and at the European level. Together they gained one seat in the European Parliament in 1984 and again in 1989. Yet there is resistance against a merger or even a loose federation, especially within the GPV and the most conservative wing of the SGP (van de Ven and Vink 1986).

The other small parties in the Netherlands lack a reference party. To some extent D'66 competes with the Liberal Party (VVD) and claims to have taken over the progressive liberal heritage from the more conservative Liberals (van Mierlo 1988). At the same time, however, the Democrats compete with the Labour Party – which has moved towards the centre and begun to show sympathy for liberal ideas as well. D'66 could even attract CDA voters. This may reflect the position of a hinge party. Democratic Socialists '70 occupied a similar position in the 1970s, though the party was set up to compete mainly with the Labour Party; by 1974 it was torn between two wings, one still oriented towards the PvdA, the other more towards the centre (Schonewille 1983: 32–9). But even a fringe party like the Boerenpartij appealed to voters from all pillars and parties, Labour, Christian Democrats and Liberals (Sociaal-Wetenschappelijk Instituut van de Vrije Universiteit, Afdeling

Politicologie 1967: 13). The same applies to the Centre Party. All these parties lack the stability of 'external conscience' (satellite) parties. They fulfil other functions: articulating and diffusing discontent, exploring new ideas or reviving old ones and representing particular interests (Herzog 1987; Lucardie 1986).

Relationship with society

According to Rochon, new small parties that respond to changing cleavage structures in society ('mobilizers') are more likely to win and maintain seats in Dutch parliaments than (new) small parties which 'challenge the legitimacy of existing parties on their own turf by claiming that they no longer properly represent the interests of their support base' (Rochon 1985: 421). The latter, called 'challengers' by Rochon, might seem identical with the 'external conscience' and *integralist* parties distinguished above. However, in our view small parties could challenge and mobilize at the same time. Rochon's operationalization of the two categories seems rather arbitrary; without specifying his criteria he defines D'66, the PSP, GPV, Boerenpartij, RPF, PPR and Centre Party as mobilizers, and only DS'70, the EVP and the RKPN as challengers. But the RPF and GPV 'challenge' the Christian Democratic Appeal as much as the EVP and RKPN did. A look at the cleavages to which (new or old) small parties respond might help to clarify this problem.

The cleavages that have shaped Dutch politics are religion and class. Regionalism, race or ethnicity and cultural values have played only a minor role. Until recently, religion was the most salient cleavage.

Religion
The first modern party in the Netherlands was the Anti-Revolutionary Party (founded in 1879), which was closely associated with the Calvinist Reformed Churches (Gereformeerde Kerken). More orthodox and pietistic Calvinists, associated with smaller reformed denominations, considered this party too secular and established the Staatkundig Gereformeerde Partij (SGP) in 1918. The other two Protestant parties GPV and RPF are associated with equally fundamentalist but less pietistic denominations. The RPF resulted partly from the fact that the GPV shows a clear preference for only one church – the Vrijgemaakt Gereformeerde Kerk (Free Reformed Church). Its modern style and its connections with the Evangelical Broadcasting System make the RPF somewhat similar to the United States Moral Majority or Christian New Right. Its religious base seems less homogeneous and solid than those of the GPV and SGP;

the RPF competes with the latter for support from fundamentalist Calvinists but attracts also Protestants from other, more evangelical denominations like Baptists. Ideologically, the three Protestant parties agree on most issues; all three favour a strong and strict Christian state that fights evil (abortion, euthanasia, pornography) but does not interfere too much with the market economy.

Unlike orthodox Protestants, orthodox Catholics have failed to develop a political party in the Netherlands. In 1972 the orthodox Roman Catholic Party of the Netherlands won one seat in parliament, but it began to fall apart soon afterwards and lost its seat in 1977. In 1986 an even more extreme traditionalist Catholic group, 'God with Us' (God met Ons), took part in the elections but failed to obtain more than 0.1 percent of the popular vote. These Catholic parties could not count on support from the Catholic Church hierarchy or from other significant Catholic organizations. As long as traditionalist Catholics are not organized as a denomination or an officially recognized current within the Catholic Church – as their Protestant counterparts are – they will probably not provide a solid base for a political party (Lucardie 1988: 92).

Progressive, modernist Catholics and Protestants face a similar problem in the Netherlands: lacking a distinct denominational base, they have failed to form a stable political party. In 1968 radical Christians from different denominations founded the Political Party of Radicals, which developed into a fairly stable but more and more secular leftist party. In 1981 progressive Christians left the Christian Democratic Appeal and set up the Evangelical People's Party (Evangelische Volkspartij), which won one parliamentary seat in 1982; so far it has managed to maintain its religious identity but not its seat, which was lost in 1986. In 1989 it joined the Green Left alliance. While belonging to different denominations, the members of this very small party seem to share a somewhat chiliastic 'political theology'; they feel inspired by the early Christians who were not yet corrupted by collaboration with worldly powers. Their ideal of a Christian state has more in common with libertarian socialism than with the authoritarian theocracy advocated by the SGP (Evangelische Volkspartij 1983).

Electorally even less successful than progressive Christians are non-Christian religious groups such as the international Humanist Party or local Muslim parties in the Netherlands.

Social class
Next to religion, social class constitutes a salient cleavage in Dutch politics. Roughly speaking, the Labour Party represents the lower classes and the Liberal Party the upper class; only the Christian

Democratic Appeal can be considered a catch-all party in the socio-economic sphere. Naturally, the small leftist rivals/satellites of the Labour Party appeal to the lower classes as well. Recently, however, their appeal seems to have fallen increasingly on deaf ears. Even the Communist Party, traditionally quite strong in proletarian quarters of Amsterdam, in industrial towns north of Amsterdam and in poor rural areas in the north-east of the country, has lost its old working-class base in recent years. Within the party, lawyers, social workers and teachers have replaced the dockers, construction workers and farm hands, but at the price of dramatic electoral losses (Fennema 1988). While the Communist Party has been turning into a new middle-class party during the 1980s, the Pacifist Socialist Party and even more clearly the Political Party of Radicals have always been new middle-class parties. The PSP has attracted workers as well, often in formerly anarchist areas, but has always been dominated by intellectuals (*Ontwapenend* 1982: 84, 221, 248; Platvoet 1985). The PPR tried to appeal to Christian workers, but soon realized it would mobilize 'the partisans of the poor' rather than the poor themselves (van Ginneken 1976: 44, 152). Hence by 1990 the only truly proletarian Dutch party may be the marginal Socialist Party, originally a Maoist splinter from the CPN, which has won a number of seats in municipal and provincial councils, but not (yet) in parliament (Voerman 1987).

Like industrial workers, farmers seem to lose political influence in a post-industrial society. Since the 1930s, farmers' parties have tried to articulate protest against the process of modernization. During the 1950s, disgruntled farmers rebelled against the corporatist reorganization of agriculture in the Netherlands; in 1958 their movement was turned into a political party, the Boerenpartij. Within a few years, its abrasive and often demagogic leader, Koekoek – himself a small farmer – became a national symbol for protest against government bureaucracy. Thus in 1966 the party won 6.7 percent of the popular vote at provincial elections; not only in rural areas, but also in working-class as well as middle-class urban districts. Yet it failed to consolidate a distinct electoral base and to develop a coherent programme or an effective party organization. Koekoek's maverick personality proved capable only of attracting media attention but not of leading a party organization; practically all his active supporters quarrelled and broke with him at some point. Nevertheless the party retained one or more seats in parliament until 1981 (Noöij 1969; Lucardie 1988).

Like workers and farmers, small businessmen have made attempts to organize a political party in the Netherlands. In 1971 a Dutch Middle-Class Party (Nederlandse Middenstandspartij) won two seats in parliament; but in 1972 it lost both and disappeared from the political scene. One of its founders made another attempt in 1986, but obtained merely 0.2 percent of the popular vote.

Hence, one might conclude that class cleavages have lost some of their salience with respect to small Dutch parties.

Region
Unlike religion and class, region does not provide a significant cleavage in Dutch politics. At provincial elections, regionalist parties have proved successful only in Frisia (Friesland) and Limburg. The Frisian National Party not only defends regional interests, but strives for a federal state in the Netherlands and for recognition of Frisian as an official language (Fryske Nasjonale Party 1982; Lucardie et al. 1987).

Race/ethnicity
Like region, race or ethnicity is not seen as a significant factor in Dutch politics. Yet in 1982 the ethnocentric Centre Party (Centrumpartij) won one seat in the parliament with slogans like 'Stop immigration' and 'Maintain Dutch culture'. In 1984 it obtained 2.6 percent of the popular vote at the European elections, campaigning under the slogan 'Europe for the Europeans'. In the same year, however, internal strife began to destroy the party from within. In 1986 it lost its parliamentary seat. In the late 1980s the party was still represented in a few municipal councils, but its representatives tended to remain isolated and inactive. Yet in 1989 its former leader, Janmaat, re-entered parliament as leader of a new party, the Centre Democrats.

Values
Perhaps a new cleavage is emerging in the Dutch party system, as in other post-industrial nations: post-materialist versus materialist values. As defined by Inglehart (1977), post-materialist values include preference for self-realization and expression, participatory democracy, ecology and social contacts, whereas materialists prefer law and order, security, economic growth and a strong defence. Van Deth found a correlation between these values and party preferences in the Netherlands: about 90 percent of potential PPR and PSP voters held post-materialist values, compared to about 60 percent of CPN supporters, over 50 percent of Democrats '66, 40 percent of Labour Party supporters and even fewer Christian Democrats or Liberals (van Deth 1984: 189–97). Thus one might regard the PPR and PSP, and to a lesser extent also the CPN and D'66, as 'new politics' parties that articulate post-materialist values. Perhaps one

could even speak of a post-materialist subculture which provides a not very stable but potentially important social base for 'new left' parties or 'new politics' (Lucardie 1980). However, the interpretation of the values cleavage is still a subject of lively academic debate in the Netherlands (Niemöller and van der Eijk 1985).

One might conclude here that small parties need an ideological or sociological niche in order to survive. Few small parties can afford to ignore these cleavages. A difficult case seems to be DS'70: without a distinct social base and with a rather vague ideology – conservatism with a socialist flag, or the other way around? – it occupied one or more seats in parliament from 1971 to 1982. From 1971 to 1972 it was part of a centre-right government coalition. Its temporary success could be attributed to various factors: well-respected leaders, a clear programme (efficient government, inflation control) and perhaps the nostalgia for consociational government among many (former) supporters of the radicalized Labour Party. By 1982 these factors had lost relevance: the leaders had quarrelled and lost respect, and the programme appeared out of date, whereas the Labour Party had shed its radicalism (Verstraaten 1981).

The above conclusion can be supplemented with a few comments on the organization of the small parties and their links with interest groups. The three religious parties SGP, GPV and RPF are formally federations of local electoral associations (*kiesverenigingen*), though their national leaders tend to enjoy considerable authority and are rarely criticized openly. Their membership ratio is very high; often membership of the party is seen as a quasi-religious duty, like church attendance, subscription to a Protestant newspaper and involvement in Protestant social and cultural organizations; in other words, the parties are highly pillarized 'parties of integration' (Neumann 1956: 404–5; Seiler 1984). Formal links with interest groups are rare, but membership and leadership of pillarized organizations often overlap. Thus, for example, members and leaders of Protestant parties have played a part in the anti-abortion movement in the Netherlands. Moreover, RPF leaders have worked for the Evangelical Broadcasting Association (Evangelische Omroep), which counted more than 300,000 members in the 1980s.

The three leftist parties lack this loyal pillarized membership and suffer from high membership turnover. Their organizations are relatively open and democratic: members have many opportunities to take part in discussions, conferences, educational programmes and committee meetings. In their structure, the small leftist parties imitate the large Labour Party; hence they have been described (not without some irony) as 'small mass parties'. Seiler (1984) might call them 'partis de militants'. Until recently, the Communist Party deviated from this pattern and preferred democratic centralism to grass-roots democracy; but since 1980 it has adapted its organization. All three parties attach importance to extra-parliamentary action, contributing actively or passively to direct action against nuclear missiles and nuclear power, for the rights of women and gay people, ethnic minorities and so forth. Hence there exist informal and occasionally formal contacts between the three parties and the so-called new social movements, that is, the feminist movement, the peace movement (in the 1980s especially the Committee against Cruise Missiles), anti-nuclear and ecological groups, squatters and organizations of unemployed people (van der Loo et al. 1984). Links between small leftist parties and trade unions seem rather rare nowadays, although party members may be active within unions, especially the public service union, teachers' unions and the union of workers in food industries. There is no broadcasting association connected with the three left-wing parties in the Netherlands, but the somewhat libertarian (formerly liberal Protestant) VPRO shows some sympathy for radical leftist ideas.

The other small parties lack a clear social base as well as links with interest groups: lacking a stable and large membership, they look more like electoralist parties (Seiler 1984: 'partis d'électeurs') than (small) mass parties. Their membership ratio tends to be low: only 2 percent of D'66 voters and 1 percent of DS'70 voters had joined their party around 1972; no data are available on members of the Boerenpartij, but it was probably more a fan club around leader Koekoek than a (small) mass party (Koole and Voerman 1986).

Conclusion

It seems difficult to generalize about small parties in the Netherlands. There is a wide gap between small Protestant parties such as the SGP and small leftist parties like the PPR; but also between these two and the Boerenpartij. All three might be considered fragments from traditional Dutch pillars, in a historical sense: they were founded by people who belonged to the Protestant or Catholic pillar. Yet they developed in different directions.

The SGP, with its companions the GPV and RPF, tried to purify and protect its Protestant heritage in a fundamentalist or *integralist* sense. It became the core of a new pillar or network of sociocultural and religious organizations, schools, newspapers, youth groups, and so forth. Its supporters tend to join mostly organizations within the pillar, thus isolating themselves from the predominantly secular society. Hence the party is highly organized, disciplined, solid, stable and loyal, but without influence on the political decision-making process.

The PPR, and to a lesser extent its companions the PSP and CPN, tried to renew and change its heritage. In a sense, it could be seen as an *integralist* party of the left; but certainly not as pillarized. And even its integralism seems questionable, as the party turns more towards 'new politics' or the 'new left' than towards 'old left' socialism or social democracy; or in Rochon's terms: it has become a mobilizer rather than a challenger. Its voters, however, continue to regard the social democratic PvdA as serious second choice; in other words, as reference party. The 'new politics' style and post-materialist values which characterize the PPR – and to a lesser extent the PSP, CPN and D'66 – have not yet really crystallized into a new political subculture which would provide a solid social base for the party; perhaps solidity would be inconsistent with 'new politics' anyhow. Hence the 'new left' parties remain unstable, conflict-ridden, dynamic, poorly organized but occasionally influential and 'agenda-setting' factors in the Dutch political system.

The Boerenpartij, finally, failed to develop a clear identity. It got stuck in the process of depillarization, clinging to a traditional, Christian heritage while articulating diffuse populist protest against consociational politics, defending *laissez-faire* liberalism and moral conservatism, appealing to pietistic Calvinist farmers as well as to secular urban workers. It was temporarily united around its leader, Koekoek; but his charisma proved insufficient to build a real party. DS'70 suffered from similar weaknesses, in spite of its different origin; founded by moderate and right-wing members from the PvdA, it remained a hybrid, socialist mainly in name, conservative or pragmatic in practice. Its initial triumph as well as its subsequent collapse were attributed to a great extent to its leader, Drees. In a different context, the same could be said about the much smaller Centre Party.

D'66 seems a different case: clearly depillarized, in style 'new politics', though not quite 'new left'; yet dependent on personal charisma for success (Van Mierlo in 1971, Terlouw in 1981, Van Mierlo again in 1986). It may be the only hinge party, in Smith's terminology; a new middle-class liberal party, similar to the British Liberals, the Italian Republicans, the French Radicals or the US Liberal Democrats – but in the Dutch context it has always been a deviant case, difficult to classify.

The diversity of small parties in the Netherlands reflects, no doubt, the pluralism and fragmentation of the political and social system. Both the electoral system and the 'consociational' political culture facilitate the rise of small parties. However, there are

Fragments from the pillars: the Netherlands 133

repressive aspects to Dutch tolerance. In the first place, small parties which are perceived as outside the pale of consociationalism – Communists during the Cold War, xenophobic groups more recently – may be boycotted or denied certain privileges. In the second place, even the most loyal and 'governmental' small party (the SGP or the GPV, for instance) enjoys very little influence in the national political system. With a few exceptions, small parties have been excluded from government coalitions. In a consociational system each pillar is normally represented by one party; rivals whether *ecumenical* or *integralist* parties, are tolerated but not included in the process of accommodation and decision-making. When consociationalism declined, exceptions were allowed – DS'70 in 1971, D'66 and PPR in 1973, D'66 again in 1981. Since 1981, the major parties have reinforced their grip on Dutch politics again and lost interest in small allies, probably. The small parties may survive only if they have captured a sociological or ideological niche, such as a religious denomination or a post-materialist or alternative subculture. Yet as the motions, questions and criticisms of small party representatives fall on deaf ears in parliament, many of these politicians without power despair and discuss dissolution of their party. Only the Calvinist parties seem immune to (self-)destruction, as they are convinced that, no matter how deaf the masters of this world may be, God will lend them a willing ear.

Notes

1. The fact that both 'small' and 'minor' are translated in Dutch as *klein* may have some significance here.
2. As of 1990 only ten signatures are required for a list in one electoral district, but signers have to be present at the election office of the district: the deposit will be dfl. 25,000 for any new party, regardless of the number of districts it wants to participate in. Furthermore, parties have to be legally incorporated associations (*verenigingen met volledige rechtspersoonlijkheid*) registered with the national Election Board (Elzinga 1989: 101–4, 124–7).

Appendix 6.1   Dutch parties represented in parliament since 1945

ARP	*Anti-Revolutionaire Partij* (Anti-Revolutionary Party) founded in 1879, merged into CDA in 1980.
BP	*Boerenpartij* (Farmers' Party) founded around 1958, renamed *Rechtse Volkspartij* (Rightwing People's Party) in 1981 but disappeared shortly after.
CD	*Centrumdemocraten* (Centre Democrats) split from Centre Party (CP) in 1985.

134 Small parties in Western Europe

CDA	*Christen Democratisch Appèl* (Christian Democratic Appeal) resulted from the merger of ARP, CHU and KVP in 1980.
CHU	*Christelijk Historische Unie* (Christian Historical Union) founded in 1908, merged into CDA in 1980.
CP	*Centrumpartij* (Centre Party) founded in 1980, broke into two parts around 1985: Centre Democrats (CD) and the more radical *Centrumpartij '86* (Centre Party '86): the latter is not represented in parliament.
CPN	*Communistische Partij Nederland* (Communist Party of the Netherlands) founded in 1909 as Social Democratic Party, renamed in 1918; joined *Groen Links* (Green Left) in 1989.
D'66	*Democraten '66* (Democrats '66) founded in 1966.
DS'70	*Democratisch Socialisten '70* (Democratic Socialists '70) broke away from PvdA in 1970, disbanded in 1983.
EVP	*Evangelische Volkspartij* (Evangelical People's Party) founded in 1981 by left-wing Christian Democrats, joined Green Left in 1989.
GPV	*Gereformeerd Politiek Verbond* (Reformed Political Association) broke away from the Anti-Revolutionary Party (ARP) in 1948.
KNP	*Katholieke Nationale Partij* (Catholic National Party) broke away from the Catholic People's Party (KVP) in 1948 but rejoined it in 1955.
KVP	*Katholieke Volkspartij* (Catholic People's Party) since 1945 the name of the major Catholic party which developed in the nineteenth century, merged into the CDA in 1980.
NMP	*Nederlandse Middenstandspartij* (Dutch Middle Class Party) founded in 1970, fell apart in 1972.
PPR	*Politieke Partij Radikalen* (Political Party of Radicals) founded in 1968 by radical members of the Catholic People's Party (KVP) and the Anti-Revolutionary Party, joined Green Left in 1989.
PSP	*Pacifistisch Socialistische Partij* (Pacifist Socialist Party) founded in 1957, joined Green Left in 1989.
PvdA	*Partij van de Arbeid* (Labour Party) resulted from a merger of Social Democrats, Liberal Democrats and left-wing Christian groups in 1946.
RKPN	*Rooms-Katholieke Partij Nederland* (Roman Catholic Party of the Netherlands) founded in 1972, disappeared after 1977.
RPF	*Reformatorische Politieke Federatie* (Reformed Political Federation) founded in 1975.
SGP	*Staatkundig Gereformeerde Partij* (Political Reformed Party) founded in 1918.
VVD	*Volkspartij voor Vrijheid en Democratie* (People's Party for Freedom and Democracy) resulted from a merger of two Liberal groups in 1948.

7
Small Parties in a Small Country: The Belgian Case

Kris Deschouwer

Smallness is in simple terms a matter of size. If one wants to classify political parties according to their smallness or largeness, it surely makes a lot of sense to go for a numerical criterion. But if one turns to international comparisons of the size of political parties, problems start crowding in. One can stick firmly to the numerical yardstick (see Mair in this volume), and it can still be defended as making sense in a comparative perspective. It offers clear-cut divisions and has the advantage of being unambiguous.

Yet, the problem is that while the numbers seem clear, they do not have the same meaning in every country. The Belgian case is very illustrative of this point. If parties with less than 15 percent of the popular vote are to be considered as small political parties, Belgium has only one large party! At the 1987 general election, the largest party, the CVP (the Flemish Christian Democrats), polled 19.5 percent. The numerical division gives a clear answer, but it is a division that in this case loses a lot of its substance. What is the ultimate use of a criterion of classification that does not classify at all? What is the use of going into further details on the political roles of small parties in a country where almost all the parties are small?

This chapter aims to deal explicitly with this problem. While searching for small political parties in Belgium, and describing their role within the Belgian party system, we have to return to the problem of definition.

The fractionalization of the Belgian party system

The difficulty of distinguishing between large and small parties in Belgium is due to the very high degree of fractionalization of the party system. Figure 7.1 shows the evolution of the fractionalization in parliament (the Lower House) since 1946. After a relatively normal period immediately following the Second World War, the fractionalization index then sky-rocketed. Since 1968 it has not dropped below 0.80. This high fractionalization is simply a matter of a

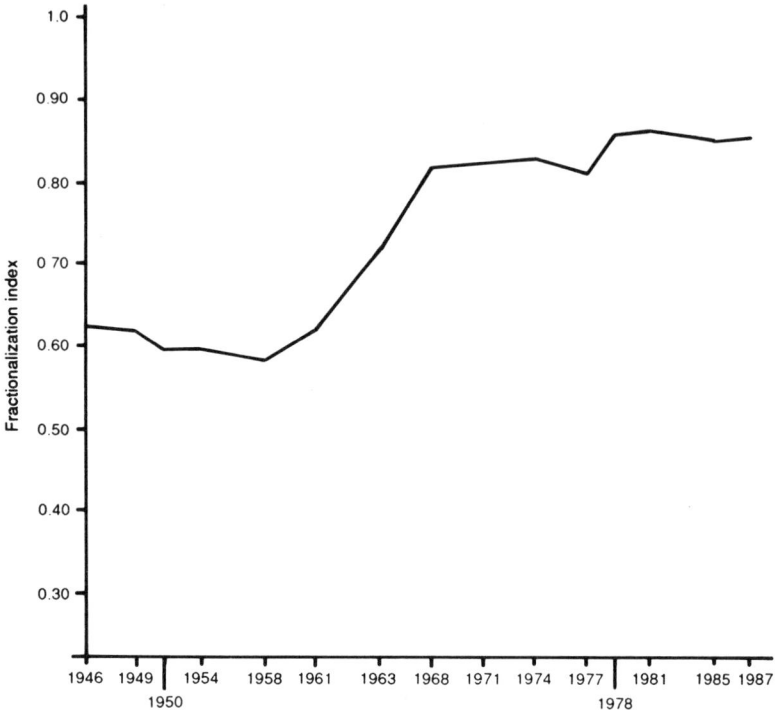

Figure 7.1 *The evolution of the fractionalization of the Belgian parliament since 1946 (Lower House)*

growing number of parties being represented in parliament. The reasons for this proliferation are fairly easy to find: it is above all the linguistic problem that has dominated Belgian politics in recent decades. It is therefore necessary to explain historical background in order to relate small parties in Belgium to the linguistic cleavage and hence put our subject in context.

The predominant linguistic cleavage
At the beginning of this century, Belgium had a rather stable three-party system. Two of the parties were larger: the Christian Democrats and the Socialists polled between 35 percent and 40 percent, while the third party, the Liberals, usually polled some 15 percent of the vote. Up to 1919 the political debate had been centred on religious and economic conflicts. From 1919 a fourth party entered the scene: the Flemish nationalist Frontpartij. The linguistic problem was then becoming quite important. It would give birth to several new parties, and ultimately be the cause of the death of the three original Belgian political parties as they were.

When Belgium reached independence in 1830, it was governed by a French-speaking élite, although the majority (some 60 percent) of the inhabitants were Flemish, that is, Dutch-speaking. Their part of the country, the North, was not so important at that time. It was a poor and largely rural area. The South, where the French-speaking Walloons lived, was much more important. That region was one of the first in Europe to industrialize.

The difference between North and South was not only a matter of language. The North was (and still is) predominantly Catholic. The Catholic Party held all the parliamentary seats in the Flemish regions. The Liberals had only some support in the South, and when the Workers' Party sent representatives to the parliament, they all came from the industrial Walloon regions. In Flanders a movement of protest slowly came into being, demanding the recognition of Dutch as an official language within the Belgian state, and later a federalization of the Belgian state, which would mean some political autonomy for the Flemings. Their demands were mostly denied, but the extension of the suffrage made the Flemish majority too important to ignore any longer. So by 1919 the linguistic problem was there to stay. The situation in Brussels, the capital, made this regional conflict even more complicated. The city had been a Flemish city, but it very rapidly Frenchified, due to the immigration of French-speaking white-collar workers involved in the ever expanding central administration, and due to the greater prestige of the French language and the better chances for upward mobility given to French-speakers in this country where French was the language of government.

It was in Brussels that the first dissidence within the traditional parties occurred. Flemish Liberals and Flemish Catholics presented separate lists in Brussels for the elections of 1919. They were not very successful, however. In that same year there was also for the first time a Flemish nationalist party that presented candidates for parliament. It was called the Frontpartij, referring to the war front, where many Flemish soldiers had given their lives but had to serve under officers who did not speak or understand their language. Some of the Flemish Nationalists had collaborated with the Germans during the First World War, trying to achieve some changes that had been refused before the war. A radical wing within the Flemish movement even proclaimed an independent Flemish state in 1917, and formed its own government. The programme of the postwar Frontpartij, however, was not that radical. The party won 2.6 percent of the vote in 1919, which meant five seats in parliament. It is important to note that a system of proportional representation was adopted (to prevent a too rapid growth of the

Socialists and to prevent a too rapid decline of the Liberals). There is no formal electoral threshold, which makes it fairly easy for new parties to win seats in parliament.

The party programme of the Frontpartij became more radical during the 1920s and the 1930s. This led the more moderate nationalists to leave the party, and to strive for the Flemish cause from within the traditional parties. Much progress was made. Dutch was now recognized as an official language in Belgium and education in the northern part of the country was in Dutch. Brussels nevertheless became more and more a city where the normal language was French.

The party-political development of Flemish nationalism slowly evolved towards a more radically separatist and much more explicitly Catholic movement, and during the 1930s the party openly sympathized with Nazi ideology. It rose to 7.1 percent of the vote at the 1936 elections, which meant about 10 percent of the Flemish vote. The party, which changed its name into Vlaams-Nationaal Verbond (Flemish National Union) or VNV, welcomed the German invasion in 1940, and managed to be recognized by the Germans as the only representative of the Flemish population. Lots of Flemish young men were persuaded to join the German army to go and fight against Bolshevism. This ideological evolution towards Fascism, and this open collaboration with the Germans during the Second World War, would seriously compromise the Flemish movement in the future (there is today still a Fascist wing within the Flemish movement, claiming the preservation of the purity of the Flemish race, whatever that may be).

This certainly does not mean that all the Belgian Fascists before and during the Second World War were Flemings. There was a French-speaking party named REX, lead by Léon Degrelle, and this party reached 11.5 percent of the vote (concentrated in Brussels) in 1936. It was seriously defeated in 1939, but Léon Degrelle played a major role during the war. He also gathered soldiers to fight in the German army.

REX did not reappear after the war. A new Flemish party was created in 1949, but it was not very successful. Another attempt was made in 1954. This time one seat in parliament was won. From that time, the Flemish Nationalists never again disappeared from parliament. The party, now named the Volksunie (the People's Union), grew rapidly to enjoy some 10 percent of the vote, which is about 15 percent of the Flemish vote. A dissident group, the Vlaams Blok, was created in 1978. It is a more radical right-wing party, claiming a still greater autonomy for the Flemish state, and advocating the expulsion of non-European immigrants living in Belgium.

In the early 1960s, a claim for more political autonomy could also be heard in the south of the country. The motivation there was not in the first place a matter of language or religion. It was an economic problem. After the Second World War a lot of new industries were created in Flanders, while the southern part of the country slowly de-industrialized. Europe's oldest industrial region was declining, and still is today. Flanders was now the richer part of the country. Furthermore, Flemish élites were clearly aware of this situation and tried to direct economic policy towards an even greater expansion of Flanders. The emancipation of Flanders forced the Walloons (the demographic minority) to react against possible political and economic discrimination.

There is no such thing as a 'Walloon movement', similar to the Flemish movement. In the first place, the Walloon movement, or the Walloon reaction, lacks the tradition of the Flemish movement. It is a movement that originated in the 1950s and 1960s. The movement is not rooted in a linguistic or cultural nationalism. It is more explicitly political and economic. While the Flemish movement was and is inspired by the Catholic religion (the dominant religion and political ideology in Flanders), the Walloon reaction grew out of the Walloon wing of the Socialist Party (the former Workers' Party) and of the socialist trade union. As a political party it never reached the importance and the impact of the Flemish nationalists. The Rassemblement Wallon (Walloon Mobilization) could only play a significant political role through its association with the Francophone party created in Brussels.

The Francophone reaction in Brussels was much more important than Walloon nationalism. This reaction, the Front des Francophones (FDF), grew out of a large protest movement against the linguistic laws of 1963. These laws made bilingualism a condition for access to higher positions in the national administration and to local (communal) positions within Brussels that involved social interaction with the public. The success of the FDF was tremendous. It caused a real impact in Brussels. In no time it controlled no less than 40 percent of the vote cast in Brussels, on a programme for a federalization of the country, within which Brussels would be an autonomous and Francophone region. At the national level this electoral result did not mean that much. As can be seen in Table 7.1 (below), the FDF and the Rassemblement Wallon (RW) together reached a maximum tally of 11.2 percent in 1971. The RW fielded candidates in Wallonia and the FDF fielded candidates in Brussels. In fact they acted as one single party. Today the RW has completely disappeared, while the FDF is reduced to a meagre 1.2 percent of the vote.

Much more important, however, than the electoral evolution of these three regional parties, one in Flanders, one in Wallonia and one in Brussels, is their political impact, and the influence they had on the three traditional parties. It is not only the rise of these new parties that caused the fractionalization of the Belgian party system (the maximum score of all regional parties together was 22.3 percent in 1971), but also their effect on the other parties. However, it is hard to tell if the problems within the three traditional national parties were directly caused by the appearance of the regionalist parties. Maybe it is more plausible to state that the ever recurring linguistic and regional conflicts opened up the possibilities for some electoral success for regionalist parties, and at the same time made the survival of the national parties difficult. The Christian Democratic Party split into two separate parties in 1968, after the troubles at the University of Louvain (this was a bilingual university, located in Flanders, and the French-speaking part of it was forced to create a new Francophone university in Wallonia, the so-called 'Louvain-La-Neuve'). Three years later the Liberal Party split, and finally in 1978 divorce was consummated in the Socialist family. Ever since then Belgium has had no more national political parties (except for the very small Communist Party).

In Brussels the fate of the traditional parties was even worse. There, the existing local party structure was really torn apart. Catholics, Liberals and Socialists now sometimes each fielded three separate lists: a Francophone list, a Flemish list and a bilingual list, put forward by the last and desparate Belgian nostalgics. Meanwhile the Front des Francophones devoured them all. In 1974, the votes for the three traditional families (at least six electoral lists), taken together, could no longer constitute a 50 percent majority in Brussels.

The other small parties
It is therefore clear that the most important new (and small) parties in Belgium are linguistic parties. The linguistic cleavage is the one and almost only cause of the high fractionalization of the party system. It is a political evolution that is idiosyncratic to the Belgian system. Other developments, like the creation of a Communist Party and the rise of a Green Party, also occurred in Belgium, but their impact was very low, compared to the impact of the linguistic cleavage.

The Belgian Communist Party was founded in 1924. It won two seats at its first attempt at legislative elections in 1925, with 1.6 percent of the vote. Its electoral score went up to 6 percent in 1936 and 5.4 percent in 1939. The party reached its highest peak during the first years after the war. It held 12.3 percent of the vote in 1946,

Small parties in a small country: Belgium   141

Table 7.1 Electoral results of Belgian parties since 1919 (parties represented in parliament)

Election	Catholics Flem.	Catholics Wall.	Socialists Flem.	Socialists Wall.	Liberals Flem.	Liberals Wall.	Flem. Nat.	Wall. Nat.	Comm.	REX	Flem. Greens	Wall. Greens	RAD/UDRT	Rest
1919	36.8		36.6		17.6		2.6							3.0
1921	41.3		34.8		17.8		3.0							3.0
1925	38.6		39.4		14.6		3.9		1.6					1.8
1929	38.5		36.0		16.6		6.3		1.9					0.7
1932	38.6		37.1		14.3		5.9		2.8					1.3
1936	28.8		32.1		12.4		7.1		6.0	11.5				2.0
1939	32.7		30.2		17.2		8.3		5.4	4.4				1.8
1946	42.5		31.6		8.9				12.3					4.3
1949	43.6		29.8		15.3		2.1		7.5					1.9
1950	47.7		34.5		11.2				4.8					1.8
1954	41.1		37.3		12.1		2.2		3.6					3.5
1958	46.5		35.8		11.0		2.0		1.9					2.8
1961	41.5		36.7		12.3		3.5		3.1					2.9
1965	34.5		28.3		21.6		6.7		4.6					2.1
1968	22.3	9.4	28.0		20.9		9.8	2.2[2]	3.3					0.1
1971	21.9	8.2	27.2		9.5	7.2	11.1	5.9[2]	3.3					0.7
1974	23.3	9.1	26.7		10.4	6.0	10.2	11.2[2]	3.0					0.2
1977	26.2	9.8	27.0		8.5	7.0	10.0	10.5[2]	3.2					2.3
1978	26.1	10.1	12.4	13.0	10.4	6.0	8.4[1]	7.1[2]	2.1				0.9	3.0
1981	19.3	7.1	12.4	12.7	12.9	8.6	10.9[1]	7.3[2]	3.3		2.3	2.2	2.7	2.4
1985	21.3	8.0	14.6	13.8	10.7	10.2	9.3[1]	4.2[2]	2.3		3.7	2.5	1.2	2.3
1987	19.5	8.0	14.9	15.7	11.5	9.4	9.9[1]	1.2	1.2		4.5	2.6	0.1	2.9

[1] The votes for the more radical Vlaams Blok (holding one seat) are included.
[2] This is the sum of the votes obtained by the Walloon Rally (RW) and by the Brussels Francophone Front (FDF).

which meant twenty-three seats and participation in the national government until 1947. After that the party declined to some 3 to 4 percent of the vote, and it lost its importance in Belgian politics. In 1985 the Communists finally disappeared from the national parliament. They managed, however, not to be torn apart by linguistic problems!

There has been one other party that was created alongside the social and economic cleavage. In 1978 a bilingual anti-tax party called 'Respect for Work and Democracy' (RAD/UDRT) was born. The party attracted most of its voters in Brussels. It gained one seat in the Lower House in 1978, three seats in 1981 and again one seat in 1985. Now, however, the party has ceased to exist.

Since the early 1980s Belgium has also had two new green parties. The existence of these two parties does not reflect ideological divergences. It only means that there is a Flemish Green Party called 'Anders Gaan Leven' ('For a Different Way of Life') or AGALEV, and a Walloon Green Party called ECOLO. The two parties have fielded candidates at legislative elections since 1981. They are both growing slowly but steadily. In 1987, the Flemish party polled 4.5 percent of the vote (six seats), while the Walloon party gained 2.6 percent (three seats).

Small and large: the numerical approach

This short historical overview of the Belgian party system during the 1960s, 1970s and 1980s leaves a first impression of some chaos. However, a classification of all these parties according to their size over time should be able to help, using the numerical criterion proposed by Peter Mair in this volume.

Table 7.2 offers a classification of the Belgian parties for three time periods. Parties are labelled as 'large' (at least 15 percent at every election), 'minor' (at least once below 1 percent) or 'small' (the others). The table offers a view of the Belgian party system, moving from a system with two large and three small parties before 1968, towards the present system with only one large party, eleven small parties and one minor party.

It is no surprise to see the nationalist parties and the green parties coming out as small parties. The other small parties, however, are of a rather special kind, at least from a comparative point of view. It is not really exceptional to see a small liberal party (or two of them), but it surely is exceptional to see a small Christian democratic party or a small socialist (social democratic) party. Actually, nobody in Belgium would ever even think of calling these parties small. Yet it is true, at least if the numerical criterion is firmly adopted. One

Table 7.2 *Classification of Belgian parties according to the numerical criterion*

Party	1946–65	1968–78	1981–7	Electoral result 1987 (% of vote)
CVP/PSC	L			
CVP		L	L	19.5
PSC		S	S	8.0
BSP/PSB	L	L		
SP			S	14.9
PS			S	15.7
PVV/PLP	S			
PVV		S	S	11.5
PRL		S	S	9.4
Volksunie	S	S	S	8.0
Vlaams Blok			S	1.9
RW		S	M	—
FDF		S	S	1.2
KPB/PCB	S	S	M	0.8
AGALEV			S	4.5
ECOLO		S	S	2.6

Abbreviations are explained in Appendix 7.1.
Large (L): at least 15% at every election.
Minor (M): at least once below 1%.
Small (S): other parties.

thing surely makes a lot of sense: the salience of the CVP as the only possible large party. Everybody will agree that it is the most important Belgian party. Its political opponents often use the word 'CVP-state' to indicate the power of the CVP, as either dominating within the Flemish part of the country or reflecting domination of the country by Flanders.

This reflection reminds us of the basic criticism of the numerical criterion, but at the same time of a possible Belgian-specific way of using it. The criterion takes electoral results as its starting point. One can hardly deny that electoral results have some importance for the comparative analysis of political parties. It looks at electoral results at the national level, and that also seems perfectly logical. However, when Belgium goes to the polls, the electoral results are not in the first place interpreted at the national level. In fact, these overall national results are really meaningless, because the political parties do not compete in the national arena. The Flemish parties put forward candidates only in Flanders, the Walloon parties only in Wallonia, and the Brussels regionalist party only in Brussels. The electoral results of a Flemish party cannot be compared with the electoral results of a Walloon party, and indeed they never are. The size of the parties, then, should be measured at the level of electoral significance, which is the regional one.

Trying again the numerical approach at the regional level, we have the classification as presented in Table 7.3. These results match the more intuitive classification of size that one would make for the Belgian parties. Six parties qualify as large: the remainders of the three traditional national political parties. The Flemish Liberals polled 14.4 percent in Flanders in 1977, and that is why they are small in 1968–78. A seventh party is labelled large, but only for the first period: the Brussels regionalist party FDF. The vote for the FDF climbed to 40 percent in Brussels during this time period. Today it has fallen to some 10 percent, and as such it is only a small party in Brussels. All the other regionalist parties qualify as small, but the Walloon Nationalists (non-existent today) lost this status, becoming a minor Walloon party. The Greens are also small political parties.

It is the absence of national political parties, and the absence of a national political arena in which national parties compete, that makes the 'normal' numerical classification problematic. If adapted to this specific Belgian feature, it is, however, useful. It also makes

Table 7.3 *Classification of Belgian parties according to the numerical criterion, measured at the regional level*

	1968–78	1981–7	Regional score 1987 (% of vote)
CVP	L	L	31.4
PSC	L	L	23.2
SP		L	24.2
PS		L	43.9
PVV	S	L	18.5
PRL	L	L	22.2
Volksunie	S	S	12.9
Vlaams Blok		S	2.7
RW	S	M	—
FDF	L	S	10.9
AGALEV		S	7.3
ECOLO		S	6.5

Large (L): at least 15% at every election.
Minor (M): at least once below 1%.
Small (S): other parties.

the Belgian classification meaningful for comparative analyses, because the unit within which the parties and their size can be compared is then the relevant electoral arena: normally the country as a whole, but in Belgium the three different regions.

Yet national politics are important, and they are surely still important in Belgium too, even if essentially controlled by regional parties. The Belgian party system as a whole, and the political system as a whole, is the most relevant level for analysing the overall role and impact of the different parties. We will analyse this impact in the next section, taking the 'modified' numerical classification of the Belgian parties and other approaches into account.

The systemic approach: the political impact of the small parties

So far we have searched for a good criterion with which to differentiate between small and large parties. The crude numerical criterion was rejected, because the resulting classification of the Belgian parties, as one large party and more than ten small parties, did not seem to make any sense. As just shown, using the numerical criterion makes sense only at the regional level. This 'making sense' has ultimately nothing to do with the size of the parties as such; rather it refers to the political importance of the different parties in Belgium. The so-called traditional parties (those that are large at the regional level) are definitely different. They are more important and have a higher political status than the (regionally) small parties. To show this is the aim of this subsequent discussion. The emphasis will be on the relations between the parties, as the most significant dimension in this particular case.

Multi-partyism normally requires the formation of coalitions. This is certainly true for Belgium. The fractionalization of the party system is so great that a minimal winning coalition needs three parties at least. No combination of two parties can ever be a winning coalition (simple 50 percent majority). The possibility of forming coalitions and the ability to form them are an important indicator of the political impact of parties in Belgium. Coalition potential is a crucial measure of their relevance.

The traditional political parties (or families) have always been, and still are, the basis of all the Belgian governments. The participation of other (small) parties is very exceptional. The Communist Party was taken into the national government immediately after the Second World War. It left the government in 1947 and has never returned to it since then. The Communists were never again invited; nor did they themselves ask for governmental participation.

In 1974 the regional and linguistic parties participated for the first time in the process of forming a national coalition government. They were invited in an attempt to solve once and for all the regional conflict by a reform of the state. Since 1970 the Constitution has recognized the relative autonomy of two cultural entities in Belgium: the Dutch-speaking and the French-speaking. This was a first step towards the federalization demanded by the Flemish. The Walloons, however, wanted a division of the country into three regions: Flanders, Wallonia and Brussels. The Flemish were not ready to accept Brussels as an autonomous region, because this would mean that two out of the three Belgian regions would be French or predominantly French, and it would deprive the Flemish of the means of preserving what was left of the Flemish language and cultural tradition in Brussels. In 1974 this problem seemed not yet ripe for a solution. A minority government was formed, with the passive help of the Rassemblement Wallon. A few months later this party acceded formally to the government. Except for the Communist Party in the early postwar period, this was the first time a non-traditional party entered the national government.

Prime Minister Tindemans dismissed the ministers of the Rassemblement Wallon in 1977 for their lack of solidarity with governmental decisions. This put an end to his government, and the political crisis led to new elections. After the elections, a new attempt was made to solve the regional conflict, which had dominated the political scene since the early 1960s. After long negotiations an agreement was reached between the Socialists, the Christian Democrats, the Front des Francophones and the Volksunie. It was a very delicate and complicated compromise, combining a division of the country into two cultural entities and into three regions. Only one year later the government, composed of the above-cited parties, collapsed, due to a lack of agreement on the interpretation of the compromise (this also meant the end for the national Socialist Party).

New elections meant significant losses for the Flemish Nationalists, and the creation of the new and more radical Vlaams Blok. The Flemish Nationalists were not very eager to participate in a new government, and the old coalition was repeated without them. The FDF was the only linguistic party remaining in the government. The radicalism of the FDF ministers torpedoed several new attempts to agree on a suitable and acceptable reform of the state, and by the end of 1979 the FDF ministers were expelled from the government.

This seemed to be the end of the participation in government of the regionalist parties. Of the three of them that have played a governmental role, only the Flemish Nationalists managed to survive. The Rassemblement Wallon disappeared, and the Brussels FDF has been reduced to a small and – even in Brussels – politically rather irrelevant party. The Volksunie, however, could recover the losses experienced in 1978, and it still represents about 10 percent of the Belgian population and 15 percent of the Flemish population. When in 1988 a new attempt was made to reach a compromise on a further reform of the state, the Volksunie again agreed to participate in the national government. The heavy losses that were experienced at the local elections in October 1988 and at the European election in June 1989 indicate that the Volksunie voters still do not want their party to compromise with other parties.

What gives a party the chance to participate in government? What are the possible sources for gaining coalition potential? To understand this, some remarks on the rules of coalition formation in Belgium are needed. In the first place, the Constitution states (since 1970) that there must be so-called 'parity' between Dutch-speaking and French-speaking ministers. This means that any government needs the participation of at least one Walloon and one Flemish party. Since two parties can never be enough to reach a normal majority, more parties are needed. Up to now, all Belgian governments have always been symmetrical. This means that the traditional political families, always composed of two parties, were never separated at the governmental level. If, for instance, the Flemish Christian Democrats participate in the government, the Walloon Christian Democrats will be in too.

The fractionalization of the party system is thus tempered by this political practice in coalition behaviour. It means that the separation between the two wings of the former national parties is principally an organizational separation, but not a political separation at all levels. It would indeed become very difficult for both parties of the same ideological family if one of them governed while the other was in opposition. The threat of this kind of terrible divorce is often heard during electoral campaigns or during the process of coalition formation, but it has never really been taken into serious consideration.

If ideological families do stay together at the governmental level, some parties can become members of the national government almost automatically. They have a coalition potential that is quite independent of their electoral strength and of their numerical size. This is especially true for the Walloon Christian Democrats. This party polls between 20 percent and 25 percent of the Walloon vote (8 percent to 10 percent of the Belgian vote), but since the Flemish Christian Democrats are the largest and dominating party in

Flanders, their Walloon counterparts cannot be left out of the government. The little Walloon brother is very happy with this situation. It gives this party a great deal of power, which it often uses to get things done. The other party that can boost its political relevance by being the counterpart of another is the Flemish Socialist Party. The Walloon Socialists are very important. They control more than 40 percent of the Walloon vote. Governing against them is possible (and it happens), but it is very difficult. And when they govern, they always bring (sometimes reluctantly) their Flemish brothers along. There is no such mechanism enhancing the chances for the liberal parties. Both liberal parties are the third political force in their own region. A government of Christian Democrats and Liberals often does not have a majority in Wallonia, and this can cause problems. The Flemish Liberals are then kept out too.

The constitutional rules exclude a one-party government (unless some new bilingual national party were to reach a majority). The fractionalization creates the need for at least a third party to allow a government to get a simple majority. The political tradition always brings in a fourth party. Four-party governments are thus the most common governments. They are oversized (minimal winning, but not minimal number or minimal weight).

Why then from time to time take the nationalist parties into the government? Because sometimes a simple majority is not enough. Belgium has been working since 1970 on an important revision of the Constitution, transforming the country slowly but steadily into a federal state. To revise the Constitution, a two-thirds majority is needed, and for some articles (those concerning the creation of separate regions and communities and the relationships between them) a majority within each language group is also needed. So what is required is a large and balanced majority. The backbone of such a majority can only be a coalition in which the Flemish (and Walloon) Christian Democrats are present, together with the Walloon (and Flemish) Socialists. Two possibilities remain to enlarge the coalition: taking in the liberal parties, or taking in one or more nationalist parties.

The possibilities for the nationalist parties of entering a governing coalition are thus clearly bound to the political agenda. If no constitutional reform is planned, the nationalist parties will not be asked. The periods during which they were in the government (1974–9 and since 1988), were periods during which important reforms were voted or planned. When in 1980 the FDF was ousted, a grand coalition of the six traditional parties was formed. It voted the new constitution of August 1980. The Liberals were out of the government again in October 1980.

During the long negotiations of 1987–8, the idea of a grand coalition was launched again. The differences between Liberals and Socialists were too important to give this formula any chance. The Flemish Nationalists were asked to enlarge the Christian Democratic/Socialist coalition, which they did. This coalition has a two-thirds majority, and a majority in each language group. It is working hard on a further revision of the Constitution.

The two green parties can be considered as small parties at present. They both poll at least 5 percent within their region. Their political relevance is extremely low (Deschouwer 1989). In the first place, they are numerically small. They cannot be the most important partner in a governmental coalition. Their only chance is to be asked by the large parties. But why should they need the Greens? There is no reason – traditional, political, constitutional or numerical – to let them govern. They are not considered as governmental parties, and they do not present themselves as such. If some coalition needs to be enlarged, the Greens will not be the first choice. The political cleavage on which they base their clear political profile is not the most relevant. Bringing in the Greens would mean incorporating many new problems and political topics (nuclear energy, peace, the Third World, etc.). Unless these topics become very salient, there is no reason to import them into government. Even if the Greens grow larger, their political relevance will remain low. In the Belgian situation, they are linked to the wrong cleavage.

Being or not being in the national government has some important consequences, besides of course the possibility of realizing some aspects of the party programme. Political parties have a firm grip on the governmental administration. They control some nominations and almost all the promotions. For an administrative career, membership of (or at least affirmed loyalty to) a political party is needed. The governing parties have their adherents nominated or promoted, while the opposition parties stand aside. Since some parties are normal governing parties (the large ones), some parties are incidental governing parties (the Nationalists) and some parties are not governing parties (Communists, Greens), their presence in the national bureaucracy is very different.

The old three-party (or six-party) system is still very visible in the administrative bodies. The (ever-governing) Christian Democrats have the largest share, while Socialists and Liberals only control a smaller number of the civil servants. When Socialists or Liberals govern, they try very hard to have a maximum of their own people nominated or promoted, since they know that after a few years they will be back in the opposition. The Nationalists are rather marginal in this game. They do not govern very often, and this also means that it is not very rewarding for a civil servant to rely on them. In this respect the traditional parties really control the state apparatus, while the others are more or less outside the state. The Greens of course are completely excluded from this political practice.

Conclusion

The Belgian party system is highly fractionalized, due to the linguistic split of the traditional national parties. The distinction between small and large is not commonly used in Belgium, for the important distinction to be made is one between traditional and non-traditional parties. The 'pure' numerical criterion does not enable us to discriminate between the parties that are 'substantially' small or large. The numerical criterion distinguishes only one large party, and a lot of small parties.

This problem was solved by using the numerical criterion on a more appropriate level: the level of the real political arena in which the parties compete, that is, the regional. If the parties are classified by a numerical criterion, according to their regional electoral score, the picture starts making sense. The important parties qualify as large parties, while the less important parties qualify as small (or minor) parties.

The political impact of the different parties varies with their size, measured in this modified way. The large or traditional parties are the normal governmental parties. Even the smaller ones have an important coalition potential, because they are still in some way linked together with their Flemish or Walloon counterparts. The small (Nationalist) parties usually do not participate in the governmental coalitions. If they do, their chance here is linked to the political agenda. The special majorities needed to change the constitutional rules, a process ongoing since 1970, make the Nationalist parties potential partners for enlarging a normal four-party government. The Greens enjoy no significant political impact at all, since they have no coalition potential and since their own cleavage position is submerged by the overriding presence of the linguistic cleavage. The consequences, therefore, of that cleavage have done much to require a redefinition of small parties in the Belgian context. This only argues for analysing small parties in Belgium with the systemic approach.

Appendix 7.1 Belgian parties

CVP (Christelijke Volkspartij): Flemish Christian Democrats
PSC (Parti Social Chrétien): Walloon Christian Democrats
PS (Parti Socialiste): Walloon Socialists
SP (Socialistische Partij): Flemish Socialists
PVV (Partij voor Vrijheid en Vooruitgang): Flemish Liberals
PRL (Parti Réformateur Libéral): Walloon Liberals
Volksunie: Flemish Nationalists
Vlaams Blok: Radical Flemish Nationalists
FDF (Front Démocratique des Francophones): Brussels Francophone nationalist party
RW (Rassemblement Wallon): Walloon Nationalists
AGALEV (Anders Gaan Leven): Flemish Greens
ECOLO: Walloon Greens
RAD/UDRT (Respect voor Arbeid en Democratie/Union Démocratique pour le Respect du Travail): anti-tax party
PCB/KPB (Parti Communiste Belge/Kommunistische Partij van België): Communists

8
They Also Serve: Small Parties in the British Political System

Jorgen Rasmussen

The incidence of small parties in Britain

Since Britain has long been considered to have one of the few two-party systems, it is not surprising that small parties are not prevalent there. Only one party – the Liberals – qualifies as an enduring small party during the period since the Second World War. Support for the Liberals has ranged from 2.5 to 19.3 percent of the vote in general elections, never falling below 1 percent and only twice surpassing 15 percent (see Table 8.1 below). Thus the party satisfies Mair's criteria quite well (see Mair in this volume).

Beyond the Liberals, however, small parties are sparse in the United Kingdom. The Social Democratic Party, founded in 1981, managed (in an electoral alliance with the Liberals) to meet the criteria for small parties in the elections of the 1980s, as Table 8.1 shows. But it fought only two elections before it disbanded in 1990.

In 1988 the Liberals and part of the SDP merged to form a new party, the Social and Liberal Democratic Party, now known as the Liberal Democrats. Some members of the SDP supported the party's leader, David Owen, in opposing this merger. They decided to continue on as the SDP. After the merger/split, the SDP had only three MPs. Finishing behind Screaming Lord Sutch of the Raving Loony Party in a 1990 by-election may well have been the final straw that broke the SDP.

No other country-wide party, even in its best single performance, has been able to gain 1 percent of the vote in parliamentary elections. In contrast to many continental countries, in Britain parties on the fringes of the spectrum have not fared well. When the extreme right-wing National Front enjoyed its greatest success in 1979, it obtained a mere 0.6 percent of the vote. While the Communists managed to elect two MPs in 1945, that was the only election in which the party was able to surpass 100,000 votes. A telling indication of its electoral futility is that when in the next election it offered five times as many candidates, its total vote declined.

Nor has Britain seen the agrarian parties that are common on the Continent. Several Conservative MPs represent rural constituencies and apparently look after the interests of the farmers with sufficient vigour to preclude the need for a separate party. Furthermore, the National Farmers' Union has sufficient legitimacy to gain access to policy-makers and implementers. While the Green Party has put forward candidates in British elections, it has gained only a handful of votes in national parliamentary elections. (While the Greens won 15 percent of the vote in 1989 in elections for the European Parliament, opinion polls show that they would be lucky to obtain even a third of that level in the next general election.)

Regional parties should not be overlooked, however, even if Mair's criteria must be relaxed to consider them. Since the Welsh electorate is only about 5 percent of the total UK electorate, a party contesting elections only in Wales would have to win 20 percent of the region's vote to qualify as a small party. That seems excessively demanding. Northern Ireland is even more of a problem. A party operating there only would need about 40 percent of the vote to be considered a small party in the entire UK system.

Since the major British parties have not fielded candidates in Northern Ireland in the last five general elections, not classifying the parties that do operate there as small parties would be to ignore an important aspect of British politics. Therefore, this study considers the Scottish Nationalists (SNP), Plaid Cymru (the Welsh Nationalists), the Ulster Unionists and the Social Democratic and Labour Party (SDLP) to be small parties.

Thus in Britain at the country-wide level, the enduring small party has been of the Liberal family, while those which operate only regionally are nationalist parties. In the 1940s and 1950s the Liberals had a strong 'libertarian' wing that believed that individual freedoms were best preserved by curtailing the role of government, limiting it to only a few welfare programmes and little regulation of free enterprise. In the 1960s the social-reform wing of the party came to predominate, moving the Liberals to the centre of the political spectrum (Rasmussen 1965).

As for the regional parties, the nationalist label is satisfactory for Plaid Cymru and the SNP. On issues other than independence for their regions, they are left of centre, Plaid Cymru perhaps more so than the SNP. The Ulster Unionists do not seek to separate Northern Ireland from the UK, but to maintain the existing union. The union which the SDLP favours is with the Republic of Ireland. The positions which these two parties take on other issues put the Unionists on the right and the SDLP on the left.

The incidence of small parties is much narrower in Britain than is

Table 8.1 Results of British elections 1945–87

	1945	1950	1951	1955	1959	1964	1966	1970	1974 Feb.	1974 Oct.	1979	1983	1987
Conservative													
% of vote	39.8	43.5	48.0	49.7	49.4	43.4	41.9	46.4	37.9	35.8	43.9	42.4	42.2
No. candidates	624	620	617	623	625	630	629	628	623	623	622	633	632
No. MPs	213	298	321	344	365	304	253	330	297	277	339	397	375
Labour													
% of vote	47.8	46.1	48.8	46.4	43.8	44.1	47.9	43.0	37.1	39.2	36.9	27.6	30.8
No. candidates	604	617	617	620	621	628	621	624	623	623	623	633	633
No. MPs	393	315	295	277	258	317	363	287	301	319	269	209	229
Liberal													
% of vote	9.0	9.1	2.5	2.7	5.9	11.2	8.5	7.5	19.3	18.3	13.8	13.7	13.1
No. candidates	306	475	109	110	216	365	311	332	517	619	577	322	327
No. MPs	12	9	6	6	6	9	12	6	14	13	11	17	17
SDP													
% of vote												11.6	9.5
No. candidates												311	306
No. MPs												6	5

They also serve: Britain 155

	1945	1950	1951	1955	1959	1964	1966	1970	Feb 1974	Oct 1974	1979	1983	1987
Plaid Cymru													
% of vote	0.1	0.1	0.0	0.0	0.2	0.3	0.3	0.2	0.6	0.6	0.4	0.4	0.4
No. candidates	7	7	4	11	20	23	20	36	36	36	36	38	38
No. MPs	0	0	0	0	0	0	0	0	2	3	2	2	3
SNP													
% of vote	0.1	0.0	0.0	0.0	0.1	0.2	0.5	1.1	2.0	2.9	1.6	1.1	1.3
No. candidates	8	3	2	2	5	15	20	65	70	71	71	72	71
No. MPs	0	0	0	0	0	0	0	1	7	11	2	2	3
Unionist													
% of vote								0.7	2.0	0.9	0.8	0.8	0.8
No. candidates								7	70	7	11	16	12
No. MPs								7	7	6	5	11	9
SDLP													
% of vote									0.5	0.5	0.4	0.4	0.5
No. candidates									12	9	9	17	13
No. MPs									1	1	1	1	3
Others													
% of vote	2.6	1.2	0.8	1.0	0.5	0.8	0.8	1.5	1.9	1.8	2.2	1.9	1.4
No. candidates	133	146	27	43	49	96	103	152	247	264	627	536	293
No. MPs	22	3	3	3	1	0	2	6	6	5	6	5	6

Sources: Butler and Butler 1986; Craig 1981; Wood 1987

typical for European countries, suggesting that the role of small parties is less fully developed than in most continental systems.

The role of small British parties

Diachronic considerations: party life-cycles
Just as individuals pass through various life-cycles, so parties may mature through stages of development. In founding a party, as distinct from a movement or interest group, political activists declare their intention of offering policy alternatives and candidates to the electorate. As for the launching of the parties in this study, the Liberals had been a major party, but were displaced by Labour during the interwar period. This period also saw the founding of both the SNP and Plaid Cymru. Thus all three parties had passed through their declaration stage well before the start of the time period covered by this study.

The same could be said for the Ulster Unionists, since they date back to the nineteenth century. Prior to 1970, however, most observers saw them simply as the British Conservative Party under another name appropriate to the region. Reports of election results typically included the Ulster Unionist vote and MPs within the Conservative totals without any qualification. When hard-line Unionists began to suspect, however, that even the Conservatives could not be trusted to guarantee that Northern Ireland would forever remain separated from the Republic of Ireland, fissures developed within the party. Factional fighting produced a kaleidoscope of groups and labels. Eventually known as the Official Unionist Party, the organization broke all links with the Conservatives in the early 1970s.

Beginning in 1943, a handful of candidates appeared at various elections in Northern Ireland under a variety of labels including the word 'Labour', although unconnected with the UK Labour Party. These were more personal candidacies than party campaigns. While similar in policies and clientele, the Social Democratic and Labour Party, founded in 1970, sought to appeal to the electorate beyond the careers of individual leaders.

The most recently launched small party is the SDP. Conflict between the left and right seems endemic to the Labour Party. The level reached in the late 1970s, however, was rare even for Labour. Many Labour moderates opposed the left's desire to take Britain out of the EEC and to have the country unilaterally dispose of its nuclear weapons. The related procedural or party-organization issues were who should draw up the electoral manifestos, who should elect the party leader and what power constituency parties should have to select parliamentary candidates. Matters came to a head at a special party conference early in 1981. Here the party's rules were altered so that Labour MPs, who had had sole power to select the party leader, were reduced to only 30 percent of the votes in a new electoral college created to make the choice. Several prominent Labour moderates responded by forming a Council for Social Democracy, which eventually became the SDP.

After a party is launched, the next step is to obtain the necessary official authorization. Some time may elapse in certain countries between the declaration and authorization stages, but in Britain parties need not officially register. Access to the ballot requires only the signatures of ten electors and submission of an electoral deposit. While the deposit is intended to deter 'frivolous' candidates, it has also curtailed the electoral efforts of small British parties. In 1950 the Liberals deliberately decided to fight on a broad front by contesting three-quarters of the constituencies (Rasmussen 1965: 13–18, 93–9). The resulting disaster – about two-thirds of their candidates lost their deposit – put a damper on subsequent campaigns. Only once during the next twenty years did the Liberals contest more than half the constituencies. None the less, the deposit is not much of a barrier to the launch of new parties.[1] None of the small parties included in this study was unable to contest the first election following the party's formation. Thus, the authorization stage quickly followed the declaration stage for all of them.

Reaching the authorization stage in Britain does not gain a party full equality with the major parties. Broadcasting time allocated to parties during campaigns depends upon their parliamentary strength and the extensiveness of candidature. Some minor parties have been limited to a single five-minute broadcast during the three-week campaign, while others have received nothing at all. The Liberals were never given as much time as were the major parties. Only in 1987 did the Alliance, the electoral pact combining the Liberals and the SDP, gain equal time.

Having been authorized to seek representation, a party's task is to convince the electorate to grant it. The barrier most commonly cited to crossing the threshold of representation in Britain is the single-member, simple-plurality electoral system. This system, however, can be an aid as well as an impediment. Only parties that dilute their support by making country-wide appeals are hampered; those that concentrate their efforts in a limited area can actually benefit from the system.

In October 1974 the SNP, with 3 percent of the national vote, obtained eleven MPs. The Liberals, with six times as many votes, received only two more. Even more to the point is the experience of the Unionists. Were they to receive representation proportional to their share of the total vote, they would have about five or six MPs; but since they confine their efforts to Northern Ireland, they usually gain two to five more. Therefore, it is not surprising that four of the six parties in this study are regional.

As a former major party, the Liberals reached the representation stage well before start of the period of this study. The SDP gained representation before contesting an election, since a number of Labour MPs joined the new group. Of the regional parties, the Ulster Unionists were quite successful in the first election which they contested and the SDLP managed in that same election to obtain a representative (see Table 8.1). In contrast, both PC and the SNP had to struggle for some time to surmount the threshold of representation, despite the benefits which parties of their type can obtain from the electoral system. Not until 1970 did the SNP win representation in a general election and manage to maintain it without a subsequent break. For PC the comparable date is February 1974. Thus these two parties – probably because early on they were more micro-parties than small ones – required forty to fifty years to pass fully into the representation stage. Electoral support for the small parties is shown in Table 8.1. While in general the two country-wide small parties have gained a much more substantial share of the vote, the SNP at its high point in October 1974 obtained a larger share of the popular vote than had the Liberals in the mid-1950s, despite its contesting only about two-thirds as many seats.

Once a party has obtained representation, its next goal is relevance. This quality will be discussed in the section on governmental relations below. As will be seen, the parties in this study attained relevance of one type or another during the postwar period.

In summary, during the first half of the postwar period, Britain had only one small party and it appeared to be declining. Not only did it lack relevance for both coalition formation and direction of competition, but its ability to continue to surmount the threshold of representation was in doubt. In the second half of the period not only did the Liberals reverse their decline, but several other parties passed through the various stages of party development all the way to relevance.

Systemic aspects: social relations

For much of the twentieth century social class has been the basic cleavage of British politics. The Liberals' unwillingness or inability to relate to that cleavage is the chief reason for their decline from major to small party status. The party has lacked a distinctive core clientele in society. More so than either of the major parties, it is literally representative of society, the proportion of its vote coming from a particular social group tending to correspond to that group's proportion of the electorate. The alliance with the SDP was expected to change this. The hope was that since the SDP was comprised of former Labour supporters, the two parties would be able to poll better among the working class than had the Liberals. This seems not to have occurred (Rasmussen 1985: 97–8).

Specifying the social bases of the regional small parties is difficult. The survey research organizations that regularly sample political opinions in Britain routinely exclude Northern Ireland. While Wales and Scotland are included, the number of respondents from either region typically is too small to permit subgroup analysis. Fortunately, during the 1987 election Market & Opinion Research International conducted three surveys in Scotland only and with samples sufficiently large to provide information about the social bases of party support.[2]

These surveys indicate little about the SNP's clientele that is distinctive. Gender, social class and union membership have little effect upon its appeal. Not even housing – a variable which has come to rival or replace class in its effect upon political behaviour generally in Britain – is important. Those who own their own homes are as likely to vote SNP as are those living in council housing. About the only background characteristic that had some influence was age – those under 24 were much more likely to favour the SNP than were those over 65 – but even this finding was not present in all three surveys.

The overwhelming majority of those intending to vote SNP were dissatisfied with the government's performance, yet they were even less likely than were Alliance supporters to think that their own party had the best policies. The SNP's main *raison d'être* is Scottish independence. Yet among those planning to vote for the party, five times as many said that unemployment was one of the two or three most important issues in 1987 as preferred devolution and a Scottish Assembly. That issue finished no better than fourth in importance in the views of SNP supporters. Of all those respondents favouring a 'completely independent Scottish Assembly separate from England', twice as many said they would vote Labour as intended to support the SNP.

In short, despite its distinctive central policy, the SNP tends to resemble the Liberal Party since it lacks a distinctive core clientele and seems to appeal to voters more on the basis of image than of specific policy. Just as the Liberal Party often gains support from those simply wanting to express a feeling of discontent with the establishment parties, so too does the SNP in Scotland. This similarity in electoral role may well explain why a majority of SNP supporters were dissatisfied with Margaret Thatcher, Neil Kinnock and David Owen, but a plurality of them were satisfied with David Steel's performance as Liberal leader.

This type of detailed information is not available for Plaid Cymru or the Northern Ireland parties, but one point can be made about the latter's relation to social cleavages. In Northern Ireland, religion, not class, is the basic cleavage. The Ulster Unionists appeal to the Protestant majority and the SDLP to the Catholic minority. Within their denominational group each must contend with other smaller parties, but the two do not compete with each other, for that would require appealing across the confessional divide.

While examining the clientele of small parties and their relation to social cleavage can reveal a good deal about the nature of their support, that focus on 'who' needs to be supplemented with some discussion of 'why'. A study of non-major parties in the United States sees them – in the words of its subtitle – as 'citizen response to major party failure'. 'Third parties are expressions of discontent with the major parties and their candidates. They are an explicit and deliberate rejection of the two dominant parties' (Rosenstone et al. 1984: 5–6).

That British voters have increasingly rejected the two leading parties is clear from Table 8.2. In the first two decades of the postwar period, two-thirds to four-fifths of the electorate voted Labour or Conservative, while since the mid-1970s only a half to

Table 8.2 *Two-party share of the electorate in postwar elections*

Election	Two-party share (%)	Election	Two-party share (%)
1945	66.3	1970	64.4
1950	75.2	1974 Feb.	59.2
1951	79.9	1974 Oct.	54.7
1955	73.8	1979	61.4
1959	73.4	1983	50.9
1964	67.4	1987	55.0
1966	68.2		

Sources: calculated from the results in Butler and Butler 1986; Craig 1981; Wood 1987

three-fifths have done so. The economic problems which began to afflict Britain in the 1960s, following as they did upon the seemingly endless prosperity of the 1950s, produced considerable disenchantment with the major parties. Voter loyalty was much attenuated, and the resultant partisan dealignment swung Britain from closed-class to open competition (Crewe et al. 1977; Franklin 1985; Rose and McAllister 1986).

As Table 8.1 shows, since the mid-1970s small and micro-parties have fielded many more candidates, have obtained more popular support and have gained greater representation. Whether the rise of small and micro-parties was cause or effect, whether they were taking advantage of an opportunity created by the major parties' apparent ineffectiveness or were helping to generate voter dissatisfaction with the leading parties, is difficult to resolve.

Some insight into the process can be obtained by distinguishing between mobilizers and challengers (Rochon 1985). Parties classified as mobilizers seek to organize voters around a new cleavage. The rise of such an alternative to existing major parties is facilitated by the entry into the electorate of sizeable new groups, because new voters have yet to develop strong partisan loyalties and can be mobilized easily by new parties. Challengers do not seek to alter the current pattern of politics, but rather fight existing parties on their turf. Challengers merely claim that they are able to do a better job.

Mobilizing has not been a very promising strategy in Britain during the postwar period. The chief opportunity to pursue it occurred in the late 1960s when the voting age was lowered from 21 to 18, thereby increasing the electorate by nearly 3.5 million. Since turnout dropped by nearly four percentage points in 1970 and the number voting rose by little more than a million, it would appear that many of these newly enfranchised voters initially did not bother to go to the polls – perhaps delaying until the next election. Between 1970 and February 1974 the electorate increased by less than half a million, but the number voting rose by three million.

That this is the time when small parties began to play a significant role in Britain may not be entirely fortuitous, even though the small parties made no special effort to target the youth vote. Some research suggests a relation between voter life-cycle and party systems; younger voters are more disposed than are older segments of the population to support minor parties (Barnes 1988; 1989). In the case of Britain, however, the data analysed are for party identification rather than for actual vote. If minor parties do enjoy relatively greater success among younger than among older voters, the support they mobilize is only transient. Barnes argues that as the voters age they tend to switch to one of the major parties. The

SNP's experience certainly does not challenge this theory. Any newly enfranchised voters that it mobilized in the early 1970s seem largely to have departed by 1987, since the party lacked any disproportional strength among those aged 35 to 45.

A mobilization strategy need not be limited simply to targeting new entrants to the electorate; a party may seek support from those who in the past have been too uninterested to vote. In Britain this was an even less sensible strategy because abstainers were not a distinct social group. Given disenchantment with the performance of the major parties, challenging was much the more plausible strategy.

The Liberals have tended to pursue the challenging strategy; they covet regaining their role as a major party. Similarly, the SDP was nothing if not a challenger, hoping to entice away enough of Labour's traditional supporters to replace it as a major party. Mobilization has not been entirely absent, however, from either party's strategies. The SDP found that, even in a period of partisan dealignment, winning over Labour's core clientele was a hard slog. At the same time, the party discovered that many of its activists were in fact people who had not been politically active before. To some extent the SDP, whatever its intentions, *was* mobilizing a new segment of the electorate.

As for the Liberals, their lack of an electoral base in any significant social group has encouraged them to make a classless appeal to the voters (Lemieux 1977; Rasmussen 1981: 162–4). While not becoming a 'new issues' party, the Liberals began in the 1970s to emphasize volunteerism and community service, themes that have some affinity to post-materialism (Cyr 1977). This has given the party something of an apolitical appeal; much of its voting support is attracted more by party image and leader personality than by issue position (Alt et al. 1977). That the Liberals have been helped by declines in the Prime Minister's popularity might be interpreted as the ability to capitalize on major-party failure (Clarke and Zuk 1986). The party has not benefited, however, from the government's inability to deal with either inflation or unemployment. Worsening of these problems tends to turn voters *away* from the Liberals, because the party is not as clearly identified with remedial action on either issue as is one or the other of the major parties. Challenging on the current issues seems to be a strategy of limited utility for the Liberals.

Mobilization efforts, however, have fared little better. While the party's increased support has been due to both mobilized abstainers and converts from the major parties, the Liberal vote has nevertheless been notoriously fickle. A much smaller proportion of the Liberals' clientele continues to vote for the party election after election compared to supporters of the major parties (Alt et al. 1977; Rasmussen 1981: 171–2).

Most of the regional small parties have also preferred to function as challengers rather than mobilizers. While both Plaid Cymru and the SNP were seeking to promote a new issue, they were more concerned to win converts from supporters of the major parties than to mobilize a new segment of the electorate. Even in Wales the number of Welsh speakers is sufficiently limited to preclude a strategy of trying to mobilize only that group. And emphasizing language, as distinct from the broader concern of culture, would be to write off any hope of support from the non-Welsh-speaking majority, not to mention even among some bilingual Welsh. In addition to the issue of independence, the SNP also challenged the major parties on North Sea oil. Its claim that it was 'Scotland's oil' meant not only that the nation would have adequate finances were it to become independent, but also that until this occurred the revenues from the oil should be spent on Scotland and not used to help keep the English economy afloat. The Ulster Unionists' challenge could hardly have been more explicit. The party's rank and file, as distinct from its leaders, were adamantly opposed to the British Conservative government's plans to give Catholics a greater voice in governing Northern Ireland and to create a council representative of the whole of Ireland.

The SDLP is the one regional small party that is best regarded as a mobilizer. Its appeal is to the Catholics of Northern Ireland. Since they are condemned to perpetual minority status under a Protestant majority that does not scruple to discriminate, many withdraw from politics into either apathy or violence. The SDLP seeks to mobilize this segment of society with an appeal emphasizing that aspirations for a united Ireland can be realized through constitutional means.

Thus, although small British parties have not ignored the mobilization strategy, the challenging strategy is clearly more preferred. That parties favouring such a strategy became significant in British politics at the time that partisan dealignment was making the major parties vulnerable to challenge is noteworthy. The preference for the role of challengers means that support for small parties in Britain is more likely to come from those becoming dissatisfied with the position and performance of major parties than from those who never found them attractive in the first place.

Systemic aspects: governmental relations
Small parties which have cleared the representation threshold next encounter obstacles to relevancy. Unlike the West German Bundes-

tag, for instance, the House of Commons does not require a minimum number of representatives for official recognition. Small party MPs are as able as those from major parties to speak, offer motions and introduce legislation. Since all MPs are quite restricted in these matters, that is not saying very much.

Special speaking privileges are granted, however, to Privy Councillors. The Commons' presiding officer recognizes privy councillors in preference to ordinary backbenchers. Since by the 1950s no Liberal MP was a privy councillor, the party was constrained even beyond its small size in presenting its views during debates. Jo Grimond served as leader of the party for five years before he was made a privy councillor. With the precedent thus established, his successors did not have to wait as long. As for the other small parties, no consistent practice exists. The success of the SNP in the 1974 elections gave it a strong case for such a concession, since its strength surpassed that of the Liberals when Grimond became a privy councillor. None the less, the SNP leader, Donald Stewart, had to wait five more years until he received this honour. None of the leaders of the other small parties has been made a privy councillor. The SDP leader, David Owen, had become one while a minister in a Labour government; thus no question arose about whether the leader of this party deserved the status. Although two Ulster Unionist MPs have been privy councillors the party leader was not, and each received the honour for reasons unrelated to the party's role in the Commons. The SDLP and Plaid Cymru have had to seek a voice in debates without any help from privy councillor status, since none of their representatives have gained that honour.

The role of most small parties in debate is curtailed in yet another way. During each session of Parliament twenty 'opposition days' are given to the government's opponents to decide what matters are to be discussed. Seventeen of these go to the major opposition party and three to the second largest opposition party. Hence, none of the other small parties are accorded any control over the agenda.

Opposition parties in the Commons are granted public funds to help pay for the expenses of their parliamentary work. They receive a set amount for each seat won in the previous general election, along with an additional payment for every 200 votes received. To receive these funds, however, a party must have at least two MPs, or one MP and 150,000 votes. This prevented the SDLP, for example, from receiving any payment until June 1987.

Some of the regional small parties do fare better in one regard. The Commons has a Scottish Grand Committee and a Welsh Grand Committee for the second reading stage of bills dealing with the one region or the other. In addition, two Scottish Standing Committees exist to handle the committee stage of legislation pertaining to Scotland, although no similar provision is made for bills concerned with Northern Ireland. For most of the twentieth century Northern Ireland had its own legislature, so no special arrangements were needed in the House of Commons.

If a small party is to be of significance, it must have either coalition or competitive relevance (Sartori 1976: 122–4). Hinge parties (those occupying the centre of the political spectrum) and detached parties (those appealing to a special clientele) – to refer to Gordon Smith's classification in this volume – are in a good position for coalition potential. Marginal parties (those at the fringes of the spectrum) are not well situated for such a role, but, because of their blackmail potential, they may be able to alter the direction of competition.

In Britain no small party had coalition relevance until the mid-1970s. Then the regional parties became as relevant as were the Liberals. Not only did their status as detached parties make them as well placed as the Liberals for coalition relevance, their parliamentary strength was roughly equivalent to that of the Liberals. While fringe parties are most likely, by virtue of their position, to have competitive relevance, the extreme wings of the political spectrum in Britain have had such minuscule support that neither has been able to alter the direction of competition. Despite their lack of influence, the direction of competition has nevertheless shifted during the postwar period.

British parties in 1945 were hardly polarized. None the less, they began to move even closer together, a process that by the late 1950s had culminated in the period known as 'Butskellism'. Although this development was the outcome of autonomous major-party change, it greatly affected the Liberals' role. Given their location at the centre of the political spectrum, they found their room for manoeuvre decreasing as the major parties converged upon them from both directions. Also significant was the major parties' ability to swing in this direction without driving voters on the wings of the political spectrum to support extreme fringe parties. Ultimately, due to developments internal to the major parties, this convergence was reversed. Towards the end of the 1970s, the Labour left wing's challenge to the party's moderate leaders, and Margaret Thatcher's reorienting of the Conservatives, directed the major parties away from the centre of the spectrum.

Now the Liberals had an opportunity to alter the direction of competition. If they could manage to win the support of those on the left wing of the Conservative Party along with those on the right wing of Labour, they might well redirect party competition from centrifugal to centripetal. When many Labour moderates broke from their party to form the SDP, and then arranged an electoral alliance with the Liberals, the competitive relevance of the parties at the centre was enhanced.

The SDLP, SNP and Plaid Cymru can all be called separatist parties; they wish to take their particular region out of the United Kingdom. Some might regard them, therefore, as anti-system parties. In the nineteenth century, when all of Ireland was part of the United Kingdom, Irish Nationalists in the Commons attempted to prevent Parliament from functioning, hoping thereby to force independence to be granted to Ireland. The MPs for the contemporary separatist parties have not chosen this strategy. Despite their desire for independence, they have served in the Commons just as have other MPs, accepting their responsibilities and not attempting to be disruptive. Thus, they have not made any concerted effort to achieve relevance through a blackmail strategy. On the other hand, the demands of the SNP for Scottish independence forced Labour to rethink its policies on devolution and pushed it into a position more divergent from the Conservatives than otherwise would have been the case. As for the Ulster Unionists, their rupture with the Conservatives can be seen as an unsuccessful blackmail attempt. While the Unionists did not alter the direction of competition in the entire system, they certainly did further polarize party competition in Northern Ireland.

Thus, small parties have not been without significance for the nature of party competition in postwar Britain. Despite the absence of any formal coalition governments during this period, British small parties have had a certain systemic relevance.

Systemic aspects: political relations
Given the important constraints which governmental structures in Britain place on the role of small parties, their ability to express societal concerns effectively may well turn on relations with other parties. Effectiveness is thus likely to be a matter of alliances. Parties relatively close together on the political spectrum should obviously be able to co-operate more easily than would parties far apart. At the same time, the party nearest, however, poses the biggest threat; it is most likely to be competing for the same electorate.

The question of linkages with other parties has become largely irrelevant to the divisive politics of Northern Ireland, although at the start of the postwar period that region offered one of the best examples. In the first quarter-century after 1945 the Ulster Unionists were tied to the Conservatives. The most revealing evidence of their relationship occurred after the 1951 election. The Conservatives had won a very narrow victory. Had the twelve Ulster Unionist MPs not been counted among the Conservatives' total, the latter would have been four seats short of a bare majority, but the Conservatives did not need to negotiate a coalition before forming a government to displace the Labour one. In the early 1970s, the Unionists severed these links. Not only were the Conservatives divorced from Northern Ireland's politics, but Labour, the Liberals and the SDP as well made no effort to be involved. (Whether the Conservatives' fielding of a candidate in a Northern Ireland by-election in 1990 presages a change in the next general election remains to be seen.) As for relations with the indigenous parties, the Ulster Unionists have at times co-operated with some of Northern Ireland's micro-parties. The principal result of these relations has been to keep the Unionists from contesting every one of Northern Ireland's constituencies in every election.

The Liberals tended to be right of centre in the early postwar period, and were rather more likely to win support of former Conservatives than of previous Labour voters. In a few instances, the Liberals went so far as to form local electoral pacts with the Conservatives, agreeing not to contest a particular seat if the Conservatives refrained from offering a candidate in another seat. These pacts came under increasing fire from those Liberals who wanted the party to move in a more progressive direction, and by the end of the 1950s they had ceased (Rasmussen 1965: 102–8). Without these pacts, however, the Liberals might have been reduced to only three or four MPs during the 1950s; whether they could have remained a viable party under such circumstances is questionable. As the Liberals moved to the centre, they began to offer as much competition to Labour as to the Conservatives.

With the founding of the SDP, the Liberals were faced with a new competitor at the centre of the spectrum. Since both parties recognized that competition between them would be mutually destructive, they quickly worked out an electoral pact in which constituencies were allocated between the two parties, so that nowhere would they oppose each other. Furthermore, they ran a joint electoral campaign, which, in turn, required some degree of joint policy-making (Rasmussen 1985: 86–92). The relations which developed out of these arrangements led the Liberals and the bulk of the SDP eventually to merge to found a new party in 1988. The competitive thrust of the Liberal/SDP Alliance was somewhat ambiguous. On the one hand, they sought to replace Labour as the major opposition party to the Conservatives, and to that extent they presented the greatest threat to the former. On the other hand,

Labour's declining electoral support made the Alliance candidate the chief challenger to the great bulk of Conservative MPs in southern England. In that sense the Alliance also threatened the Conservatives.

The nationalist parties have not faced the Liberals' and SDP's need for co-operative arrangements, since they have contested elections in different regions. None the less, prior to the 1987 election Plaid Cymru and the SNP did sign a formal pact. They agreed upon a programme for negotiation if the forthcoming election gave no party a majority in Parliament. Furthermore, they ruled out any coalition or deal with the Conservatives. (Since the Conservatives won the election with a sizeable majority, these plans proved to be irrelevant.) In terms of the search for voting support, both the SNP and Plaid Cymru compete with Labour and the Alliance parties for the middle to the left of the spectrum in their respective regions.

The matter of relations between parties is one of relative strength as well as of location. The Liberals were irrelevant to the arithmetic of government formation for over a quarter of a century into the postwar period. When the February 1974 election failed to give any party a majority, however, Prime Minister Edward Heath briefly discussed the possibility of coalition with Liberal leader Jeremy Thorpe, but no agreement was reached (Steel 1980: 13–16). Labour then formed a minority government without seeking any Liberal help. Since in the next election, a few months later, Labour won a majority, albeit a tenuous one, the Liberals continued to be ignored. In less than two years, however, by-election defeats made Labour a minority government once again and the small parties became highly relevant. Surprisingly, given their positions on the political spectrum, Labour turned first to the Ulster Unionists. Only when the Unionists refused to guarantee Catholics a significant voice in governing Northern Ireland, were the region once again to be given a legislature with substantial powers, did Labour decide that the price was too high and seek Liberal support (King 1981: 50; but see also Donoughue 1987: 159).

Instead of a formal coalition, with the Liberals taking seats in the cabinet, a 'pact' was made in which the Liberals agreed to support Labour in the Commons so that it could remain in office. This arrangement lasted for a year and a half, at which point the Liberals let it lapse. Liberal gains from the pact were rather modest. The 1978 Budget provided for profit-sharing by employees, a long-time Liberal panacea for improving industrial relations. The Labour government dropped plans for taking more enterprises into state ownership. The party's leaders had wanted to drop them in any event but were afraid this would alienate their left wing. And a mechanism for consultation with the Liberals on government policy and legislation was established (Steel 1980: 152–7). The Liberals had pressed for proportional representation in elections for the European Parliament. While the government introduced such legislation, it did not whip its MPs. Although a majority of them voted for the bill, enough voted against so that it was defeated (Steel 1980: 107–11). Thus the potentially most significant prize of the Liberals' new relevance was lost.

With the pact ended, Labour was forced to reconsider support from the regional parties. The government's refusal to proceed with devolution legislation for Scotland so angered the SNP that it introduced a motion of no confidence. Only after it had done so did the Conservatives press the issue with a similar motion. Since Labour could expect no support from the Liberals or the SNP, that left Plaid Cymru, the SDLP and the Ulster Unionists. The votes of the former were bought fairly cheaply – compensation for quarrymen suffering from respiratory diseases (King 1981: 86–7). The Northern Ireland situation was more complicated. Labour had agreed that inasmuch as Northern Ireland's legislature had been abolished the region should have substantially greater representation in the House of Commons (Donoughue 1987: 159). Despite this concession, the Unionists were unhappy with the government over its failure to reintroduce some measure of self-government for the region. While this delay did not dissatisfy the SDLP (since it was caused by a concern to ensure that the rights of Catholics were protected), that party's lone MP was disillusioned with Labour's willingness to increase the number of Northern Ireland seats and to seek deals with the Unionists (House of Commons Debates 1979: 515–22).

All of the Liberals and of the SNP voted against the government in support of the no confidence motion, while Plaid Cymru voted with the government. The SDLP MP abstained, while the Ulster Unionists split with five of them voting against the government but two supporting it. The government lost the division by a single vote. *All* the small parties – even the SDLP with but one MP – were therefore relevant at this point. Labour was forced to call an election a few months earlier than it had intended, an election that Margaret Thatcher won as the first of a string of three consecutive victories.

Although the most dramatic, the division of 28 March 1979 was not the only example of small party relevance. In the United States, for instance, third parties have served to initiate and popularize new ideas and issues, which major parties then adopt in order not to lose their dominant position due to a shifting ground swell of public opinion. The increased interest in Welsh and, especially, Scottish nationalism which Plaid Cymru and the SNP were able to generate in the 1970s forced the major parties to respond.

Granted that in the end the devolution plans proposed by the Labour government were not implemented and would have fallen far short of what the nationalist parties desired even if they had been. None the less, the government was forced to modify its position on devolution in the direction of greater autonomy for Wales and Scotland. Furthermore, 'the devolution legislation passed only because the Liberals and the nationalist parties . . . supported it' (King 1981: 77–8). Small parties clearly were relevant to the policy process in this respect, even though they did not succeed in achieving their full aims. Had it not been for their efforts the Welsh and Scottish electorates never would have had an opportunity to express their views on whether the existing institutional arrangements adequately recognized any national distinctiveness they felt. The parties had forced the government to pay attention to an issue of importance to their clientele – an issue which both major parties had been ignoring.

The government also has been forced to respond once more to the Northern Ireland situation. As was the case with Scotland and Wales, however, the response was not what the small parties in question preferred. The Anglo-Irish agreement negotiated by the Thatcher government can be seen as an attempt to move towards solving the problem reflected in the growth of small party prevalence in Northern Ireland.

Thus, while none of the small parties entered a formal coalition during the postwar period, they have had in given situations to be taken into account for majority control of the Commons. They have influenced the content of government policy and they have so popularized new policies that the major parties have not been able to continue to ignore them.

Conclusion: assessing the value of small British parties

For more than a quarter of a century following the Second World War, small parties in Britain were of negligible significance. The last decade and a half, however, has seen several small parties progress through the various stages of party development identified in this volume all the way to relevance. The period of relevance proved to be short-lived; whether any British small party had relevance by the end of the 1980s was questionable.

The small parties that developed in Britain challenged the major parties on their own ground or by raising new issues. Their main aim was not to mobilize new segments of the electorate, as the Labour Party had done early in the century. Furthermore, small party growth occurred not at the fringes of the political spectrum, but at the centre or from a detached position. While these 'detached' parties could be given a location on the spectrum, their fundamental aims were largely irrelevant to the left–right cleavage of the major party system. Their basic purpose was either to seek to separate a particular region from the existing governmental system or to ensure that it remained forever as tightly bound to that system as it currently was. Most of the small parties to arise in Britain during this period were regional, not country-wide, ones.

In terms of impact upon the direction of competition, their coalition potential and their relevance to government policy-making, these regional parties played as significant a role as did the country-wide small parties. Inasmuch as the country-wide parties clearly were stronger in terms of popular support and, to some extent, parliamentary representation, this is a surprising conclusion. Why should regional small parties have been as prevalent as they have in Britain and have enjoyed such relative success?

Despite having to surmount the obstacles which major parties erect to hamper the growth of new parties, regional parties, because of their concentrated support, are better able to cope with Britain's electoral system. Once small parties gain representation, the constraints they encounter in Parliament do not all cut the same way. Some disadvantage regional parties more than country-wide ones, but other institutional arrangements facilitate expression of regional concerns.

Furthermore, the way in which the British system functions tends to stimulate the development of regional parties more than country-wide ones. The parliamentary system as operated in Britain for the bulk of the twentieth century has stressed party cohesion and highly disciplined legislative voting. Unless the desires and needs of constituents are to be ignored totally, such a system is practicable only in a quite homogeneous country. Canada illustrates what happens to a party system when a country tries to operate the British parliamentary system in an environment that is geographically and culturally diverse. Unless stringent party discipline is relaxed, fragments break off from major parties as some parliamentarians find they cannot conform and still represent their districts, or major parties are driven from some areas because indigenous political groupings can voice regional demands in a way that legislators toeing the policy line of a country-wide major party cannot.

United States parties are coalitions of disparate interests and areas. They have proven durable by eschewing legislative cohesion.

Britain may not be as varied as is the United States, but it fails to correspond to the traditional textbook portrait of homogeneity from Land's End to John o'Groats. The country is too diverse to incorporate adequately the various demands of all its people within only two tightly disciplined parties. The UK has failed to balance party discipline with diversity at a point that can maintain a two-party system as pure as that in the USA. Since the major British parties are concerned to develop policies for the entire country, it is not surprising that interests that matter only to a region tend to be ignored. By definition only a small minority care about such topics; they are of little moment to a relatively inflexible party seeking to make a country-wide appeal to all people of a particular social type.

Since the British party system tends not to represent regional interests adequately, the development of small parties to fill the void is no real surprise.[3] Whatever the Liberals may claim about the inadequacy of the choice offered by Labour and the Conservatives on a country-wide basis, the alternatives are not so clearly deficient in addressing the full range of the electorate's concerns as they are in the case of regional matters. For that matter, although the Liberals have sought to make a country-wide challenge (even in those elections in which they contested a minority of the constituencies), much of their success in surmounting the threshold of representation has been regionally based. A disproportionate number of Liberal MPs have been elected in Scotland, Wales and the West Country – the 'Celtic fringe' (Rasmussen 1981: 174–5). While in terms of their objectives the Liberals have been a country-wide party, in terms of their accomplishments they, too, have been something of a regional party.

Given this pattern of Liberal representation, why was it not until the rise of the nationalist parties that the devolution issue was put on the political agenda? Obviously, having three parties pressing for something is likely to have greater impact than having only one doing so. And the Liberals were an essential element in the grouping that managed to get legislation passed that led to the devolution referendum.

But a further consideration is relevant as well. The nationalist parties focus primarily on a single issue. By doing so they are likely to have a greater impact upon agenda setting than would a party that dilutes its effect by forwarding a range of issues. Regional concentration of *policy* objectives is likely to be an asset to effectiveness just as regional concentration of *electoral* support gains maximum representation for any given level of popularity. In this way again the political process seems tilted to favour the regional small party over the country-wide one.

In recent years, party cohesion in the Commons has declined somewhat, but not so far as to eliminate the attractiveness of small regional parties for representing the neglected concerns of some segments of the electorate. Small parties may drop from relevance or return to it, but they seem unlikely to disappear from Britain until such time as the major parties totally restructure themselves and alter their conceptions of the way in which to operate the British parliamentary system.

Notes

I am happy to acknowledge partial financial support for this study from the Ralph Dorfman Memorial Fund. Additional aid was received from the University of Glasgow and the European Consortium for Political Research.

1. From 1918, when it first was required, until 1987, the electoral deposit was £150. The substantial increase in the number of candidates in the 1970s showed that this sum had ceased to be much of a deterrent. So for the 1987 election it was increased to £500. The share of the vote which a candidate had to win to get the deposit returned was reduced, however, from 12.5 percent to only 5 percent.

2. These surveys were commissioned by *The Scotsman*. Access to the results is by courtesy of Robert Worcester of MORI.

3. Labour has a single, unified party structure throughout Britain; no Scottish Labour Party exists. The Labour Party in Scotland is simply one of eleven regional party organizations. While the Conservatives do have a separate Scottish Conservative Party, its autonomy from the country-wide party is questionable. Interestingly, the Scottish and Welsh Liberal Democrats do enjoy a good deal of autonomy. None the less, even they are not as distinctly separate as are the SNP and Plaid Cymru.

9

The Decline of Small Parties and the Emergence of Two-Partyism in Greece

Yannis Papadopoulos

Despite recent scholarly interest in the Greek party system (Mavrogordatos 1983a; 1983b; Nicolacopoulos 1984; Papadopoulos 1989b), and its emphasis on the features of the 'new' system that emerged after the restoration of democracy in 1974,[1] the field of small parties remains a *terra incognita*. It is true that since 1974 and until the election of June 1989 no direct impact of small parties could be observed on governmental formation. After four national legislative elections, no coalition had proved to be necessary for the formation of a government. Each of these governments has been majoritarian, composed of only one party – the conservative New Democracy (ND) in 1974 and 1977, the socialist PASOK in 1981 and 1985[2] – although the parliamentary majorities were all, save the first one, 'manufactured' (Rae 1967: 74–7), in the sense that the ruling party had a minority of popular votes. Those 'majorities simply became an extension of the government' (Katsoudas 1987: 24), ratifying its acts, indicating an executive dominance over the legislative that may also be measured by the impressive durability of the cabinet (Lijphart et al. 1988: 20). This situation changed after the June 1989 election with the advent of a coalition between the conservatives and the far left. However, this government was not expected to be viable in the long run, because of the ideological differences of the partners on social and economic issues. It had a limited mandate for three months, until new elections were held, and its main purpose was to ensure 'catharsis' (investigations into corrupt politicians) and democratization after eight years of socialist rule. The November 1989 election did not result in a majority either; the three major parties (ND, PASOK and the far left) then formed a grand coalition. Yet this too was a provisional solution until the new election of April 1990, which brought ND to power, although with a narrow majority.

The simplest way to approach small parties is the numerical one. Although quantitative thresholds may seem arbitrary, it must be said to their credit that they are at least clear ones. Peter Mair, for example, in his contribution to this volume, uses the parties' electoral score to distinguish small parties from both 'micro-' and large parties. This electoral perspective, however, while obviously suitable for cross-national comparison since it relies on homogeneous criteria, does not seem accurate enough to handle country specificities evident in monographic studies. Regarding the Greek case, it does not help very much because:

1. The time-span since the emergence of the present party system is rather short and therefore few elections were held during this period; thus, the number of cases is perhaps not sufficient.
2. There are in some cases tremendous fluctuations in the electoral score of individual parties: in its initial phase, the new party system was indeed a very fluid one and was constantly reshaped (for example, PASOK was only the third party in 1974).
3. According to Gordon Smith's contribution (this volume) 'smallness' is above all a systemic and thereby a relative quality, dependent upon the particular format of each party system; parties cannot but be defined in relation to each other and not in absolute terms, a point particularly applicable to Greece.
4. Organizational discontinuity is observable within the ideological streams, and the parties that periodically expressed them did not all possess the same degree of systemic relevance.

Let us therefore turn to qualitative variables, related to the functions performed by small parties within the party system. In fact, according to Fisher (1974: 8), 'many scholars seem to agree that account must be taken not only of the number of votes won by a party, but also of its influence on the roles and positions of the major parties in the system'. In other words, preference will be given to criteria of relevance, although the latter is likely to be influenced by party size. The criteria for inclusion in the analysis will therefore be the following:

First, *presence in parliament*, a threshold which distinguishes small parties from totally marginal ones. The threshold is to some extent arbitrary, since some parties which were not actually represented in parliament may have had 'blackmail' potential (Sartori 1976: 123) and thus have been relevant, but this is an unsolved problem caused by the heterogeneity of those minor parties without parliamentary representation. In any case, it definitely makes no sense to include those 'proto-parties' which have passed the formal thresholds of declaration and authorization (250 Greek parties have been created since 1974), but not the higher and far more effective ones of representation and relevance, which are generally the only ones to denote some sort of political significance.

Secondly, *parties with or without coalition potential*: this criterion enables us to distinguish smaller parties from the third party, the communist KKE, whose coalition potential is uncertain. KKE should be seen as distinct from small parties: it fits Epstein's (1967: 64) definition of the third party, since it is constantly 'threatening to win enough offices to influence control of the government'. KKE (or rather, the 'Alliance of the Left and Progress', electorally dominated by this party) recently acquired coalition potential in the 'historical compromise' government that resulted from the June 1989 election, where despite a conservative relative victory no party won a majority of seats. Yet, as mentioned above, this provisional government had a limited mandate, and only two members of the left participated, besides non-members of KKE. The 'Alliance' also took part in the grand coalition government (the first one under normal circumstances since 1926, when the communists had remained in opposition) that was formed after the November 1989 election. Yet the logic both of electoral behaviour (bipolarization) and of government formation (a transitional process until new elections were held) remained majoritarian. It cannot be ruled out, however, that 'progressive' coalitions may emerge in the future, as the socialists find it more and more difficult to attain power without the help of a partner. Besides, the vote of Communist MPs has been required during dramatic parliamentary events, such as the controversial presidential election by the parliament in 1985, or the constitutional amendments that followed it.

Thirdly, *parties which remain relevant*, either because of blackmail potential (parties may contribute to altering the direction of competition), or for some other reasons specific to the Greek setting, which remain to be defined.

The above criteria must be tempered by three restrictions which again stem from some characteristics of the Greek party system, such as its initial fluidity, personalism or the tensions between tradition and change. The following will therefore be excluded from discussion:

(a) Parties which are only transitionally small, falling into another category in the subsequent elections.
(b) Mere parliamentary splinters which persist during one sole legislature and may thus be assimilated to 'proto-parties' with a parliamentary origin, but which fail to develop at the societal level.

(c) 'Satellite' parties which do not elect their parliamentarians autonomously.

The logic is therefore largely exclusive, and only four parties really deserve full attention as being 'small' in a strict sense: the National Front, the Party of Neo-Liberals, 'Democratic Renewal' (DIANA) and the Eurocommunist party KKE-essoterikou (KKE-es, Communist Party of the Interior). The first two are ephemeral, short-lived parties, which eventually vanish, absorbed by ND, which progressively consolidates its hegemony over the conservative camp. DIANA is a 'small party of personalities' (Duverger 1976: 323), issued from a split in New Democracy. KKE-es can on the contrary be portrayed as a durable, 'permanent minority party' (Duverger 1976: 323); or at least, because of recent changes in the party labels, as a permanent minority *force*, which is an expression of a marginal but persisting culture. For each of these parties it will be suitable to determine its electoral strength and social basis, its organizational pattern and its ideological profile, its resources and its role in both the party system and the political system. A systemic analysis is thus preferred for Greece, focussing on the three dimensions of the small parties' relations to their environment: relationship with society, with other parties and with institutions.

Finally, it may sound somewhat paradoxical to analyse the impact of small parties, at first sight negligible, if not insignificant, in Greece. This chapter intends to show nevertheless that *some* small Greek parties are or have been neither totally irrelevant[3] nor mere parentheses before the 'freezing' of party cleavages when these parties became ephemeral. It may be argued that, even in a party system with a limited format like the Greek one, small parties are likely to fulfil some functions – which should of course not be overemphasized – and to play a certain role, however modest it may be. The Greek case is useful also in throwing light on why in certain countries small parties have had less impact than in others.

Small parties and society

A historical flashback to the postwar and pre-1967 'old' and exclusivist party system may be illuminating with regard to the evolution of the small parties' relationship with society. The emergence of small parties was no more than sporadic, their success fluctuating, with most of them quite ephemeral. This was despite the personalistic dimension in Greek politics: the latter is a factor not just of atomization, but also of the fluidity of the party system.

The notable exception of EDA (Unitary and Democratic Left) should, however, be mentioned. This was a front for banned Communists which was irrelevant because it was a 'pariah', but which can be counted as neither actually small nor short-lived. Its minimum score was 9.6 percent in the first election it contested in 1952, held under the plurality system, and it even reached a peak of 24.4 percent in 1958, becoming the first opposition party. EDA still exists, recently split in two, although practically only on paper. Only one among the small parties elected deputies under the same name and by itself (without combining with other parties or merging with them) in more than one election, and this was in the first two postwar elections (the right-wing National Party of Greece: 6.0 percent and twenty MPs in 1946, 3.7 percent and only seven MPs in 1950).

To be sure, this fluidity was not specific to small parties but, as a correlate of personalism, it also affected more successful parties. Nevertheless, small parties started forming alliances as soon as the first postwar election, and started declining significantly in the early 1960s. As we shall see in due course, both in the old and in the new party system, consolidation of the party system meant at the same time its oligopolization. Although the persistence of personalism delayed the freezing of a tripolarity which is linked to effective two-partyism, it did not impede it. It first appeared clearly in the 1961 election, and was not interrupted thereafter with the exception of the first two post-junta elections, which must be viewed as atypical and transitional, still marked by the cataclysmic events that preceded them (Papadopoulos 1989b: 59–60). After the 1961 election and prior to the royal coup of 1965, and *again* after the dictatorship since the 1981 election, we find the three ideological families united as a result of the two major cleavages that have marked recent Greek history (the 'national schism' between royalists and liberal republicans, and the civil war between a bourgeois coalition and the Communists): the right, the centre (now centre-left) and the communist left.[4]

In the very early period of transition to democracy after 1974, a plethora of minor parties and groups emerged (for example, seven communist parties were counted); there was a temporary resurgence of civil society common to moments following prolonged abnormal periods. No less than thirty-six parties, for example, contested the first postwar election, despite the abstention of the left (a similar proliferation can be found, for instance, in post-revolutionary Portugal).[5] Ephemeral minor groups of this initial stage may therefore be depicted as themselves transitional, that is, not so much functionally relevant for the transition process but rather indicators of it.

In the first election after the restoration of democracy, however, which took place in November 1974, New Democracy,[6] founded by the 'swing man' (Diamandouros 1984) of the transition and then Prime Minister, Karamanlis, won an overwhelming majority of 54.4 percent of the vote. Table 9.1 presents the outcomes of the legislative elections of 1974, 1977, 1981, 1985, 1989 and 1990 as well as those of the European elections of 1981, 1984 and 1989.

During the first legislature (1974–7), there was a dominant-party phenomenon,[7] the hegemony of ND not being brought into question by the fragmented centre and the left opposition. The place of the first opposition party was occupied by the moderate centrist party EK–ND (Centre Union–New Forces). Andreas Papandreou's PASOK had to content itself with third place, its score having been far lower than its expectations; nevertheless, it had already outdistanced the communist left. Hence, this election fulfilled a function of legitimation and institutionalization of a transition process where the predominant will was to regulate all sorts of excess 'variety'. Except PASOK, which later became a pillar of the party system, the only party that could be considered a small one was the United Left alliance, which was the fourth political force in competition to elect deputies, without any coalition potential, however. This alliance had no blackmail potential by itself either, since its components split immediately after the election (the orthodox CP, the Eurocommunist party and EDA, the already mentioned legal cover of the CP during the exclusivist period when this party was banned, and which refused to merge with the Communists after their legalization in 1974).

The election of November 1977 was also devoid of a power contest, since the opposition to ND had remained divided and had not managed to form an alliance. Yet, this election prepared the ground for two-partyism, with PASOK's dramatic rise, the decline of the centrist party EDIK (formerly EK–ND) and the relative stagnation of the left. None the less, and despite some losses (41.9 percent), ND preserved its absolute majority in seats, thanks to the electoral system the effects of which will be discussed more in detail later. In 1977, competition was high in each of the ideological spaces of the right, the centre (including the centre-left) and the communist left, but this type of conflict was resolved during this election (Mavrogordatos 1983a: 72): ND remained hegemonic over the right at the expense of the extreme-rightist National Front, while PASOK acquired hegemony over the centrist clienteles at the

Table 9.1 Electoral outcomes in Greece since 1974, national and European elections

Party	National Nov 1974 % of vote	National Nov 1974 No. of seats	National Nov 1977 % of vote	National Nov 1977 No. of seats	National Oct 1981 % of vote	National Oct 1981 No. of seats	Eur. Oct 1981 % of vote	Eur. June 1984 % of vote	National June 1985 % of vote	National June 1985 No. of seats	National June 1989 % of vote	National June 1989 No. of seats	Eur. June 1989 % of vote	National Nov 1989 % of vote	National Nov 1989 No. of seats	National April 1990 % of vote	National April 1990 No. of seats
Extreme right[1]	1.1		6.8	5	1.7		2.8	2.5	0.6		0.3		1.5	0.1		0.1	
New Democracy	54.4	220	41.8	171	35.9	115	31.3	38.1	40.9	126	44.3	145	40.4	46.2	148	46.9	150
Neo-Liberals			1.1	2													
Centre Union[2]	20.4	60	12.0	16	0.4												
Minor centre parties[3]					1.2												
PASOK	13.6	12	25.3	93	48.1	172	40.1	41.6	45.8	161	39.2	125	36.0	40.7	128	38.6	125
United Left[4]	9.5	8									13.1	28	14.3	11.0	21	10.3	21
KKE			9.4	11	10.9	13	12.8	11.6	9.9	12							
KKE-es[5]			2.7	2	1.4		5.3	3.4	1.8	1							
Extreme left			0.5		0.2			0.4	0.3		0.6		1.1	0.2		0.4	
Other parties and candidates[6]	1.0		0.4		0.2			0.5	0.3		1.1		4.3	1.8	3	3.2	3

[1] EDE in 1974, National Front in 1977, Progressive Party in 1981, EPEN in 1984, 1985 and 1989.
[2] EK-ND in 1974, EDIK in 1977 and 1981.
[3] Including DIANA in June 1989 and 1990.
[4] KKE + KKE-es + EDA in 1974, 'Alliance of the Left and Progress' since 1989 (KKE + EAR + EDA + six minor parties).
[5] Symmachia (Alliance): KKE-es + four minor parties in 1977.
[6] Including 'Greens' and candidates of the Muslim minority since 1989.

Sources: Mavrogordatos 1983a: 71, 81; Kathimerini 5.6.85., 8.10.85., 22.6.89., 8.11.89.; Messimvrini, 10.4.90

expense of the declining EDIK, and KKE consolidated its own hegemony over the communist space. Two short-lived small parties among those which contested this election proved to be important through the effects of their presence on party competition or through the future implications of their existence: the aforementioned National Front and the Party of Neo-Liberals.

The extreme-rightist National Front polled 6.8 percent of the vote in this election, quite an unusual score for an ideological stream which in other elections has oscillated between 0.1 and 2.8 percent. This party was a coalition of all sorts of reactionary notables, monarchists and former supporters of the military dictatorship. The geographical distribution of the National Front electorate was quite uneven: the Front polled up to 27.3 percent of the vote in the constituency of Rodopi in Thrace, where it was the second party and where the Muslim population voted massively for it; however, it oscillated between 0.4 and 1.7 percent in the constituencies of the island of Crete, one of the main strongholds of liberalism and republicanism. In general, the Front performed much better than its national average in the strongholds of the right, like the constituencies of the southern Peloponnese (it came second in Lakonia), and was systematically under-represented in the large urban areas (Athens, Piraeus, Salonica) as well as on the Aegean Islands.

The second relevant small party of the 1977 election, the Party of Neo-Liberals, was founded by Mitsotakis, one of the Centre Union leaders (the party in power from 1963 to 1965) who had supported the royal coup of July 1965 by quitting their party, a manoeuvre which led to the overthrow of the then centrist government. Considered since the traumatic events of that period as one of the leading 'turncoats' or 'apostates', he was unable to find a place in any existing party, and even after 1974 his efforts to integrate with ND by offering allegiance to Karamanlis were rejected. He decided then to found his own party, a genuine 'small party of personalities', corresponding to the traditional pattern of political mobilization in Greece. The Neo-Liberals were a 'cadre' party with a personalistic-clientelistic basis and a vague ideology: in the Greek political semantics of that time, 'neo-liberal' had not at all the current anti-*étatist* and rightist connotation, but denoted rather the party's wish to appear as heir to the centrist liberal tradition. Anyway, the party took root only regionally, on the island of Crete, one of the strongholds of Greek liberalism, going back to E. Venizelos, a charismatic leader native of the island. Though party candidates contested the election in more than half the constituencies, the party registered its best scores in two of the four Cretan constituencies (its average score in Crete was 13.4 percent, whereas its national average was only 1.1 percent): Rethymno (26.0 percent) and Chania (25.7 percent), where it gained its two MPs, even managing to be the second party after ND in Rethymno and the first in Chania. (In a third Cretan constituency, Lassithi, the Neo-Liberals polled 7.9 percent of the vote.) The clientelistic and personalistic bases of the party are confirmed by the fact that Mitsotakis, who was elected in Chania, had already polled 18.3 percent of the vote there as an independent candidate in 1974, and also by the fact that the second Neo-Liberal MP had already polled 22.3 percent of the vote in Rethymno in 1974, also running as an independent.

In the 1981 election, not a single small party survived, a pattern which seems practically unchanged since then: only the three major parties have preserved parliamentary representation. This was the first election after 1974 where the question of alternation in power appeared on the agenda in real terms of competition between two parties (Mavrogordatos 1983b). Alternation took place indeed as PASOK, once more doubling its votes (48.1 percent) replaced ND (35.9 percent) in government. The strong duopolistic concentration was partly due to the effects of the electoral system. But it was above all the product of the situation that reinforced the 'wasted vote' argument, which admittedly acts in turn as a self-fulfilling prophecy against small parties.

In the national election of 1985, held in a climate of unprecedented bipolarization, the two-party system was strengthened: PASOK and ND reached together an even higher score (86.7 percent) than that of 1981 (84.0 percent). Simultaneously, the small parties collapsed: the extreme right vote fell to 0.6 percent and the centre to 0.2 percent. Only the Eurocommunist KKE-es succeeded in having its leader elected and in increasing its vote compared with the national election of 1981 (1.8 percent instead of 1.4 percent); yet, this result remained far lower than that in the European elections of 1981 and 1984. The persistence of this force – whose fortunes fluctuated the least despite the trend towards the consolidation of tripolarity – argues for paying particular attention to it in order to explain its marginality *and* durability, its electoral failure *and* survival. For example, in the June 1989 election which was held under conditions of polarization similar to those of 1985 but under an electoral law which was much closer to proportionality (with a bonus for parties that polled between 2 and 3 percent!), the left Alliance emerged as a third force with coalition potential, although PASOK and ND combined still polled 83.5 percent. The Eurocommunist 'new left' tendency within the Alliance, although electorally smaller, then established a certain ideological hegemony by imposing its line on the pro-Soviet KKE, torn between the orthodoxy of its members (in disarray over Gorbachev's reforms) and the constraints of local pragmatism.

The only small party that gained one seat in parliament by itself in June 1989 was DIANA, whose leader C. Stephanopoulos was elected in Athens. Although ten deputies had followed him when he had left ND after the defeat of 1985, DIANA suffered a constant erosion of its membership, absorbed by its big conservative rival, and failed to win wider support (1.0 percent). Although the party had candidates in almost all constituencies, its only score much above the average was in Achaia (3.5 percent), Stephanopoulos's fief. Yet, the poor electoral score of DIANA probably sufficed to prevent the formation of a conservative majority in Parliament. And its leader, who is considered a moderate centre-right politician, was already being mentioned as a possible Prime Minister after those elections, which resulted in no clear majority. DIANA did not take part in the election held in November of the same year, discouraged by its poor results in the previous one. In April 1990 this party elected one sole deputy, who ironically enough provided the conservative government with the single vote they needed to get a majority in Parliament. In short, DIANA's key ideological location between ND and PASOK is largely counterbalanced by the party's precarious condition. Its absorption by ND, or at least its satellitization seem to be the most probable outcomes.

The results of the November 1989 election did not differ much from the outcome of the election held five months before. The two major parties strengthened their respective positions, thus bipolarization became even more acute. The Alliance of the left underwent some losses, for many communist voters had not been sympathetic to the summer governance with the conservatives. The Alliance could no longer afford to continue as a coalition partner of ND and ignore PASOK, which is ideologically much closer to her. On the other hand, ND again missed a majority in Parliament in spite of its electoral gains, because of the electoral system. No minimal winning coalition was possible any more: the left could not renew its co-operation with the conservatives and its support for PASOK would not be sufficient either. The stalemate was perfect and long negotiations finally resulted in the formation of a grand coalition (ND-PASOK-Alliance). The latter had to content itself with caretaker functions, for all governmental parties made an extensive use of their veto right, paralysing thereby any legislative activity.

It is striking that the majoritarian logic continued to prevail; the Greeks came to vote for the third time in less than a year. The election of April 1990 did not cause major shifts either, but this time ND reached a majority in Parliament, although a marginal one dependent in the beginning upon the support of the DIANA deputy. As far as small parties are concerned, we noticed in both November 1989 and April 1990 the emergence of one Green deputy and of two parliamentarians who explicitly represent the Muslim minority; nevertheless, those new forces should not for the time being be viewed as relevant. The Greens are fragmented into numerous minor parties and their MP was elected under the banner of a loose and heterogeneous confederation that encompasses only some of them. Besides, the fact that Muslim deputies were for the first time not members of national parties was due to the tactical choices of the Turkish government which backs them and in large part controls the Muslim electorate which is concentrated in Northern Greece, close to the Turkish border. Last but not least, such marginal streams are at the mercy of a harsher electoral system, which cannot be excluded for the next elections.

After having reviewed elections, let us examine in more detail KKE-essoterikou (the Greek Communist Party of the Interior), which persisted throughout the whole time-span under consideration. It originated from a split within the Greek communist movement that occurred during the dictatorship, in February 1968 (the label 'of the Interior' results from the fact that the Politbureau members who created KKE-es had first organized in Greece an illegal and unofficial interior bureau of the Communist Party) (Kapetanyannis 1979). The new party leaders opposed the Soviet invasion of Czechoslovakia, which took place soon after the party's formation, and later adopted the Eurocommunist doctrine, taking inspiration from theoretical developments in the Italian PCI.

Nevertheless, the communist label and affiliation impeded the party's progress among other progressive strata of society. This 'sin' was not counterbalanced by the adoption of a very moderate line, which often contrasted sharply with the maximalism of PASOK in opposition and of KKE: the party was harshly criticized for acting in this way as a pawn of the bourgeoisie. On the contrary, the mobilizing discourse of PASOK's charismatic leader Papandreou, who combined strong nationalistic and populistic elements, was most likely to appeal to the radicalized *petit bourgeois* strata of Greek society (Papadopoulos 1989a: 91–104), especially because PASOK was not handicapped by any communist origin, since it was rooted in the centre-left tendency that was present before the military coup (Lyrintzis 1983; Mavrogordatos 1983b). The change of name from KKE-es into 'EAR' (Greek left) institutionalized the decline of official Eurocommunism in Greece too: in a congress held in April 1987, the majority of the delegates opted for the creation of a new left party devoid of any communist label.[8] More recently a debate was initiated within EAR on the adoption of a social democratic platform.

The social impact of KKS-es – and now of EAR ('Greek left'), – remains considerable, however. This is mainly because this party has undeniable political visibility, mostly due to its leader, L. Kyrkos, who, though not really as charismatic as Karamanlis or Papandreou, is rather popular: he is perceived as the most moderate among ten prominent politicians (Behrakis and Nicolacopoulos 1988: 91). Hence, the party enjoys a source of sympathy which is nevertheless not translated into votes. Although we lack empirical evidence to prove the following assumption, it is highly probable that, through the leader's and the party's image of responsibility and democratic outlook, EAR would be a second preference for many PASOK or even some ND voters (who might prefer the more leftist but moderate EAR to PASOK which has a strong 'anti-right' ideological core). The higher scores registered in the European election of 1981 and 1984 tend to prove that KKE-es lost a part of its potential electoral capital in national elections because of its marginality, which makes the 'wasted vote' argument work. Simultaneously, it is unlikely that EAR was also a second preference for orthodox KKE voters if we take into account that the latter's score also increased in European elections. As mentioned earlier both parties decided to create an Alliance with the prospect of the June 1989 election, and this 'Alliance of the Left and Progress' also includes other minor parties of the left.

EAR is also a laboratory for political ideas. Though its relationship with society is rather loose (KKE-es registered its best scores in 1985 in the urban areas of Athens, Piraeus and Salonica, as well as in some communist strongholds such as the islands of Lefkada and Samos), the party is the strongest at the cultural level and the one in which intellectuals are the most influential. Its élitism is therefore undeniable, and the risk of assimilation to a club rather than to a party is obvious. But it is also true that EAR is certainly the most open-minded among Greek parties, the least inclined to suffocate mass movements, the only one to allow and to have institutionalized internal democracy and the expression of different tendencies. Despite its small size, EAR displays some characteristics of a modern mass party, influenced by the communist pattern but having liberalized it.

In a somewhat authoritarian environment – the case of Greece highlights the gap that may exist between the democratic form of a regime and the authoritarian structure of political organizations (von Beyme 1986: 3) – EAR may be seen as an 'avant-gardist' exception. Moreover, this is the party most open to the demands of social and cultural minorities as well as to new social movements: it performs in Greece functions similar to those of, say, Partito Radicale in Italy. In that sense KKE-es already was more a 'new left' party, open to non-party adherents of the left, rather than a communist one, and this despite the communist outlook of its leadership.

To summarize the evolution of the party system from its creation in 1974 onwards, we may qualify it as *transitional* until the 1984 European election, since when the system has stabilized, and the dealignments have become weaker. PASOK's landslide victory in 1981 and the rise to power for the first time in the country's history of a party calling itself 'socialist' also inaugurated a new phase in Greek party politics. The consolidation of democracy (Diamandouros 1984) seems therefore to go together with the consolidation of the party system, which may be measured by aggregate electoral volatility (cumulative gains for the winning parties: Pedersen 1983: 32–3), obviously lower at the recent election – see Table 9.2.[9]

We may therefore also speak of the parallel consolidation of a marginal role to which small parties are confined, since significant space was left to them only during the initial transitional phase. Small parties do not seem very optimistic themselves: the decision of the left parties to merge is a case in point. Yet, 'small' might be more beautiful after a reshaping of the party system which may still occur, but this will be discussed later in this essay.

In a systemic account of the relationship of small parties with

Table 9.2 *Aggregate electoral volatility*

Election	National or European	Compared with	Aggregate volatility
Nov 1977	National	1974 Nat. el.	20.6
Oct 1981	National	1977 Nat. el.	22.8
Oct 1981	European	1981 Nat. el.	12.9
June 1984	European	1981 Nat. el.	6.2
June 1984	European	1981 Eur. el.	7.0
June 1985	National	1981 Nat. el.	5.1
June 1985	National	1984 Eur. el.	7.0
June 1989	National	1985 Nat. el.	6.3
June 1989	European	1984 Eur. el.	3.6
June 1989	European	1989 Nat. el. (June)	4.0
Nov 1989	National	1989 Nat. el. (June)	3.4
Apr 1990	National	1989 Nat. el. (Nov)	1.6

society, the parties can also be classified according to the political families they belong to, with two underlying assumptions: first, that the more complex the cleavage structure, the more possibilities are available for their emergence; and secondly, that their success may be unevenly distributed according to the interests they succeed in aggregating. Thus, 'detached' parties which cannot be reduced to the left-right dimension are likely to introduce into the political arena specific agrarian, ecologist or regionalistic demands which are not satisfactorily encompassed by the left–right scheme. Now, since ethnic, linguistic and religious cleavages are practically absent from a country as homogeneous as Greece, obviously no parties are required to express them. As to post-materialist sets of values (in Greece mainly pacifism, feminism and to a lesser extent ecology), these are not very strong,[10] and in any case the major parties have an extraordinary capacity for absorbing them.[11]

It is important to recall here the atrophy of Greek civil society (Diamandouros 1983) and that it is a political culture marked by what Gramsci called 'statolatry'. In sum, the left–right cleavage is practically the only salient one, not to say the only relevant one, although it is more strictly political and not so much social: class borders are blurred and the *petite bourgeoisie* is the majority class, so that one should speak about a polarization on the non-structural 'system' issue rather than on the social one (Lane and Ersson 1987: 262). In other words, since the cleavage structure is rather simple and the partisan conflict relies on overall simple bases, not much attention can be paid to small parties as vectors of ignored dimensions; such a role has indeed very little significance in Greece. In fact, their electoral and parliamentary marginality is also related to the fact that all of them (right, left-wing or centrist) can be placed on the left–right axis. Small parties are permanently squeezed by large parties in this unidimensional space and are more likely to be ephemeral than permanent or, when they do not undergo 'infant mortality', to remain moribund.

Small parties and the party system

As noted earlier, the systemic role and functions of four small parties will be considered more elaborately, as an example of small parties' possibilities either in a party system under formation – as is the case for the two ephemeral parties – or in an already oligopolized system – as has more recently been the case for the 'permanent minority party'.

The 1977 election was the only one where the extreme right achieved autonomous representation in parliament under the banner of the National Front. And in a party system that had not yet been consolidated, the 'ghost' of this small party even haunted the 1981 election, although ND had in the meantime absorbed its parliamentary élite. As a matter of fact, PASOK's victory over ND may also be explained in spatial terms. PASOK succeeded in capturing the centrist electorate, whereas ND failed in this task because of a too-right-wing profile, resulting *precisely* from its intention to recapture the disappointed right-wing voters who had opted for the National Front in 1977.

The Front thereby acted as a sort of blackmail party, although we should use that concept very cautiously and only for convenience's sake, for reasons it is now time to mention. Strictly speaking, the term 'blackmailing' would imply that the party in question threatens to punish its rival if the latter does not submit to its demands. However, neither in reality nor in Sartori's mind are things like this, but the author devotes much less room in his argument to the blackmail than to the coalition potential of a party: according to him, the blackmail party merely affects (centrifugally as an anti-system party) the direction of the competition. Moreover:

1 It is doubtful whether the blackmail party actually prefers its 'victims' to conform to its wishes, or on the contrary to remain intransigent, so that the blackmailer draws the expected electoral benefits.
2 In party competition, the 'blackmailer' does not necessarily express any threats, for two reasons: he may prefer his rival to remain unaware of the risk of losing a part of his electorate; and he does not have enough resources himself to control the latter completely.
3 What Sartori means by 'blackmailing' looks like an objective element underlying electoral competition and cannot be assimilated to an intentional illegal action, something that makes the metaphor inappropriate (the concept of 'intimidation' sounds more correct). Each party knows well, whatever the subjective attitudes of other parties, that if it does not adapt its appeal to the preferences of its less firm supporters, the latter are likely to be captured by those rivals which are ideologically close to them: the fear of 'blackmailing' therefore renders the act itself useless.

Hence, 'blackmailing' seems to affect interactions between all parties (at least during electoral campaigns) and not just at the margins of the party spectrum. For Sartori, it is in fact just a correlate of the anti-system character of a party, otherwise the latter would 'in all likelihood' (Sartori 1976: 123) have coalition potential. Whatever the relevance of the anti-system concept itself for parties eager to legitimize both electoral competition and parliamentarism through their participation, coalition and blackmail potential can no more be viewed as mutually exclusive if 'blackmailing' is considered as a normal component of competition. Because 'blackmailing' is not only an alternative to coalition potential for extremists, it is therefore more suitable to talk about objective mutual pressure and stress, which are ubiquitous because they are intimately related to the very notion of *competition*. Thus, we require a broader approach to this type of interaction than Sartori's one, which is itself inspired by a few pages written by Downs (1957: 127–32), although the former pays attention to parliamentary whilst the latter to electoral competition, considering blackmail parties as newcomers acting as pressure groups with respect to established parties.[12]

Coming now to the second short-lived small party, it is thanks to his entry to parliament as a leader of a party, albeit a small one, that Mitsotakis, the Neo-Liberals' leader, was able to negotiate further on his adhesion to ND, which was trying at the time to absorb the centre-right. In 1978, Mitsotakis joined the ND government, and successively held the important portfolios of Co-ordination and of Foreign Affairs. Later on, after ND's failure in the European election of 1984 – which in the Greek case may be considered as a 'mid-term' one (Reif 1984) – Mitsotakis seized the opportunity of a leadership crisis. He managed to be elected by ND's parliamentary group as the party leader; thus, since then he has headed one of the two major parties. Hence, the small and short-lived Neo-Liberal Party has been important because it was a mere vehicle and an instrument for the personal ambitions of its leader, for its creation may be perceived as a future-oriented tactical manoeuvre of his.

Mitsotakis increased in this way his leverage for exerting pressure on ND, in order to legitimize himself as a prominent personality, no more an intruder or a 'pariah'. The Neo-Liberals were neither a party with autonomous governing potential (they merged into ND when they obtained portfolios), nor one with blackmail potential, but rather a pressure group created in order to safeguard and promote their leader's interests, by providing him with additional resources. Nevertheless, given the persistent role of notables and personalities in the conservative area, this party can by no means be discounted as irrelevant: it is not only an indicator of the fluidity of the transitional period, but also an actor whose presence influenced the course of subsequent party developments.

As to the more durable 'new left', it should first be discussed why Eurocommunism did not make an impact in Greece. KKE-es had to compete inside the ideological space of the communist left with the well-organized orthodox KKE. The latter is perceived there as a revolutionary party, whereas KKE-es is considered an élitist club, disconnected from the masses. It took much time for the majority of this party to understand that the game within the communist space was already lost, at least from the 1977 election whose most prominent feature was intra-area competition. The party persevered in its attempt to establish itself in this space, whereas KKE had already acquired a quasi-monopolistic position in it. KKE-es waited until very recently to draw conclusions from the way things were going and to revise its strategy by abandoning the communist label and adopting the more neutral (and more ambitious!) name of 'Greek Left' (EAR). But it is probably too late now, since the space of the non-communist left has long since been occupied by Papandreou's PASOK, and may still be covered by the heirs of the latter if Papandreou retires from politics.

Nevertheless, the relevance of a party not only depends on its size but is also a function of its relative position, with regard to its ideological proximity to large parties. Thus, EAR has acted as a blackmail party, especially after the rise to power of PASOK and because of the inevitable compromises that it has had to make. EAR could depict itself as the guardian of the abandoned principles of the 'third way to socialism' and (as well as the orthodox KKE) exert pressure on the Socialists to return to a radical path. Despite the fact that PASOK often tried to distance itself from KKE-es (in the opposition period by condemning its moderation; after the rise to power by condemning its extremism), and the fact that some 'new left' intellectuals in their turn despise PASOK's populism,[13] the two parties are nevertheless ideologically close.

Hence, although the size of KKE-es/EAR is minor, this party embarrasses PASOK: this small party is therefore relevant *vis-à-vis* its giant neighbour. The latter cannot ignore it, simply because a rival (even a marginal one) which 'sells' a similar ideological 'product' in the political market forces PASOK to react. For the risk remains that this competitor might encroach upon a part of PASOK's electorate, however small this part may be. Pressure may be a rational strategy for those parties which, without necessarily being extremist, are unnecessary for coalition building but whose ideological proximity to major parties represents a real threat for them. In fact, according to *Eurobarometer 25* (spring 1986), KKE-es was the closest party to PASOK on a left–right scale ranging from 1 to 10 (3.1 for KKE-es and 4.3 for PASOK).[14]

We know that the impact of small parties decreased in Greece with the trend towards the consolidation of a two-party system similar to the Westminster model. The pattern of change in Greece is indeed opposite to that of other Western European party systems, where fragmentation has increased in recent years, mainly with the advent of new-politics, single-issue and regionalist parties. Hence, the Greek case seems to be a deviant one, but this is probably a pattern common to 'new' democracies (except Spain, where nationalist parties are regionally important, not to say dominant in their particular regions).

The values of Rae's fractionalization index based upon legislative seats (1967) are as shown in Table 9.3, according to seat distribution in the seven national elections. Fragmentation is generally very low in a system marked by the presence of a dominant party in 1974 and 1977 and a two-party one since 1981. It is indeed important for estimating the role of small parties to underline the fact that the present Greek party system is in fact a two-party one, not a 'two-and-a-half' one (Blondel 1969: 155–60) nor a case of 'limited but polarized pluralism' as Mavrogordatos (1984: 168) classifies it. It is noticeable that, according to the Laakso–Taagepera (1979) index, which measures the number of parties tempered by their share of seats, the value for Greece is 2.1, very similar to the most typical cases of two-partyism (Lijphart et al. 1988: 10–11, 20–2).

It is true that such quantitative measures do not say much about the systemic properties of the system; on the other hand, 'limited pluralism' implies at least three relevant parties and coalition government. In this type, 'all the parties are governing oriented, that is available for cabinet coalition', according to Sartori (1976: 179). Now, if the third Greek party, KKE, is indeed available for coalition, its effective coalition potential is highly precarious and this party does not play a permanent pivotal role: this is rather the exception to the rule. Again, according to Sartori (1976: 186), 'we have a two-party format whenever the existence of third parties does not prevent the two major parties from governing alone, i.e.

Table 9.3 *Fractionalization index based on legislative seats*

Election	Index
November 1974	0.421
November 1977	0.666
October 1981	0.523
June 1985	0.543
June 1989	0.584
November 1989	0.570
April 1990	0.577

whenever coalitions are unnecessary', 'whenever third parties do not affect, *in the long run* and at the national level, the alternation in power of the two major parties' or whenever they are not strategically located. In this sense, the Greek party system is a two-party one, a genuine duopoly, nevertheless featuring the peculiarity of being highly polarized. Again according to the *Eurobarometer 25* data (spring 1986), the ideological distance between the two major parties in Greece was of 4.1 on the left–right scale (New Democracy: 8.4; PASOK: 4.3), and was among the highest in the twelve EC member countries. This bipolarization prevents small parties from becoming vehicles for popular discontent against the established parties.

It is worth noting that, unlike Sartori, F.L. Wilson (1971: 17) admits the possibility of 'polarized dualism', yet this concept differs from the Greek case as it implies that one side must be dominant. Seferiades's (1986) argument on the nature of the Greek party system also deserves some attention here, in so far as it may be frankly misleading for understanding the latter's functioning, because it overemphasizes practically non-existent pluralist trends. According to him, the Greek party system would be 'extreme and polarized pluralism' (1986: 87). The author's concern is the inconsistency between the limited number of parties and the extent of the ideological spread, an important one indeed. His concept of party relevance is, however, a very extensive one: he includes in his counting of parties party factions during the pre-dictatorship period and small parties without coalition potential during the post-1974 era. This no doubt biases the party-system format: for example, party factions are not particular to Greece, and they are less visible there than in systems with more institutionalized party organizations. The system's mechanics are also distorted by Seferiades, for he lays too much stress – always thinking comparatively – on intra-party competition and on the centrifugal impact of blackmail parties as the key explanation of polarization.

Small parties and the institutions

In majoritarian democracies like the Greek one, small parties essentially lack the legitimacy that encourages their participation in state affairs. Besides, since no mechanisms of direct democracy exist save those controlled by the executive power (never used since the plebiscite on the monarchy in 1974), small parties also lack a channel that could have favoured their promotion. In Switzerland, for example, which is the prototype of the opposite model to Greece, the consensual one (Lijphart 1984: 23–32), and also the country with by far the greatest number of referendums held in the world (Butler and Ranney 1978: 6), coalitions of small parties not represented in the federal government often mobilize much more than their own electorate in referendum votes and they even manage to win in 20 percent of the cases (Ossipow 1981: 47–50). In that sense, they possess a certain 'veto power' indicated by their role here.

There has been another institutional problem for the Greek small parties: the 'reinforced proportionate' electoral system, a variation of the Hagenback–Bischoff method that favoured major parties and handicapped small ones by prescribing a quorum of 17 percent (25 percent for coalitions) in order to participate in the second distribution of seats (Vegleris 1981). This law still remained in force in 1981 and was only marginally amended by the Socialist government in spite of PASOK's promises for the 1985 election. The electoral system, meant to favour governmental stability, constituted a fierce obstacle to the parliamentary representation of small parties. It 'ensures a systematic and organic over-representation of the larger parties and under-representation or non-representation of the smaller ones' (Vegleris 1981: 35).

It is well known, however, that the electoral system is by no means the sole independent variable that shapes the party system: for example, Wolinetz (1979: 23–4) finds only a weak relationship between the permissiveness of electoral laws and party systems fragmentation. It may therefore be argued that this institutional variable is not the decisive obstacle to small parties' viability: at worst it distorts, as is often the case in Greece, the popular will. For example, when local personalism still persisted, independent candidates were still elected even under a plurality system. That was the case in 1952 in Crete, although the two MPs joined major centrist parties later. On the other hand, once the process of concentration had begun or resumed after the military interlude, and despite the relatively kinder electoral system, no parliamentarian was elected to represent a small party in 1961, 1964 or 1981. It is true that such a system may ensure small parties' presence in parliament and, even better, favour their pivotal role under certain additional conditions. Yet this is not to say that the electoral system is of much help for the deepening of small parties' social roots. In any case, Table 9.4 shows the gap between the combined shares of votes and seats for the *two* large parties in each election, which has been narrower since the advent of two-partyism.

Now, as to the effect of the 'wasted vote' argument, which also contributes to the weakness of small parties, this can hardly be considered as a defect of the electoral system. Obviously, there is an

Table 9.4 *Cumulated share of votes and seats for the two bigger parties*

Election	Percentage of votes	Percentage of seats
November 1974	74.8	93.3
November 1977	67.1	88.0
October 1981	84.0	95.7
June 1985	86.7	95.7
June 1989	83.5	90.0
November 1989	86.9	92.0
April 1990	85.5	91.7

effect, since voters know that small parties are handicapped by the electoral rules, but this is an indirect one. The argument is not just a Machiavellian and rhetorical device coined by the major parties, it is above all the outcome of a rational cost/benefit analysis on behalf of the voters.[15] Since 1981, that is, since elections became competitive, the argument has worked in favour of those parties which appeared as governing-oriented – the major parties – and with serious chances of access to the state institutions.

Nevertheless, it may be argued that parties are likely to emerge – especially when statism prevails – for the promotion of clientelistic interests (such as the allocation of private goods). Patronage has a long-term tradition in Greece but, although it undoubtedly persists (significantly and optimistically called *paléokommatismos* – 'old-partyism'), it implies today the mediation of the big centralized parties' mass organizations. The latter are 'collective patrons' (Mouzelis 1987) which have replaced the traditional small personalistic party. In clientelism, access to the state – which is the main factor in the allocation of private goods – is an imperative precondition for the creation of a relationship to society; and politicians who are not sustained by powerful organizations nowadays lack the necessary resources to obtain this access by themselves. This again operates against small parties.

Three qualifications should, however, be made with respect to the general impotence of small parties in Greece. The success of their élites in gaining access to the state has been greater than their ability to find a social audience. One very tangible effect of the National Front's blackmailing was that politicians of the extreme right were integrated in New Democracy when in power. This was anything but useless, for it ensured their own parliamentary survival after their party was dismantled. As to the Neo-Liberal leader, he is today the Greek Prime Minister, heading the ND government that came into office following the April 1990 election. Besides, several cadre members of the 'new left' were given appointments in the state apparatus by the Socialists after 1981, because of the latter's need for 'cultural capital' and their relative ideological proximity to that 'think-tank'. Others were appointed during the 'historic compromise' formula of summer 1989 and remain in place.

Besides, despite the apparent simplicity of the two-party format, the Greek parliament preserves for several reasons some complexity and variety. First, some MPs resign during the legislature if they happen to disagree with their party (voting discipline is very strong), but this has no impact on the composition of parliament, for they are immediately replaced by another member of the party list. MPs sometimes also break away from their party, make a statement of independence and remain in parliament: there were four such cases in the 1985–9 legislature, all affecting ND, which suffers from the role of notables, one of the dissenters being the former Prime Minister. To be sure, before the end of the legislature these politicians generally seek to join a new party, which is necessary for their re-election because of the electoral law and the stabilization of two-partyism. The fact remains, however, that such cases of dissidence have led to the creation of new parties or rather parliamentary caucuses. For example, this happened after the break-up of the centrist EDIK following its defeat in 1977, and after the defeat of New Democracy in 1985 with the creation of DIANA, and following the disagreement of 'purists' with the abandonment by PASOK of its initially radical goals. (The most prominent case is that of the former Minister of the Economy, who created the Greek Socialist Party which polled only 0.2 percent of the vote in the June 1989 election and returned to PASOK thereafter.)

Moreover, numerous minor parties are represented in the parliament via the election of one or a few MPs following a pact with one of the major parties. For example, elected with PASOK in 1981 and 1985 were: the leader of EDA, which practically lost its *raison d'être* with the Communists' legalization; one MP from Christian Democracy; and one of the leaders of the centrist party who had in the meantime created his own party, PARKE. In 1985 a second centrist leader, who claimed the official centrist legacy, was also elected. Yet those among them who participated by themselves in the June 1989 election did not gain parliamentary representation again. Prominent politicians of KODISO (Party of Democratic Socialism) joined the New Democracy ticket; and the KKE included in its lists the leader of AKE (Agrarian Party of Greece) as well as two former PASOK MPs, one of them having also created a minor party, ESPE (other PASOK dissidents were not elected). In June 1989, some KODISO personalities rejoined ND (one being at the head of its European elections list), while the official party entered the left Alliance, without getting any of its members elected. The far left again accepted PASOK dissenters, one of them (a former vice-minister) heading the list of the state deputies who are elected on a national basis; AKE's and ESPE's leaders were not re-elected, however; finally, one part of EDA also joined the Alliance, and its candidates were more successful.

In order to have more idea of the extent of this phenomenon, it suffices to compare the size of major parties' parliamentary groups immediately after the election of June 1985 and right before the June 1989 election: 161 PASOK MPs in 1985, 157 in 1989; 126 for ND in 1985, 111 in 1989; 12 for KKE in 1985, 9 in 1989.

Nevertheless, it should not be overlooked that these parties have not won their seats autonomously and their popular representation is nil. Their parliamentary survival therefore depends on the good will of major parties. Undoubtedly, the integration of some prominent leaders of small parties into major parties provides the latter with a 'surplus value' during electoral campaigns; it has a symbolic effect since it enables them to appear able to attract visible political personalities, even if the latter no longer have a wide social base. On the other hand, backing by major parties also means satellitization of the 'dwarf' party and the creation of a 'clientelist' dependence relationship towards the 'patron': the client party is no doubt artificial and irrelevant, it has only a figurative role in the party system (therefore those parties were not taken into consideration earlier in this chapter with regard to party interactions).

There is also a significant difference in small parties' performance in the European elections, compared with their poor scores in the national ones. In the 1981 election, the first one after Greece's accession to the EC, which took place the same day as the national one, small parties re-emerged and all increased their score greatly in comparison with the national election. As to the two major parties, together they polled only 71.4 percent of the vote that time. The extreme right gained 2.8 percent of the vote instead of 1.7 percent, the centrist parties (mainly the KODISO) jumped from 1.2 percent to 7.6 percent and the Eurocommunist KKE-es from 1.4 percent to 5.3 percent. Each of these three parties elected one MP to the European Parliament from a total of 24, whereas none was elected to the Greek Parliament which has 300 members. This gap may be explained by different factors – firstly, by the fact that this election was perceived as insignificant by public opinion, in comparison with the dramatically important national election of the same day; and secondly, by the electoral system, which was 'pure' and not 'reinforced' proportionate. It may be hypothesized that small parties benefited from the combined effect of two factors: voters ideologically close to them felt free to vote according to their party preferences (least distance axiom since the 'wasted vote' argument became meaningless), *and* major party voters probably voted in their turn according to a 'second best' choice rationale. The underlying assumption here is of course that those who behave that way count among the best informed citizens.

The performance of the small parties in the 1984 European election is also highly significant: they all scored lower than in the European election of 1981, but all kept their MPs in the European Parliament and won more votes than in the national elections of 1981 and 1985 (the extreme right, 2.5 percent; the centre, 1.9 percent; the Eurocommunists, 3.4 percent). The major parties polled together 79.7 percent of the vote, an aggregate score which was better than in the previous European election, but worse than in both national elections of 1981 and 1985. This situation reflects the fact that this election was more important than the European one of 1981 (as a mid-term election), and less than the national ones of 1981 and 1985. The 1984 election was not a mere European one: the conservative ND opposition party called for a protest vote against the PASOK government, which accepted the challenge. Nevertheless, even if PASOK had lost this election, this would not have automatically led to the government's resignation. In sum, this was an ambiguous election, in so far as it gave to the electorate the chance to sanction PASOK's performance in office, but this feedback was mainly symbolic and could not provoke any direct institutional effects.

In June 1989, national and European elections were held on the same day. The eleven small and minor parties that participated in both elections *all* did better in the European than in the national one. The vote for the extreme right jumped from 0.3 to 1.5 percent, but it lost its seat in the European Parliament to the benefit of DIANA, which progressed from 1.0 to 1.4 percent. The left Alliance also increased its vote by 1.2 percent, while the aggregate score of the two major parties, by contrast, fell by 7 percent. Finally, for their first emergence on the Greek scene, the various 'Greens' (practically absent from the national contest) won altogether 2.6 percent of the vote; had they unified, they would have easily elected one deputy.

The strength of small parties grew *in inverse proportion* to the importance of the election at national level (local elections are disregarded here): in what may be depicted as non-governmental, second-order or in any case not really competitive elections, the share of the vote for small parties performing an expressive function increased at the expense of support for parties with governmental potential.

Conclusion and prospects

Before coming to the prospects for small and minor parties (at this level the distinction no longer makes sense) it is meaningful to classify them with respect to their origin and functions in the party system. The *origins* of these parties are a relevant indicator of their relationship (or absence of one) to society: they may emerge from either organizational or mere parliamentary splits, be remnants of old larger parties or just personalistic, or be new parties which fill an ideological vacuum. Their functions illuminate their role in the Greek party system and in electoral competition, usually as an expressive or a personalistic one: they may be minor components of an intra-area competition, just political vehicles for the promotion of politicians when they are 'parties of personalities', transitionally small (either subsequently increasing their relevance or, on the contrary, vanishing), satellites of major parties or ephemeral parliamentary caucuses without any wider audience.

The variety of origins and functions highlights the complexity of the landscape of these 'dwarfs', which is usually overlooked when emphasis is laid on the two-party mechanics of the system. The essential question to be raised, however, is whether small parties are henceforth practically sentenced to death or whether they have any chances to grow. Their fate seems to depend upon four variables: two of them are concerned with the relationship of small parties to society and institutions, and two of them with intra- and interparty competition.

First, there is the underlying social and cultural substratum, which itself may be divided into two dimensions: ideological cleavages and utilitarian motivations related to resource allocation from the state (patronage). We know that unidimensionality is likely to prejudice against the proliferation of parties, because not much space remains available away from the established parties to be covered by newcomers. It follows that the cleavage structure itself is not favourable to parties outside the established constellation. It is also impossible to argue that small parties are likely to represent clientelistic interests, since access to the state nowadays requires the mediation of centralized organizations. The mass character of current patronage in Greece is a key variable for the understanding of voters' preference for governing-oriented parties. It doesn't only favour organizations at the expense of notables, it also contributes to the perpetuation of two-partyism, to the extent that it entails a vote for 'safe values' as to spoils allocation.

Secondly, there is the aforementioned electoral law, which has represented a serious obstacle for small parties. Yet the electoral system is admittedly one *variable* in Greece, in the etymological sense of the concept: an *ad hoc* measure, manipulated by parties in power according to their interests (Clogg 1983). This lack of institutionalized electional rules is not due to the fact that Greece is a 'new' democracy, as Rose argues (1983: 20); it has been a constant element of the country's turbulent political life. The Socialist government, for instance, suddenly decided, probably anticipating its electoral defeat, to reinforce the representation of small parties in the June 1989 election for tactical reasons, in order to weaken its main rival and to prevent the formation of a conservative single-party government. This could be assimilated to a 'mini-max' strategy in game theory, designed to provoke stress in the adversary.

Thirdly, there is the consolidation of the party system itself, which in its turn is a function of the depersonalization of party alignments. If two-partyism settles, the only path of survival for small parties seems to be their satellitization, or at best their marginalization, also perhaps some kind of peripheral access to the state apparatus for those among their élites who are eager to collaborate on an individual and subordinate basis with whichever party is in power. Small parties are also likely to re-emerge periodically in, say, 'platonic' elections where they serve as vehicles of expression for popular discontent with the major parties' performance and with polarization. Hence, the future of these parties does look rather gloomy to the extent that two-partyism takes root in Greece.

Consideration of the degree of consolidation of two-partyism itself is, however, also necessary: the settling of the two-party configuration does not seem absolutely certain, because of the personalism which persists within the two protagonists. Both major parties have undergone serious internal divisions, although these are not institutionalized and cohesion is enforced through repressive measures. Despite its autocratic character, however, personalism in the long run reinforces centrifugal tendencies within the major parties, because the leader is often the sole common point of reference for the rank and file in PASOK, while notabilism favours the existence of personal clientele networks inside ND. Besides, personalism impedes the routinization of party structures and renders party identification more precarious: to summarize, it is a potential factor of fluidity.

Fourthly, there are the electoral outcomes themselves, which have already introduced a change in the principle of government formation: in the two national elections of 1989 no party won a parliamentary majority. Although Greece returned to one-party government following the April 1990 election, and thereby to a 'pure' two-party system, the parliamentary majority of ND is a very weak one.

In any case, coalition government enhances the role of small parties. By the same token it revitalizes parliament and contributes to the consolidation of the rules of the game, something the Greek political system badly needs. Attempts by a party in power to change the rules would in all likelihood be hindered by its coalition partners. In addition, coalitions may cause splits between pragmatists and purists (Denardo 1985) within all parties, as well as leading to the creation of new parties.

To be sure, the majoritarian logic still prevails in Greece: the spate of elections held recently until a one-party cabinet could be formed, as well as the persisting bipolarization during them, prove the existence of a widespread opinion among the political classes that coalitions are prejudicial to good government. Multi-party cabinets are viewed as weak, either because of programme differences among the relevant parties, or because dominant parties feel close enough to a majority to find it worth calling for new elections.

Nevertheless, if we ultimately hold not only that the initial fragmentation of the new Greek party system was transitional, but also that this may well be the case for two-partyism, because of its precarious personalistic foundations, then the party system is only prima facie stable. All in all, though it is not actually predictable that growing complexity and fluidity could open doors to small and new parties, thereby reintroducing fragmentation into the system, it cannot be excluded either, even in the near future. Needless to say, this might be a remedy for the bad-quality democracy ('Democracy Greek Style'!) in polarized two-partyism.

Notes

This contribution (written before the election of June 1989) is a revised version of a paper presented to the workshop on 'The Role of Small Parties in Western European Party Systems – a Comparative Analysis', ECPR Joint Sessions, Amsterdam, 10–15 April 1987. The initial title was 'Greece: Small Parties in a Process of Consolidation of the Party System'. The elections of November 1989 and April 1990 have been only marginally included because of time constraints, but their outcomes do not affect the argument presented in this chapter. I am indebted to Geoffrey Pridham and to

Nikiphoros Diamandouros for their very useful comments. All errors remain mine, however.

1. Although elements of 'continuity in the alternatives' (Lipset and Rokkan 1967: 52–3) between the pre-1967 (military coup) and the post-1974 party system were often mentioned in the literature, the organizational expressions of social cleavages considerably differ between the two periods. For this reason, and also because the rules of party competition were not fully democratic in the 'old' system, the post-1974 system should be viewed as a new and distinct one, and cannot but be treated as an object of analysis *per se*. This raises, on the one hand, problems as to cross-national comparison with other democracies; on the other hand, it is by no means specific to Greece, but is common to 'new' Southern European democracies, such as Spain and Portugal.

2. And all governments emanating from elections have been single-party ones since 1952.

3. On the concept of party relevance, see Sartori 1976: 121–2.

4. See Nicolacopoulos 1984. There is, however, a universal shift to the left after the dictatorship within each of these families: the right got rid of its fascist elements; in the centre it is the centre-leftist PASOK which became predominant, and within the communist left the more orthodox KKE.

5. 'In the months immediately following the *golpe* of April 25, 1974, more than fifty groups sprang up in Portugal calling themselves political parties . . . This great proliferation of political parties can be seen as the birth of the political infrastructure of popular control. As such, it represents an attempt to break through the confining conditions of the New State and to resolve the participation crisis which Salazar's corporative infrastructure had failed to do' (Opello 1985: 83).

6. For monographs on ND, PASOK and the communist left, see Penniman 1981; and the more recent Featherstone and Katsoudas 1987.

7. A party may be considered as dominant if it polls 10 percent more votes than the second party; see Sartori 1976: 193–4.

8. A minority wanted to safeguard this label and founded the 'Communist Party of the Interior – Reformist Left', thus generating a new split, this time inside the Eurocommunist movement. Even the most stable of the small parties looks today much more vulnerable than the big parties. Yet the splinter party did not manage to poll more than 0.3 percent of the vote in national elections.

9. It does not make sense to measure volatility in the 1974 election, since the previous election had taken place ten years before, in 1964, prior to the military dictatorship. Besides, despite the ties of the parties that emerged after 1974 with the traditional ideological families, no party kept the same name before and after the dictatorship. Because even between 1974 and 1990 no small party participated in all the elections (different parties successively represented the same ideological orientation; parties changed their names in the meantime or sometimes merged with other parties), it was more realistic to measure volatility on the basis of the scores of ideological 'areas' (Mair 1983): extreme right, moderate right, centre, socialist, communist and extreme left, although this overlooks intra-area competition. Finally, European election outcomes were also included, not only because of the overall low number of elections but also because volatility between these elections and the national ones is significant in itself. Volatility would be lower if we were to aggregate broader blocks (e.g. right, centre and left), but much higher if we counted individual parties.

10. Only 9.3 percent of the Greek sample (*Eurobarometer 25*, spring 1986) were

post-materialists. Only Portugal has a lower score among the EC-countries (5.8 percent).

11. All major parties (and the new left) have their own women's or pacifist organizations.

12. Some other objections may be made to Sartori's development of the idea of blackmail potential, which lacks serious measurement, as the author himself admits (1976: 304). Is, for example, the 'veto power' of a party in parliamentary votes an indicator of anti-system blackmailing (1976: 123–4)? Does it affect competition or does it imply that such a party is coalitionable (*koalitionsfähig*), if not at governmental level at least on some critical issues of decision-making?

13. See as an example Elephantis's contribution in Penniman 1981: 105–29.

14. The values for KKE-es should be treated cautiously, however. They cannot be considered as strictly representative, given the small proportion of the sample that declared to vote for this party.

15. See on this subject the developments by Downs (1957: 47–50).

References

Aagaard, F. (1949) *Venstres Historie*. Copenhagen.
Aarebrot, F. (1988) 'A Serpent in Paradise? A Contribution to the Political Sociology of Norway's Progress Party'. Paper delivered at the IPSA Congress, Washington, DC.
Aasland, T. (1977) 'The Norwegen Agrarian Party', pp. 83–124 in H. Gollwitzer (ed.), *Europäische Bauernparteien im 20. Jahrhundert*. Frankfurt: Fischer Verlag.
Aghina, G. and Jaccarino, C. (1977) *Storia del PR '55–'77*. Milan: Gammalibri.
Allden, L. (1980) 'Medlemmene i Sosialistisk Folkeparti'. Dissertation, University of Oslo.
Allum, P.A. (1973) *Italy: Republic without Government?* London: Weidenfeld & Nicolson.
Alt, J., Crewe, I. and Sarlvik, B. (1977) 'Angels in Plastic: The Liberal Surge in 1974', *Political Studies*, 25: 343–68.
Andersen, J. (1988) 'Groen politik – perspektiver og Forklaringer', *Politica*, 20: 382–92.
Andersen, J.G. (1977) 'Småborgerskabet og Fremskridtspartiet'. Thesis, Aarhus University.
Andersen, P.C. (1975) *Kristen Politik*. Odense: Odense Universitetsforlag.
Andeweg, R.B. (1982) *Dutch Voters Adrift: On Explanations of Electoral Change*. Meppel: Krips.
Arter, D. (1979) 'The Finnish Centre Party: Profile of a Hinge-Group', *West European Politics*, 2: 108–27.
Arter, D. (1987) 'The 1987 Finnish Election: The Conservatives Out of the Wilderness', *West European Politics*, 10: 171–6.
Arter, D. (1988) 'Liberal Parties in Finland: From Perennial Coalition to an Extra-Parliamentary Role', pp. 326–55 in E. Kirchner (ed.), *Liberal Parties in Western Europe*. Cambridge: Cambridge University Press.
Balsom, D. (1979) 'Plaid Cymru: The Welsh National Party', pp. 131–55 in H.M. Drucker (ed.), *Multi-Party Britain*. London: Macmillan.
Barbagli, M., Corbetta, P., Parisi, A. and Schadee, H. (1979) *Fluidita Elettorale e Classe Sociali in Italia, 1969–1976*. Bologna: Il Mulino.
Barnes, S. (1988) 'Why Small Parties Stay Small: An Inquiry into Party Systems and the Life Cycle'. Paper presented at the 1988 meeting of the American Political Science Association.
Barnes, S. (1989) 'Partisanship and Electoral Behavior', pp. 235–72 in M.K. Jennings and J.M. van Deth (eds), *Continuities in Political Action*. New York: de Gruyter.
Bartolini, S. (1982) 'The Politics of Institutional Reform in Italy', *West European Politics*, 5: 203–21.
Bartolini, S. and Mair, P. (1990) *Identity, Competition and Electoral Availability: The Stabilization of European Electorates, 1885–1985*. Cambridge: Cambridge University Press.
Baumgarten, J. (ed.) (1982) *Linkssozialisten in Europa*. Hamburg: Junius Verlag.
Beernink, H.K. (1953) *Geschiedenis enbeginsel van de Christelijk-Historishe Unie*. The Hague: Christelijk Historische Unie.
Behrakis, Th. and Nicolacopoulos, E. (1988) 'Party Choice and Evaluation of

Politicians: A Crucial Dimension of Electoral Competition', *Greek Review of Social Research*, 69A: 82–125.
Beith, A. (1983) *The Case for the Liberal Party and the Alliance*. London: Longman.
Beyer, H. (1984) 'Finnlands Kommunisten vor großen Problemen – die finnische KP und die Parlamentswahlen von 1983', *Osteuropa*, 5: 352–64.
Beyme, K. von (1986) 'European Perspectives on Links between Parties and Interest Groups'. Paper presented to the Roundtable 'Les Groupes d'intérêt en Europe du Sud et leur insertion dans la Communauté Européenne', University of Geneva.
Beyme, K. von (1988) 'Right-Wing Extremism in Post-War Europe', *West European Politics*, 11: 1–18.
Bille, L. (1989) 'Denmark: The Oscillating Party Systems', *West European Politics*, 12: 42–59.
Bjorn, C. (1977) 'Venstre – the Party of the Rural Population in Denmark', pp. 147–68 in H. Gollwitzer (ed.), *Europäische Bauernparteien im 20. Jahrhundert*. Frankfurt: Fischer Verlag.
Blackmer, D.M. and Tarrow, S. (eds) (1975) *Communism in Italy and France*. Princeton, NJ: Princeton University Press.
Blondel, J. (1969) *An Introduction to Comparative Government*. London: Weidenfeld & Nicolson.
Bochel, J.M. and Denver, D.T. (1972) 'The Decline of the Scottish National Party: an Alternative View', *Political Studies*, 20: 311–16.
Bogdanor, V. (ed.) (1983) *Liberal Party Politics*. Oxford: Clarendon Press.
Borre, O. (1980) 'Electoral Instability in Four Nordic Countries 1950–77', *Comparative Political Studies*, 13: 141–71.
Borre, O. et al. (1976) *Vælgere i 70'erne*. Copenhagen: Akademisk Forlag.
Borre, O. et al. (1983) *Efter vælgerskredet – analyser af folketingsvalget 1979*. Aarhus: Politica.
Bouw, C., Donselaar, J. van and Nelissen, C. (1981) *De Nederlandse Volks-Unie: portret van een racistische partij*. Bussum: Wereldvenster.
Bovenkerk, F. et al. (1978) 'De verkiezingsaanhang van de Nederlandse Volksunie', in F. Bovenkerk (ed.), *Omdat Zij Anders Zijn*. Meppel: Boom.
Boy, D. (1981) 'Le vote écologiste en 1978', *Revue française de science politique*, 31: 394–416.
Bridgford, J. (1978) 'The Ecologist Movement and the French General Election 1978', *Parliamentary Affairs*, 31: 314–23.
Broughton, D. and Kirchner, E. (1984) 'The FDP in Transition – Again?', *Parliamentary Affairs*, 37: 183–98.
Broughton, D. and Kirchner, E. (1986) 'The FDP and Coalition Behaviour in the Federal Republic of Germany', pp. 72–92 in G. Pridham (ed.), *Coalitional Behaviour in Theory and Practice*. Cambridge: Cambridge University Press.
Bürklin, W. (1987) 'Governing Left Parties Frustrating the Radical Non-Established Left: The Rise and Inevitable Decline of the Greens', *European Sociological Review*, 3: 109–26.
Busteed, M.A. and Mason, H. (1970) 'Irish Labour in the 1969 Election', *Political Studies*, 18: 373–9.
Butler, D. and Ranney, A. (eds) (1978) *Referendums: A Comparative Study of Theory and Practice*. Washington, DC: American Enterprise Institute.
Butler, D. and Butler, G. (1986) *British Political Facts 1900–1985*, 6th edn. London: Macmillan.

Byrne, P. (1989) 'Great Britain: The "Green Party"', pp. 101–12 in F. Müller-Rommel (ed.), *New Politics in Western Europe*. Boulder, Co, and London: Westview Press.

Caciagli, M. (1988) 'The Movimento Sociale Italiano Destra Nazionale and Neo-Fascism in Italy', *West European Politics*, 11: 19–33.

Castles, F.G. and Mair, P. (1984) 'Left–Right Political Scales: Some "Expert" Judgements', *European Journal of Political Research*, 12: 73–88.

Chafer, T. (1984) 'Ecologists and the Bomb', pp. 217–32 in P. Chilton and J. Howorth (eds), *Defence and Dissent in Contemporary France*. London: Croom Helm.

Christensen, A.J. (1977) 'Nye politiske partier i Danmark 1920–1977'. Thesis, Odense University.

Christian, R. (1982) 'Die Grünen – Momentaufnahme einer Bewegung in Österreich', pp. 55–81 in A. Khol and A. Stirnemann (eds), *Österreichisches Jahrbuch für Politik*. Munich and Vienna: Oldenbourg Verlag.

Christian, R. and Ulram, P. (1988) 'Grün-Alternative Parteien in österreichischen Gemeinden', pp. 509–39 in A. Khol and A. Stirneman (eds), *Österreichisches Jahrbuch für Politik*. Munich and Vienna: Oldenbourg Verlag.

Clarke, H. and Zuk, G. (1986) 'The Dynamics of Third Party Support: The British Liberal Party, 1951–79'. Unpublished paper.

Clogg, R. (1983) 'Greece', pp. 190–208 in V. Bogdanor and D. Butler (eds), *Democracy and Elections – Electoral Systems and their Political Consequences*. Cambridge: Cambridge University Press.

Coakley, J. (1983) 'Minority Parties in Ireland', National Institute for Higher Education, Limerick: mimeo.

Colliander, R. (1926) *Svenska folkpartiet i Finland 1906–1926*. Helsingfors.

Cook, C. (1976) *A Short History of the Liberal Party*. London: Macmillan.

Corbetta, P. and Parisi, A. (1984) *Il Voto Repubblicano: alle Origini del 26 Guigno*. Bologna: Istituto Carlo Cattaneo.

Cornell, R. (1975) 'The Communist Parties of Scandinavia', *Survey*, 21: 107–20.

Craig, F.W.S. (1981) *British Electoral Facts 1832–1980*. Chichester: Parliamentary Research Services.

Crewe, I. (1982) 'Is Britain's Two-Party System About to Crumble?', *Electoral Studies*, 1: 275–313.

Crewe, I., Alt, J. and Sarlvik, B. (1977) 'Partisan Dealignment in Britain 1964–1974', *British Journal of Political Science*, 7: 129–90.

Criddle, B. (1971) 'The Parti Socialiste Unifié: An Appraisal after Ten Years', *Parliamentary Affairs*, 24: 140–65.

Curtice, J. (1983) 'Liberal Voters and the Alliance Realignment or Protest?' pp. 99–121 in V. Bogdanor (ed.), *Liberal Party Politics*. Oxford: Clarendon Press.

Curtice, J. (1988) 'Great Britain – Social Liberalism Reborn', pp. 93–123 in E. Kirchner (ed.), *Liberal Parties in Western Europe*. Cambridge: Cambridge University Press.

Cyr, A. (1977) *Liberal Party Politics in Britain*. New Brunswick: Transaction Books.

Daalder, H. (1965–6) 'De kleine politieke partijen – een voorlopige poging tot inventarisatie', *Acta Politica*, 1: 172–96.

Daalder, H. (1987) 'The Dutch Party System: From Segmentation to Polarization – and Then?', pp. 193–284 in H. Daalder (ed.), *Party Systems in Denmark, Austria, Switzerland, the Netherlands, and Belgium*. London: Frances Pinter.

Daalder, H. and Irwin, G.A. (eds) (1989) 'Politics in the Netherlands: How Much Change?', *West European Politics*, 12: whole issue.

Daalder, H. and Koole, R. (1988) 'Liberal Parties in the Netherlands', pp. 151–77 in E. Kirchner (ed.), *Liberal Parties in Western Europe*. Cambridge: Cambridge University Press.

Daalder, H. and Mair, P. (eds) (1983) *Western European Party Systems*. London: Sage.

Dachs, H. (1988) 'Bürgerlisten und grün-alternative Parteien in Österreich', pp. 181–208 in F. Plasser and A. Pekinka (eds), *Das österreichische Parteiensystem*. Vienna: Böhlau.

Daloze, J. (1966) 'La réorientation de PSC', *Revue Générale Belge*, 5: 106–11.

Dalton, R., Flanagan, S. and Beck, P. (eds) (1984) *Electoral Change in Advanced Industrial Societies*. Princeton, NJ: Princeton University Press.

Damgaard, E. (1974) 'Stability and Change in the Danish Party System over Half a Century', *Scandinavian Political Studies*, 9: 104–25.

Damgaard, E. (1977) *Folketinget under forandring*. Copenhagen: Samfundsvidenskabeligt Forlag.

Damgaard, E. (1982) *Partigrupper, repræsentation og styring*. Copenhagen: Schultz.

Damgaard, E. et al. (1979) *Folketingsmedlemmer på arbeide*. Aarhus: Politica.

Denardo, J. (1985) *Power in Numbers: The Political Strategy of Protest and Rebellion*. Princeton, NJ: Princeton University Press.

Denver, T.D. (1984) 'The SDP–Liberal Alliance: The End of the Two-Party System?', pp. 75–102 in H. Barrington (ed.), *Change in British Politics*. London: Frank Cass.

De Preux, E. (1974) *Servitude et grandeur du PSU*. Paris: Syros.

Deschouwer, K. (1987) *Politieke partijen in Belgie*. Antwerp: Kluwer.

Deschouwer, K. (1989) 'Belgium: The Ecologists and AGALEV', pp. 39–54 in F. Müller-Rommel (ed.), *New Politics in Western Europe*. Boulder, Co, and London: Westview Press.

De Schryver, A. (1946) 'The Social Christian Party in Belgium', pp. 5–11 in *Annals of the American Academy of Political and Social Sciences*.

Deth, J.W. van (1984) *Politieke Waarden*. Amsterdam: CT Press.

Dewachter, W. (1987) 'Changes in a Particratie: The Belgian Party System from 1944 to 1986', pp. 285–363 in H. Daalder (ed.), *Party Systems in Denmark, Austria, Switzerland, the Netherlands and Belgium*. London: Frances Pinter.

Diamandouros, P.N. (1983) 'Greek Political Culture in Transition: Historical Origins, Evolution, Current Trends', pp. 43–70 in R. Clogg (ed.), *Greece in the 1980s*. London: Macmillan.

Diamandouros, P.N. (1984) 'Transition to, and Consolidation of, Democratic Politics in Greece, 1974–83: A Tentative Assessment', pp. 199–241 in G. Pridham (ed.), *The New Mediterranean Democracies: Regime Transition in Spain, Greece and Portugal*. London: Frank Cass.

Dill, W.R. (1965) 'Business Organizations', pp. 1071–114 in J.G. March (ed.), *Handbook of Organizations*. Chicago: Rand McNally.

Dittberner, J. (1987) *FDP – Partei der zweiten Wahl*. Opladen: Westdeutscher Verlag.

Dittmer, L. (1969) 'The German NPD: A Psycho-Sociological Analysis of Neo-Nazism', *Comparative Politics*, 2: 79–110.

Donolo, C. (1980) 'Die Rolle der Radikalen Partei (Partido Radikale) im Politischen System Italiens', pp. 192–206 in R. Roth (ed.), *Parlamentarisches Ritual und politische Alternative*. Frankfurt: Campus.
Donoughue, B. (1987) *Prime Minister*. London: Jonathan Cape.
Downs, A. (1957) *An Economic Theory of Democracy*. New York: Harper & Row.
Downs, A. (1967) *Inside Bureaucracy*. Boston, Mass: Little, Brown.
Drucker, H.M. (1979) 'Crying Wolfe: Recent Divisions in the SNP', *Political Quarterly*, 50: 503–8.
Duverger, M. (1959) *Political Parties*. London: Methuen.
Duverger, M. (1976) *Les Partis politiques*. Paris: A. Colin.
Ebbinghausen, R. and Kirchhoff, P. (1973) 'Die DKP im Parteiensystem der Bundesrepublik', pp. 427–68 in J. Dittberner and R. Ebbinghausen (eds), *Parteiensystem in der Legitimationskrise*. Opladen: Westdeutscher Verlag.
Edgar, D. (1977) 'Racism, Fascism, and the Politics of the National Front', *Race and Class*, 19: 111–31.
Eijk, C. van der (1987) 'Het kiezersgedrag in 1986', pp. 73–82 in *Jaarboek 1986 DNPP*. Groningen: Documentatiecentrum Nederlandse Politieke Partijen.
Elder, N. and Gooderham, R. (1978) 'The Center Parties of Norway and Sweden', *Government and Opposition*, 13: 218–35.
Elklit, J. (1986) 'Det klassiske danske partisystem bliver til', pp. 21–38 in J. Elklit and O. Tonsgaard, *Valg og vælgeradfærd – studier i dansk politik*, 2nd edn. Aarhus: Politica.
Elzinga, D.J. (1989) *Het Nederlandse kiesrecht*. Zwolle: Tjeenk Willink.
Emanuel, P. (1974) *DKP-organisation og rolle*. Copenhagen.
Epstein, L.D. (1967) *Political Parties in Western Democracies*. New York: Praeger.
Evangelische Volkspartij (1983) *Evangelische vreedzame wereldpolitiek – samen leven en samen overleven*. Amersfoort: Evangelische Volkspartij.
Eysell, M. (1979) 'Geschichte, Programmatik und Politik der Dänischen Linken', pp. 201–92 in H. Rühle and H.J. Veen (eds), *Sozialistische und Kommunistische Parteien in Westeuropa*. Opladen: Leske Verlag.
Falter, J. and Schumann, S. (1988) 'Affinity towards Right-Wing Extremism in Western Europe', *West European Politics*, 11: 96–110.
Farneti, P. (1985) *The Italian Party System*. London: Frances Pinter.
Farrell, B. (1970) 'Labour and the Irish Party System: A Suggested Approach to Analysis', *Economic and Social Review*, 1: 477–89.
Farrell, D. (1989) 'Ireland: The "Green Alliance"', pp. 123–30 in F. Müller-Rommel (ed.), *New Politics in Western Europe*. Boulder, Co, and London: Westview Press.
Featherstone, K. and Katsoudas, D.K. (eds) (1987) *Political Change in Greece – before and after the Colonels*. London: Croom Helm.
Fennema, M. (1988) 'The End of Dutch Bolshevism? The Communist Party of the Netherlands', pp. 158–78 in M. Waller and M. Fennema (eds), *Communist Parties in Western Europe: Decline or Adaptation?* Oxford: Basil Blackwell.
Fisera, V.C. and Jenkins, P. (1982) 'The Unified Party (PSU) since 1968', pp. 108–19 in D.S. Bell (ed.), *Contemporary French Political Parties*. London: Croom Helm.
Fisher, S.L. (1974) *The Minor Parties of the Federal Republic of Germany – toward a Comparative Theory of Minor Parties*. The Hague: Martinus Nijhoff.
Fisher, S.L. (1980) 'The Decline-of-Parties Thesis and the Role of Minor Parties', pp. 609–13 in P. Merkl (ed.), *Western European Party Systems*. New York: Free Press.

Flanagan, S.C. and Dalton, R. (1984) 'Parties under Stress', *West European Politics*, 7: 7–23.
Folketingets Håndbog, 1977 and 1987. Copenhagen: Schultz.
Folketingstidende – Årbog og Registre 1986–87 (1988) Copenhagen: Schultz.
Frankland, G. (1989) 'Federal Republic of Germany: "Die Grünen"', pp. 61–80 in F. Müller-Rommel (ed.), *New Politics in Western Europe*. Boulder, Co, and London: Westview Press.
Franklin, M. (1985) *The Decline of Class Voting in Britain: Changes in the Basis of Electoral Choice 1964–1983*. Oxford: Clarendon Press.
Frischenschlager, F. (1974) 'Die Freiheitliche Partei Österreichs', *Liberal*, 7: 535–46.
Frischenschlager, F. (1981) 'Wie liberal ist die FPÖ', pp. 135–81 in *Österreichisches Jahrbuch für Politik 1980*.
Fryske Nasjonale Party (1982) *Friesland en de FNP*. Leeuwarden: Fryske Nasjonale Party.
Fürnberg, F. (1977) *Geschichte der KPÖ: 1918–1955*. Vienna: Globus Verlag.
Fusaro, A. (1979) 'Two Faces of British Nationalism: The Scottish National Party and Plaid Cymru Compared', *Polity*, 11: 363–78.
Gaay-Fortmann, B. de (1983) 'PPR, Niet Verder! Groene Politiek', *Radikale Notities*, 1: 2–6.
Gabrielsen, B.V. (1970) *Menn og Politikk. Sentexpartiet 1920–1970*. Oslo: Aschehong.
Gahrton, P. (1970) *Folkpartist*. Stockholm.
Gahrton, P. (1972) *Kan folkpartiet spela nagon roll?* Stockholm.
Gallagher, M. (1982) *The Irish Party in Transition, 1957–1982*. Manchester: Macmillan and Manchester University Press.
Galli, G. (1966) *Il Bipartitismo Imperfetto*. Bologna: Il Mulino.
Gärtner, H. (1978) 'Eine sowjetorientierte KP – Die Kommunistische Partei Österreichs – ein Vergleich', *Österreichische Zeitschrift für Politikwissenschaft*, 7: 43–54.
Gärtner, H. (1979) *Zwischen Moskau und Österreich. Analyse einer sowjetabhängigen KP*. Vienna: Böhlau.
Garvin, T. (1981) *The Evolution of Irish Nationalist Politics*. Dublin: Gill & Macmillan.
Gerretsen, R. and Linden, M. van der (1982) 'Die Pazifistisch-Sozialistische Partei (PSP) der Niederlande', pp. 85–106 in J. van der Baumgarten (ed.), *Linkssozialisten in Europa*. Hamburg: Junius Verlag.
Gibowski, W.G. (1987) 'Liberals and Greens – Smaller Parties' Perspectives in the West German Party System'. Paper for the Midwest Political Science Meeting, Chicago, Ill.
Gilberg, T. (1973) *The Soviet Communist Party and Scandinavian Communism. The Norwegian Case*. Oslo: Universitetsforlaget.
Gilg, P. (1972) 'Der Erfolg der neuen Rechtsgruppen in den Nationalratswahlen von 1971', *Schweizer Zeitschrift für Volkswirtschaft und Statistik*, 4: 591–622.
Ginneken, F. van (1976) *De PPR van 1968 tot en met 1971*. Breda.
Giovana, M. (1972) 'Italy's Neo-Fascists – the MSI Gains', *Wiener Library Bulletin*, 25: 29–32.
Godschalk, J.J. (1969–70) 'Enige politieke en sociale kenmerken van de oprichters van D'66', *Acta Politica*, 5: 62–74.
Gollwitzer, H. (1977) *Europäische Bauernparteien im 20 Jahrhundert*. Stuttgart: Fischer Verlag.
Gouldner, A.W. (1959) 'Organizational Analysis', pp. 400–28 in R.K. Merton, *Sociology Today*. New York: Basic Books.

Greene, T. (1971) 'The Electorates of Nonruling Communist Parties', *Studies in Comparative Communism*, 4: 68–103.
Greenhill, H.G. (1962) 'The Norwegian Agrarian Party – a Case Study of a Single-Interest Party'. PhD dissertation, University of Illinois.
Grimond, J. (1963) *The Liberal Challenge*. London: Hollis & Carter.
Gronner, A. (1984) 'VGÖ and ALÖ – grün-alternative Gruppierungen in Österreich', *Umdenken*, 3: 79–96.
Gronner, A. and Kitzmüller, E. (eds) (1988) *Grüne Ausblicke: Beiträge zu einer Politik der Grünen*. Vienna: Juning.
Haerpfer, C. (1989) 'Austria: The "United Greens" and the "Alternative List/Green Alternative"', pp. 23–38 in F. Müller-Rommel (ed.), *New Politics in Western Europe*. Boulder, Co, and London: Westview Press.
Hahn, K.J. (1975) *Histoire, structure, action de la démocratie chrétienne en Europe*. Rome: Centre International DC de Documentation.
Hallet, J. (1958) 'Le Parti social chrétien en pouvoir', *Dossier de l'action sociale politique*, 6: 485–7.
Hanning, J. (1981) 'The Italian Radical Party and the "New Politics"', *West European Politics*, 4: 267–81.
Harrop, M., England, J. and Husbands, C.T. (1980) 'The Basis of National Front Support', *Political Studies*, 28: 271–83.
Hartmann, J. (1978) 'Strukturprobleme christdemokratischer Parteien in Europe', *Zeitschrift für Politik*, 25: 175–93.
Haubrich, W. (1978) 'Die Kommunistische Partei Spaniens', pp. 123–54 in H. Timmermann (ed.), *Euro Kommunismus*. Frankfurt: Fischer TB Verlag.
Hauss, C.S. (1978) *The New Left in France: The Unified Socialist Party*. Westport, Conn.: Greenwood Press.
Heffron, F. (1989) *Organization Theory and Public Organizations*. Englewood Cliffs, NJ: Prentice-Hall.
Heimann, S. (1983) 'Die Deutsche Kommunistische Partei', pp. 901–82 in R. Stöss (ed.), *Parteien Handbuch*, Vol. 1. Opladen: Westdeutscher Verlag.
Hermann, P.W. (1976) *The Communist Party of Great Britain*. Meisenheim: Hain Verlag.
Hermansson, J. (1984) *Kommunism på Svenska?* Uppsala: Acta Universitatis Upsaliensis.
Hermet, G. (1974) *The Communist in Spain*. Lexington, Mass: Lexington Books.
Hermet, G. (1977) 'Die Kommunistische Partei Spaniens', pp. 214–34 in A. Kimmel (ed.), *Euro Kommunismus*. Cologne: Böhlau Verlag.
Herzog, H. (1987) 'Minor Parties: The Relevancy Perspective', *Comparative Politics*, 19: 317–29.
Hirdman, Y. (1974) *SKP 1939–1945*. Stockholm: Liber.
Hodgson, J.H. (1967) *Communism in Finland*. Princeton, NJ: Princeton University Press.
Holmgaard, B. (1966) 'Die Kommunistische Partei Dänemarks', pp. 51–74 in A. Sparring (ed.), *Kommunisten im Norden*. Cologne: Verlag Wissenschaft und Politik.
Holsteyn, J.J.M. van, Irwin, G.A. and Eijk, C. van der (eds) (1987) *De Nederlandse Kiezer '86*. Amsterdam: Steinmetzarchief.
Horner, F. (1981) *Konservative und Christlich Demokratische Parteien in Europa*. Vienna: Herold Verlag.
Houben, R. (1963) *Le PSC contesté*. Brussels: CEPESS.
House of Commons Debates (1979) 965: 515–22, 28 March.

Husbands, C.T. (1979) 'The National Front: What Happens to It Now?', *Marxism Today*, 9: 268–75.
Husbands, C.T. (1981) 'Contemporary Right-Wing Extremism in Western European Democracies: A Review Article', *European Journal of Political Research*, 9: 75–99.
Idenburg, P. (1971) 'De Christen-Radikalen en de partijverieuwing', *Civis Mundis*, 10: 313–20.
Iivonen, J. (1986) 'State or Party? The Dilemma of Relations between the Soviet and Finnish Communist Parties', *Journal of Communist Studies*, 2: 5–30.
Inglehart, R. (1977) *The Silent Revolution in Europe: Changing Values and Political Styles among Western Publics*. Princeton, NJ: Princeton University Press.
Irwin, G. and Dittrich, K. (1984) 'And the Walls Came Tumbling Down: Party Dealignment in the Netherlands', pp. 267–97 in R.J. Dalton, S.C. Flanagan and P.A. Beck (eds), *Electoral Change in Advanced Industrial Democracies: Realignment or Dealignment?* Princeton, NJ: Princeton University Press.
Irwin, G. and Holsteyn, J.J.M. van (1988) 'CDA, naar voren! Over de veranderende verkiezingsstrategie van het CDA', pp. 66–98 in *Jaarboek 1987 DNPP*. Groningen: Documentatiecentrum Nederlandse Politieke Partijen.
Irving, R.E.M. (1979) *The Christian Democratic Parties of Western Europe*. London: Allen & Unwin.
Janda, K. (1980) *Political Parties – a Cross-National Survey*. New York: Macmillan.
Janse, C.S.L. (1985) *Bewaar het pand*. Houten: Den Hertog.
Johansen, J.O. (1966) 'Die Kommunistische Partei Norwegens', pp. 75–122 in A. Sparring (ed.), *Kommunisten im Norden*. Cologne: Wissenschaft und Politik.
Johansen, L.N. (1982) 'Denmark', pp. 29–57 in G. Hand, G. George and C. Sasse (eds), *European Electoral Systems Handbook*. London: Butterworths.
Johnson, D. (1980) 'The New Right in France', *New Society*, 6: 206–8.
Jonasson, G. (1977) 'Schwedische Bauernparteien', pp. 125–46 in H. Gollwitzer (ed.), *Europäische Bauernparteien im 20. Jahrhundert*. Frankfurt: Fischer Verlag.
Jong, J.P. de and Verduyn-Lunel, J.A. (1983) 'PPR, Samen Verder! Rode Politiek', *Radikale Notities*, 1: 7–16.
Jongeling, P. (1975) 'SGP en GPV', *Partij en politiek*, 3: 31–6.
Jonge, de A.A. (1972) *Het communisme in Nederland: de geschiedenis van een politieke partij*. The Hague: Kruseman.
Journés, C. (1979) 'Les dées politiques du movement écologique', *Revue française de science politique*, 29: 230–54.
Juling, P. (1977) *Programmatische Entwicklung der FDP 1946–1969*. Meisenheim: Anton Hain Verlag.
Junker, B. (1977) 'Bauernparteien in der Schweiz', pp. 507–23 in H. Gollwitzer (ed.), *Europäische Bauernparteien im 20. Jahrhundert*. Frankfurt: Fischer Verlag.
Junker, B. and Maurer, R. (1968) *Kampf und Verantwortung, Bernische Bauern-, Gewerbe- und Bürgerpartei 1918–1968*. Berne: Komm. v. Verbandsdr.
Jurgens, E. (1971) 'De PPR en de politieke vernienwing', *Civis Mundi*, 10: 307–13.
Kaack, H. (1979) *Die FdP*. Meisenheim: Anton Hain Verlag.
Kapetanyannis, B. (1979) 'The Making of Greek Eurocommunism', *Political Quarterly*, 50(4): 445–60.
Katsoudas, D.K. (1987) 'The Constitutional Framework', pp. 14–33 in K. Featherstone and D.K. Katsoudas (eds), *Political Change in Greece – before and after the Colonels*. London: Croom Helm.
Keller, F. (1982) 'Die Spaltung der KPÖ 1969/70', pp. 149–58 in J. Baumgarten (ed.), *Linkssozialisten in Europa*. Hamburg: Junius Verlag.

Kellmann, K. (1988) *Die Kommunistischen Parteien in Westeuropa*. Stuttgart: Klett Cotta.
Kendall, W. (1974) 'The Communist Party of Great Britain', *Survey*, 20: 118–31.
Kergoat, J. (1982) 'Die Parti Socialiste Unifie (PSU) in Frankreich', pp. 107–29 in J. Baumgarten (ed.), *Linkssozialisten in Europa*. Hamburg: Junius Verlag.
King, A. (1981) 'Politics, Economics, and the Trade Unions, 1974–1979', pp. 30–94 in H. Penniman (ed.), *Britain at the Polls, 1979*. Washington, DC: American Enterprise Institute.
Kirchheimer, O. (1966) 'The Transformation of Western European Party Systems', pp. 177–200 in J. LaPalombara and M. Weiner (eds), *Political Parties and Political Development*. Princcton, NJ: Princeton University Press.
Kirchner, E. and Broughton, D. (1988) 'The FDP in the Federal Republic of Germany: The Requirements of Survival and Success', pp. 62–92 in E. Kirchner (ed.), *Liberal Parties in Western Europe*. Cambridge: Cambridge University Press.
Kitschelt, H. (1989) *The Logics of Party Formation. Ecological Politics in Belgium and West Germany*. Ithaca, NY: Cornell University Press.
Klingemann, H.D. and Pappi, F.U. (1972) *Politischer Radikalismus*. Munich: Oldenbourg Verlag.
Kogan, N. (1983) *A Political History of Italy: The Postwar Years*. New York: Praeger.
Kolding, K. (1958) *Danmarks Retsforbund*. Copenhagen: Danskerens Forlag.
Kolinsky, E. (ed.) (1989) *The Greens in West Germany*. Oxford: Berg.
Koole, R.A. (1986) 'Politieke partijen', pp. A1100/1–131 in *Compendium voor Politiek en Samenleving in Nederland*. Alphen: Samsom.
Koole, R.A. and Voerman, G. (1986) 'Het lidmaatschap van politieke partijen', pp. 115–76 in *Jaarboek 1985 DNPP*. Groningen: Documentatiecentrum Nederlandse Politieke Partijen.
Kragh, J. (1976) *Opbrud pa venstreflojen 1956–1960. Striden i DKP og SFs dannelse*. Copenhagen.
Kühnl, R., Rilling, R. and Sager, C. (1969) *Die NPD: Struktur, Ideologie und Funktion einer Neofaschistischen Partei*. Frankfurt: Edition Suhrkamp.
Laakso, M. and Taagepera, R. (1979) 'Effective Number of Parties: A Measure with Application to West Europe', *Comparative Political Studies*, 12: 3–27.
Lagasse, A. (1968) 'Les petits partis sont-ils utiles?', *Res Publica*, 10: 59–75.
Land, van der L. (1962) *Het ontstaan van de Pacifistisch Socialistische Partij*. Amsterdam: De Bezige Bij.
Lane, J.-E. and Ersson, S. (1987) *Politics and Society in Western Europe*. London: Sage.
Lange, P. and Vannicelli, M. (eds) (1981) *The Communist Parties of Italy, France, and Spain: Post-War Change and Continuity. A Casebook*. London: Allen & Unwin.
Langguth, G. (1986) *The Green Factor in German Politics*. Boulder, Co: Westview Press.
Lanzalaco, L. (1985) 'Evoluzione organizzativa e modello di partido', pp. 67–118 in A. Parisi and A. Varni (eds), *Organizzazione e Politica nel PRI: 1946–1984*. Bologna: Istituto Carlo Cattaneo.
Larsen, B.V. (1978) 'En studie af Fremskridtspartiets organisation', *Politica*, 9: 59–84.
Larsen, D. (1975) *Politiske proceshastigheder – Partidannelser foruod for folketingsvalg 1915–75*. Aarhus: Institut for Presseforskning.
Larsen, H. (1980) Det radikale Venstre i medvind og modvind 1955–1980. Copenhagen: Tidens Tankers Forlag.

Larsson, H.A. (1980) *Partireformationen fran bondeförbund till centerparti*. Lund: Studentenvorlaget.
Layton-Henry, Z. (ed.) (1982) *Conservative Politics in Western Europe*. London: Macmillan.
Leiphart, J. and Svasand, L. (1988) 'The Norwegian Liberal Party: From Political Pioneer to Political Footnote', pp. 304–25 in E. Kirchner (ed.), *Liberal Parties in Western Europe*. Cambridge: Cambridge University Press.
Lemieux, P. (1977) 'Political Issues and Liberal Support in the February 1974 British General Election', *Political Studies*, 25: 323–42.
Letamendia, F. (1977) *Historia de Enzkadi. El nacionalismo vasco y ETA*. Barcelona.
Levie, J. (1962) *Michel Levie et le movement chrétien-social de son temps*. Lonvain: Nanwelaerts.
Levy, R. (1988) 'Third Party Decline in the UK: The SNP and the SDP in Comparative Perspective', *West European Politics*, 11: 57–74.
Lichtblau, A. and Winter, M. (1986) 'Die Entwicklung der KPÖ im Spiegel ihrer Parteitage', pp. 91–108 in P. Gerlich and W. Müller (eds), *Zwischen Koalition und Konkurrenz*. Vienna: Böhlau.
Lijphart, A. (1984) *Democracies*. New Haven, Conn.: Yale University Press.
Lijphart, A. (1988) 'The Political Consequences of Electoral Laws, 1945–1985'. Paper presented at the XIVth Congress of the International Political Science Association, Washington, DC, August.
Lijphart, A., Bruneau, T.C., Diamandouros, P.N. and Gunther, R. (1988) 'A Mediterranean Model of Democracy? The Southern European Democracies in Comparative Perspective', *West European Politics*, 11: 7–25.
Lindström, U. and Wörlund, I. (1988) 'The Swedish Liberal Party: The Politics of Unholy Alliances', pp. 252–78 in E. Kirchner (ed.), *Liberal Parties in Western Europe*. Cambridge: Cambridge University Press.
Lipset, S.M. and Rokkan, St. (1967) 'Cleavage Structures, Party Systems and Voter Alignments: An Introduction', pp. 1–64 in S.M. Lipset and St. Rokkan (eds), *Party Systems and Voter Alignments. Cross-National Perspectives*. New York: Free Press.
Lomeland, A.R. (1971) *Kristelig Folkeparti blir til*. Oslo and Bergen: Universitetsforlaget.
Loo, H. van der, Snel, E. and Steenbergen, B. van (1984) *Een wenkend perspektief? Nieuwe sociale bewegingen en culturele veranderingen*. Amersfoort: De Horstink.
Lorenz, E. (1982) 'Linkssozialisten in Norwegen', pp. 33–57 in J. Baumgarten (ed.), *Linkssozialisten in Europa*. Hamburg: Junius Verlag.
Lucardie, A.P.M. (1980) 'The New Left in the Netherlands (1960–1977)'. PhD dissertation, Queen's University, Kingston, Canada.
Lucardie, A.P.M. (1986) 'Dwergen, splinters en eendagsvliegen', pp. 68–93 in *Jaarboek 1985 DNPP*. Groningen: Documentatiecentrum Nederlandse Politieke Partijen.
Lucardie, A.P.M. (1988) 'Conservatism in the Netherlands: Fragments and Fringe Groups', pp. 78–97 in B. Girvin (ed.), *The Transformation of Contemporary Conservatism*. London: Sage.
Lucardie, A.P.M. (1990) 'Politici in de periferie', pp. 126–43 in *Jaarboek 1989 DNPP*. Groningen: Documentatiecentrum Nederlandse Politieke Partijen.
Lucardie, A.P.M., Meijer, H. and Voerman, G. (1987) 'Friese en Groningse federalisten falen en Limburgse regionalisten slagen', *Namens*, 2: 327–32.

Lucius, W. and Metzner, M. (eds) (1982) *Die Radikale Partei Italiens*. Heidelberg: Wunderhorn Verlag.
Lund, B. (1982) 'Sozialistische Volkspartei (SF) und Linkssozialisten (VS) – Dänische Parteien zwischen Sozialpartnerschaft und Klassenkampf', pp. 58–84 in J. Baumgarten (ed.), *Linkssozialisten in Europa*. Hamburg: Junius Verlag.
Luther, K.R. (1988) 'Die Freiheitliche Partei Österreichs: Protest Party or Governing Party?', pp. 213–51 in E. Kirchner (ed.), *Liberal Parties in Western Europe*. Cambridge: Cambridge University Press.
Lyrintzis, C. (1983) 'Between Socialism and Populism: The Rise of PASOK'. PhD dissertation, University of London.
McAllister, I. (1981) 'Party Organization and Minority Nationalism: A Comparative Study in the United Kingdom', *European Journal of Political Research*, 9: 237–55.
McInnes, N. (1975) *The Communist Parties of Western Europe*. London: Oxford University Press.
Mackie, T. and Rose, R. (1982) *The International Almanac of Electoral History*. London: Macmillan.
Maclean, I. (1970) 'The Rise and the Fall of the Scottish National Party', *Political Studies*, 18: 357–72.
Mair, P. (1979) 'The Marxist Left', pp. 157–81 in H.M. Drucker (ed.), *Multi-Party Britain*. London: Macmillan.
Mair, P. (1983) 'Adaption and Control: Towards an Understanding of Party and Party System Change', pp. 405–29 in H. Daalder and P. Mair (eds), *Western European Party Systems: Continuity and Change*. London: Sage.
Mair, P. (1987) *The Changing Irish Party System: Organization, Ideology, and Electoral Competition*. London: Frances Pinter.
Mansbach, R.W. (1973) 'The Scottish National Party: A Revised Political Profile', *Comparative Politics*, 5: 185–210.
Marcuse, H. (1969) 'Repressive Tolerance', pp. 81–123 in *A Critique of Pure Tolerance*. Boston, Mass: Beacon Press.
Matheson, D.K. and Sänkiaho, R. (1975) 'The Split in the Finnish Rural Party: Populism in Decline in Finland', *Scandinavian Political Studies*, 10: 217–23.
Matti, B. (1966) 'Die Kommunistische Partei Finnlands', pp. 123–62 in A. Sparring (ed.), *Kommunisten im Norden*. Cologne: Wissenschaft und Politik.
Mavrogordatos, G. Th. (1983a) 'The Emerging Party System', pp. 70–94 in R. Clogg (ed.), *Greece in the 1980s*. London: Macmillan.
Mavrogordatos, G. Th. (1983b) *Rise of the Green Sun. The Greek Election of 1981*. London: King's College, Centre for Contemporary Greek Studies, Occasional Paper No. 1.
Mavrogordatos, G. Th. (1984) 'The Greek Party System – a Case of "Limited but Polarised Pluralism"?', pp. 156–69 in St. Bartolini and P. Mair (eds), *Party Politics in Contemporary Western Europe*. London: Frank Cass.
Mayer, L.C. (1980) 'A Note on the Aggregation of Party Systems', pp. 515–20 in P. Merkl (ed.), *Western European Party Systems*. New York: Free Press.
Merkl, P. (1980) 'The Study of Party Systems', pp. 1–13 in P. Merkl (ed.), *Western European Party Systems*. New York: Free Press.
Merli, F. and Handstanger, M. (1984) 'Die Alternative Liste Graz als Erweiterung des Kommunalpolitischen Systems', pp. 295–318 in *Österreichisches Jahrbuch für Politik 1983*. Vienna: Oldenbourg Verlag.
Mewes, H. (1983) 'The West German Green Party', *New German Critique*, 28: 51–85.
Meynaud, J. and Korff, A. (1967) *Die Migros und die Politik: Der Landesring der Unabhängigen*. Zurich.

Mierlo, H.A.F.M.O. van (1988) 'Liberalisme: waarheen?', *Idee*, 66(9): 4–6.
Milotte, M. (1984) *Communism in Modern Ireland*. Dublin and New York: Magill.
Miltra, S. (1988) 'The National Front in France – a Single Issue Movement?', *West European Politics*, 11: 47–64.
Møller, P. (1974) *Politik på vrangen*. Copenhagen: Stig Vendelkærs Forlag.
Monrad, J.H. (1970) *Et land bygges op Venstre i 100 år 1901–1936*. Copenhagen.
Morass, M. and Reischenböck, H. (1988) 'Populismus als Programm – die FPO unter Jörg Haider', *Zukunft*, 43: 12–17.
Morgan, R. and Silvestri, S. (eds) (1982) *Moderates and Conservatives in Western Europe*. London: Heinemann.
Mouzelis, N. (1987) 'Continuities and Discontinuities in Greek Politics', pp. 271–87 in K. Featherstone and D.K. Katsoudas (eds), *Political Change in Greece – before and after the Colonels*. London: Croom Helm.
Müller-Rommel, F. (1985a) 'Social Movements and the Greens: New Internal Politics in West Germany', *European Journal of Political Research*, 13: 53–67.
Müller-Rommel, F. (1985b) 'New Social Movements and Smaller Parties: A Comparative Perspective', *West European Politics*, 8: 41–54.
Müller-Rommel, F. (ed.) (1989) *New Politics in Western Europe: The Rise and the Success of Green Parties and Alternative Lists*. Boulder, Co, and London: Westview Press.
Müller-Rommel, F. (1990) 'New Politics Parties and New Social Movements in Western Europe', in R. Dalton and M. Küchler (eds), *Challenging the Political Order*. Oxford: Oxford University Press.
Mullin, R.W.A. (1979) 'The Scottish National Party', pp. 109–30 in H.M. Drucker (ed.), *Multi-Party Britain*. London: Macmillan.
Naerbøvik, J. and Grepstad, O. (eds) (1984) *Venstres Hundre Ar*. Oslo: Gyldendal.
Nagle, J. (1970) *The National Democratic Party: Right Radicalism in the Federal Republic of Germany*. Berkeley, Calif: University of California Press.
Nania, G. (1966) *Un parti de la gauche, le PSU*. Paris: Librairie Gedalge.
Nannestad, P. (1986) 'Dimensioner i valgernes opfattelse af partisystemet', pp. 167–94 in J. Elklit and O. Tonsgaard (eds), *Valg og vælgeradfærd – studier i dansk politik*. 2nd edn. Aarhus: Politica.
Neumann, S. (ed.) (1956) *Modern Political Parties*. Chicago: University of Chicago Press.
Nick, R. (1986) 'Rahmenbedingungen und Entwicklung der grünalternativen Szene in Voralberg', *Österreichische Zeitschrift für Politikwissenschaft*, 15: 157–69.
Nicolacopoulos, E. (1984) 'Géographie électorale de la Grèce depuis 1945: vers la nationalisation du vote'. Paper presented at ECPR Joint Sessions, Salzburg, April.
Nielsen, H.J. (1975) *Fremskridtspartiet – et højreorienteret protestparti for hvem?* Copenhagen: Copenhagen University, Institut for Samfundsfag.
Niemöller, B. and Eijk, C. van der (1984) 'Het potentiële electoraat van de Nederlandse politieke partijen', *Beleid en Maatschappij*, 11: 192–204.
Niemöller, B. and Eijk, C. van der (1985) 'Links-rechts, post-materialisme en stemgedrag in Nederland'. Paper presented at the Dutch Political Science Conference, Amersfoort.
Niezing, J. (1963) 'De kleine politieke partij – enkele hypothesen', *Sociologische Gids*, 10: 264–72.
Nooïj, A.T.J. (1969) *De Boerenpartij: desorientatie en radikalisme onder de boeren*. Meppel: Boom.
Nugent, N. and King, R. (eds) (1977) *The British Right: Conservative and Right-Wing Politics in Britain*. London: Saxon House.

Nullmeier, F., Rubert, F. and Schultz, H. (1983) *Umweltbewegungen und Parteiensystem: Frankreich – Schweden*. Berlin: Quorum.
Oberndörfer, D. (ed.) (1978) *Sozialistische und Kommunistische Parteien in Westeuropa. 1. Südländer*. Opladen: Leske Verlag.
Olsen, E. and Pedersen, R. (1976) *Fremskridtspartiet – ikke realistisk ikke sympatisk*. Copenhagen.
Olsson, S.E. (1986) 'Swedish Communism Poised: Between Old Reds and New Greens', *Journal of Communist Studies*, 2: 359–72.
Ontwapenend (1982) *Ontwapenend: geschiedenis van 25 jaar PSP*. Amsterdam: Wetenschappelijk Bureau PSP.
Opello, W.C. Jr (1985) *Portugal's Political Development – a Comparative Approach*. Boulder, Co, and London: Westview Press.
Orridge, A. (1977) 'The Irish Labour Party', pp. 153–75 in W.E. Paterson and A. Thomas (eds), *Social Democratic Parties in Western Europe*. London: Croom Helm.
Ossipow, W. (1981) 'Concurrence politique et démocratie directe', pp. 1–62 in W. Ossipow and J. Papadopoulos, *Deux études sur la démocratie directe en Suisse*. Geneva: University of Geneva, Department of Political Science, Etudes et Recherches No. 14.
Panebianco, A. (1982) *Modelli di Partito: organizzazione e potere nei partiti politici*. Bologna: Il Mulino.
Papadakis, E. (1983) 'The Green Party in Contemporary West German Politics', *Political Quarterly*, 54: 302–7.
Papadakis, E. (1984) *The Green Movement in West Germany*. New York: St Martin's Press.
Papadopoulos, Y. (1989a) *Dynamique du discours politique et conquête du pouvoir – le cas du PASOK: 1974–81*. Frankfurt and Berne: Peter Lang Verlag.
Papadopoulos, Y. (1989b) 'Parties, the State and Society in Greece: Continuity within Change', *West European Politics*, 12: 55–71.
Parisi, A. and Varni, A. (eds) (1985) *Organizzazione e Politica nel PRI: 1946–1984*. Bologna: Instituto Carlo Cattaneo.
Pasquino, G. (1983) 'Sources of Stability and Instability in the Italian Party System', *West European Politics*, 6: 93–110.
Paterson, W. and Campbell, I. (1974) *Social Democracy in Post-War Europe*. London: Macmillan.
Paterson, W. and Thomas, A. (eds) (1977) *Social Democratic Parties in Western Europe*. London: Croom Helm.
Paterson, W. and Thomas, A. (eds) (1984) *The Future of Social Democracy*. London: Oxford University Press.
Payne, S. (1974) *El nacionalismo vasco*. Barcelona: Dopesa.
Pedersen, M.N. (1967) 'Consensus and Conflict in the Danish Folketing 1945–65', *Scandinavian Political Studies*, 2: 143–66.
Pedersen, M.N. (1982) 'Towards a New Typology of Party Lifespans and Minor Parties, *Scandinavian Political Studies*, 5: 1–16.
Pedersen, M.N. (1983) 'The Dynamics of European Party Systems: Changing Patterns of Electoral Volatility in European Party Systems: Explorations in Explanation', pp. 29–66 in H. Daalder and P. Mair (eds), *Western European Party Systems*. London: Sage.
Pedersen, M.N. (1987a) 'The Danish Working Multiparty System: Breakdown or Adaptation?', pp. 1–60 in H. Daalder (ed.), *Party Systems in Denmark, Austria, Switzerland, the Netherlands, and Belgium*. London: Frances Pinter.

Pedersen, M.N. (1987b) 'Skyggebilleder? – Nogle kommentarer til validitetsdiskussionen omkring Søren Risbjerg Thomsens metode til økologisk inferens', *Politica*, 19: 333–42.

Pedersen, M.N. (1988) 'The Defeat of All Parties: The Danish Folketing Election 1973', pp. 257–81 in K. Lawson and P.H. Merkl (eds), *When Parties Fail – Emerging Alternative Organizations*. Princeton, NJ: Princeton University Press.

Pelinka, A. (1980) *Sozialdemokratie in Europa*. Vienna: Herold Verlag.

Pelinka, A. (1982) 'Die KPÖ – eine Kleinpartei in der Isolierung', pp. 143–57 in *Österreichisches Jahrbuch für Politik*. Vienna: Oldenbourg Verlag.

Pelling, H. (1975) *The British Communist Party*. London: Black Press.

Penniman, H.R. (ed.) (1977) *Italy at the Polls: The Parliamentary Elections of 1976*. Washington, DC: American Enterprise Institute.

Penniman, H.R. (ed.) (1981) *Greece at the Polls*. Washington, DC: American Enterprise Institute.

Perching, B. (1983) 'National oder Liberal: Die FPÖ', pp. 69–90 in P. Gerlich and W. Müller (eds), *Zwischen Koalition und Konkurrenz. Österreichs Parteien seit 1945*. Vienna: Böhlau Verlag.

Pérez Calvo, A. (1977) *Los partidos politicos en el Pais Vasco*. Madrid: Ediciones Tucar.

Piringer, K. (1982) *Die Geschichte der Freiheitlichen: Beitrag der Dritten Kraft zur österreichischen Politik*. Vienna.

Plasser, F. and Sommer, F. (1985) 'Eine "grüne" Premiere. Analyse der Voralberger Landtagswahl 1984', pp. 55–65 in *Österreichisches Jahrbuch für Politik*. Vienna: Oldenbourg Verlag.

Platvoet, L. (1985) 'PSP-kongresgangers doorgelicht', *Socialistisch Perspektief*, 25: 29–37.

Poguntke, Th. (1989) 'The New Politics Dimension in European Green Parties', pp. 175–94 in F. Müller-Rommel (ed.), *New Politics in Western Europe*. Boulder, Co, and London: Westview Press.

Potter, T. (1982) 'Il Manifesto and Il Partido di Unità Proletaria (PDuP), Linke Kritik an der Kommunistischen Partei Italiens', pp. 1–32 in J. Baumgarten (ed.), *Linkssozialisten in Europa*. Hamburg: Junius Verlag.

Prendeville, B. (1989) 'France: "Les Verts"', pp. 87–100 in F. Müller-Rommel (ed.), *New Politics in Western Europe*. Boulder, Co, and London: Westview Press.

Pridham, G. (1976) 'Christian Democracy in Italy and West Germany: A Comparative Analysis', pp. 142–77 in M. Kolinsky and W. Paterson (eds), *Social and Political Movements in Western Europe*. London: Croom Helm.

Pridham, G. (ed.) (1986) *Coalition Behaviour in Theory and Practice: An Inductive Model for Western Europe*. Cambridge: Cambridge University Press.

Pridham, G. (1988) 'Two Roads of Italian Liberalism: The Partito Repubblicano Italiano (PRI) and the Partito Liberale Italiano (PLI)', pp. 29–61 in E. Kirchner (ed.), *Liberal Parties in Western Europe*. Cambridge: Cambridge University Press.

Pridham, G. (ed.) (1990) *Securing Democracy: Political Parties and Democratic Consolidation in Southern Europe*. London: Routledge.

Pridham, G. and Whiteley, P. (1986) 'Anatomy of the SDP', *Government and Opposition*, 21: 205–17.

Pyne, P. (1970) 'The Third Sinn Fein Party', *Economic and Social Review*, 1: 29–50, 229–57.

Rae, D. (1967) *The Political Consequences of Electoral Laws*. New Haven, Conn. Yale University Press.

Ramseier, H.G. (1973) 'Die Entstehung und Entwicklung des Landesringes der Unabhängigen (LDU)'. Dissertation, University of Zurich.
Rasmussen, E. (1972) *Komparativ Politik II*, 2nd edn. Copenhagen: Gyldendal.
Rasmussen, E. and Skovmand, R. (1955) *Det radikale Venstre 1905–1955*. Copenhagen: Det Danske Forlaget.
Rasmussen, J. (1965) *The Liberal Party: A Study in Retrenchment and Revival*. London: Constable.
Rasmussen, J. (1981) 'David Steel's Liberals: Too Old to Cry, Too Hurt to Laugh', pp. 159–76 in H. Penniman (ed.), *Britain at the Polls*. Washington, DC: American Enterprise Institute.
Rasmussen, J. (1985) 'The Alliance Campaign, Watersheds, and Landslides: Was 1983 a Fault Line in British Politics?', pp. 81–107 in A. Ranney (ed.), *Britain at the Polls, 1983*. Washington, DC: American Enterprise Institute.
Reif, K. (1984) *Ten European Elections*. London: Gower.
Reinthaler, E. (1985) 'Die Parteikrise der KPÖ'. DPhil. dissertation, University of Salzburg.
Reiter, E. (1982) *Programm und Programmentwicklung der FPÖ*. Vienna: Braumüller.
Rhode, P. (1973) 'The Communist Party of Denmark', pp. 15–39 A. Lipton (ed.), *Communism in Scandinavia and Finland*. New York: Anchor Press.
Riesen, R. (1972) *Die Schweizerische Bauernheimatbewegung*. Berne.
Rocard, M. (1969) *Le PSU*. Paris.
Rochon, T.R. (1985) 'Mobilizers and Challengers: Toward a Theory of New Party Success', *International Political Science Review*, 6: 419–39.
Rooney, E. (1984) 'From Republican Movement to Workers' Party: An Ideological Analysis', pp. 79–98 in C. Curtin, M. Kelly and L. O'Dowd (eds), *Culture and Ideology in Ireland*. Galway: Officira Typographica.
Rose, R. (1983) 'Elections and Electoral Systems: Choices and Alternatives', pp. 20–45 in V. Bogdanor and D. Butler (eds), *Democracy and Elections – Electoral Systems and their Political Consequences*. Cambridge: Cambridge University Press.
Rose, R. and McAllister, I. (1986) *Voters Begin to Choose: From Closed-Class to Open Elections in Britain*. London: Sage.
Rosenbaum, P. (1975) *Neofaschismus in Italien*. Frankfurt: Europäische Verlagsanstalt.
Rosenstone, St., Behr, R. and Lazarus, E. (1984) *Third Parties in America*. Princeton, NJ: Princeton University Press.
Rothhacker, A. (1984) 'The Green Party in German Politics', *West European Politics*, 7: 109–16.
Rowold, M. (1974) *Im Schatten der Macht. Zur Oppositionsrolle der nicht-etablierten Parteien in der Bundesrepublik*. Dusseldorf: Droste Verlag.
Rüdig, W. and Lowe, P.D. (1986) 'The Withered Greening of British Politics: A Study of the Ecology Party', *Political Studies*, 34: 262–84.
Rühle, H. and Veen, H.J. (eds) (1979) *Sozialistische und Kommunistische Parteien in Westeuropa. Nordländer*. Opladen: Leske Verlag.
Sänkiaho, R. (1971) 'A Model of the Rise of Populism and Support for the Finnish Rural Party', *Scandinavian Political Studies*, 6: 27–47.
Sartori, G. (1966) 'European Political Parties: The Case of Polarized Pluralism', pp. 137–76 in J. LaPalombara and M. Weiner (eds), *Political Parties and Political Development*. Princeton, NJ: Princeton University Press.
Sartori, G. (1976) *Parties and Party Systems: A Framework for Analysis*, Vol. 1. Cambridge: Cambridge University Press.

Sassoon, D. (1986) *Contemporary Italy: Politics, Economy and Society since 1945*. London: Longman.
Schain, M.A. (1987) 'The National Front in France and the Construction of Political Legitimacy', *West European Politics*, 10: 229–52.
Schaller, C. (1988–9) 'Zur Rolle von Kleinparteien im politischen System Österreichsseit 1960', *SWS-Rundschau*, 1(28): 415–30; 11(29): 5–26.
Schiltz, H. (1977) *Volksunie: Identiteit – Geschiedenis – Programma*. Deurne: VK.
Schmid, C. (1987) 'The Green Movement in West Germany: Resource Mobilization and Institutionalization', *Journal of Political and Military Sociology*, 15: 33–46.
Schmiederer, U. (1969) *Die sozialistische Volkspartei Dänemarks*. Frankfurt: Neue Kritik.
Schonewille, P. (1983) 'Democratisch Socialisten '70: het vierde alternatief'. MA thesis, University of Groningen.
Schüttemeyer, S. (1989) 'Denmark: "De Gronne"', pp. 5–60 in F. Müller-Rommel (ed.), *New Politics in Western Europe*. Boulder, Co, and London: Westview Press.
Seferiades, S. (1986) 'Polarization and Nonproportionality: The Greek Party System in the Postwar Era', *Comparative Politics*, 19: 69–93.
Seiler, D. (1988) 'Liberal Parties in Switzerland', pp. 356–75 in E. Kirchner (ed.), *Liberal Parties in Western Europe*. Cambridge: Cambridge University Press.
Seiler, D.-L. (1984) 'Une généalogie des organisations de partis', *Res Publica*, 26: 119–41.
Selle, P. (1983) *Norges Kommunistische Parti 1945–1950*. Bergen: Universitetesforlaget.
Sidjanski, D. and Inglehart, R. (1974) 'Dimension gauche-droite chez les dirigeants et électeurs suisses', *Revue française de science politique*, 24: 994–1025.
Sjoblom, G. (1968) *Party Strategies in a Multiparty System*. Lund: Studentlitteratur.
Smith, G. (1978) 'Trends in Western European Party Systems', *Parliamentary Affairs*, 21: 37–51.
Smith, G. (1984) *Politics in Western Europe*, 4th edn. London: Heinemann.
Smith, G. (1987) 'The Changing West German Party System: Consequences of the 1987 Election', *Government and Opposition*, 22(2): 131–44.
Smith, G. (1989) 'Core Persistence: System Change and the "People's Party"', pp. 157–68 in P. Mair and G. Smith (eds), *Understanding Party System Change in Western Europe*. London: Frank Cass.
Sociaal-Wetenschappelijk Instituut van de Vrije Universiteit, Afdeling Politicologie (1967) *De Nederlandse kiezers in 1967*. Amsterdam: Agon Elsevier.
Soe, C. (1985) 'The Free Democratic Party', pp. 112–86 in P. Wallach and G. Romoser (eds), *West German Politics in the Mid-Eighties*. New York: Prager.
Sparring, A. (ed.) (1966) *Kommunisten im Norden*. Cologne: Verlag Wissenschaft und Politik.
Sparring, A. (1973) 'The Communist Party in Sweden', pp. 49–62 in A.F. Upton (ed.), *Communism in Scandinavia and Finland*. New York: Anchor Press.
Spira, L. (1984) 'Wie grün ist die KPÖ?', *Umdenken*, 4: 72–8.
Spotts, F. and Wieser, T. (1986) *Italy: A Difficult Democracy*. Cambridge: Cambridge University Press.
Stam, W. (1966) *De Boerenpartij*. Amsterdam.
Steed, M. (1979) 'The Liberal Party', pp. 76–108 in H. Drucker (ed.), *Multi-Party Britain*. London: Macmillan.
Steed, M. and Hearl, D. (1985) *Party Families*. London: Liberal European Action Group.

Steel, D. (1980) *A House Divided: The Lib–Lab Pact and the Future of British Politics*. London: Weidenfeld & Nicolson.
Steiner, K. (1968) *Die kommunistische Partei Österreichs von 1918–1933*. Meisenheim: Anton Main Verlag.
Stettler, P. (1980) *Die Kommunistische Partei der Schweiz*. Berne: Francke.
Steyer, B. (1981) 'Plaid Cymru', pp. 149–63 in R.S. Elkar (ed.), *Europas unruhige Regionen*. Stuttgart: Klett Verlag.
Stirnemann, A. (1986) 'Das neue Parteiprogramm der FPÖ – eine Kritische Analyse', pp. 657–94 in *Österreichisches Jahrbuch für Politik*. Vienna: Oldenbourg Verlag.
Stouthysen, P. (1983) 'De politieke identität van de Vlaamse Groene Partij AGALEV', *Res Publica*, 25: 349–75.
Sturm, R. (1981) *Nationalimus in Schottland und Wales*. Bochum: Brockmeyer Verlag.
Svasand, L. (1987) *The Norwegian Conservative, Christian, and Progressive Parties: Uneasy Neighbours in Non-Socialist Politics*. Bergen: Department of Comparative Politics, mimeo, University of Bergen.
Tannahill, R.N. (1978) *The Communist Parties of Western Europe. A Comparative Study*. Westport, Conn.: Greenwood Press.
Tarrow, S. (1977) 'The Italian Party System between Crisis and Transition', *American Journal of Political Science*, 21: 193–224.
Tarschys, D. (1974) 'The Unique Role of the Swedish CP', *Problems of Communism*, 23: 36–44.
Taylor, S. (1979) 'The National Front: Anatomy of a Political Movement', pp. 33–58 in R. Miles and A. Phizacklea (eds), *Racism and Political Action in Britain*. London: Routledge.
Teodori, M., Ignazi, P. and Panebianco, A. (1977) *I Nuovi Radicali*. Milan: Mondadori.
Terlouw, J. (1976) 'Algemene Politieke en Financiële Beschouwingen', *Handelingen Tweede Kamer*, 3: 311–16.
Thomas, A. (1988) 'Liberalism in Denmark: Agrarian, Radical and Still Influential', pp. 279–303 in E. Kirchner (ed.), *Liberal Parties in Western Europe*. Cambridge: Cambridge University Press.
Thomsen, S.R. (1987) *Danish Elections 1920–79. A Logit Approach to Ecological Analysis and Inference*. Aarhus: Politica.
Thorndahl, U. (1984) *Højforræderi – Fremskridtspartiets storhed og undergang*. Copenhagen: Chr. Erichsen.
Timmermann, H. (1979) *Die Kommunistischen Partein Südeuropas. Länderstudien und Queranalysen*. Baden Baden: Nomos Verlag.
Turf, J. (1978) *Une Identité politique pour les Communistes*. Brussels.
Ullrich, H. (1987) 'Servitu'e Grandezza. Zu Wirken und Rolle der liberaldemokratischen Parteien in der italienischen Republik', *Zeitschrift für Parlamentsfragen*, 18: 536–54.
Upton, A.F. (1973) *The Communist Parties of Scandinavia and Finland*. New York: Anchor Press.
Van den Wijngaert (1976) *Outstaan en stichting van de CVP/PSU*. Brussels: IPOUO.
Vedung, E. (1989) 'Sweden: The "Miljöpartiet de Gröna"', pp. 139–54 in F. Müller-Rommel (ed.), *New Politics in Western Europe*. Boulder, Co, and London: Westview Press.
Vegleris, Ph. (1981) 'Greek Electoral Law', pp. 21–48 in H. Penniman (ed.), *Greece at the Polls*. Washington, DC: American Enterprise Institute.

Veivaag, K. (1977) *Venstre. Politikk og Organisasjon*. Oslo: Venstres opplysningsorganisasjon.
Ven, W. van de and Vink, B. (1986) 'Het geloof der vaderen', *Intermediair*, 22: 7–15.
Verbrught, H.J. (1959–63) *Politieke Richtlijnen en de Politieke Partijen in Nederland*, Vols 1–3. Rotterdam: Groenendijk.
Veremis, T. (1981) 'The Union of the Democratic Center', pp. 84–104 in H.P. Penniman (ed.), *Greece at the Polls, 1974/1977*. Washington, DC: American Enterprise Institute.
Verney, D. (1972) 'The Foundation of Modern Sweden: The Swift Rise and Fall of Swedish Liberalism', *Political Studies*, 20: 3–17.
Verstraaten, H. (1981) 'DS'70: de ondergang van het deugdzame socialisme', *Haagse Post*, 51: 49–51.
Visscher, G. (1988) 'Het risico van het vak', *Namens*, 7: 15–16.
Voerman, G. (1987) 'De rode Jehova's: een geschiedenis van de Socialistiese Partij', pp. 124–50 in *Jaarboek 1986 DNPP*. Groningen: Documentatiecentrum Nederlandse Politieke Partijen.
Vulperhorst, L. (1986) *Gemeentepolitiek en burger*. Zutphen: Thieme.
Wagner, U. (1971) *Finnlands Kommunisten*. Stuttgart: Kohlhammer Verlag.
Walker, M. (1977) *The National Front*. London: Fontana.
Waller, M. (1989) 'The Radical Sources of the Crisis in West European Communist Parties', *Political Studies*, 37: 39–61.
Waller, M. and Fennema, M. (eds) (1988) *Communist Parties in Western Europe*. Oxford: Basil Blackwell.
Walter, G. (1973) *Theoretischer Anspruch und politische Praxis der DKP*. Meisenheim: Anton Hain.
Warnecke, S. (1976) 'The Future of Rightist Extremism in West Germany', pp. 67–90 in M. Kolinsky and W.E. Paterson (eds), *Social and Political Movements in Western Europe*. London: Croom Helm.
Weissenberger, H. (1977) 'Die Südtiroler Volkspartei', *Europäische Rundschau*, 3: 87–110.
Whiteley, P. (1979) 'The National Front in the 1977 GLC Elections: An Aggregate Data Analysis in British', *British Journal of Political Science*, 9: 370–80.
Wickmann, J. (1977) *Fremskridtspartiet. Hvem og Hvorfor?* Copenhagen: Akademisk Forlag.
Wilde, de J.A. and Smeenk, C. (1949) *Het volk ten baat. Geschiedenis van de Anti-Revolutionaire Partij*. Deventer.
Wilson, F.L. (1971) *The French Democratic Left 1963–1969*. Stanford, CA: Stanford University Press.
Wolinetz, St.B. (1979) 'The Transformation of Western European Party Systems Revisited', *West European Politics*, 2: 4–28.
Wood, A.H. (1987) *The Times Guide to the House of Commons*. London: Times Books.
Zariski, R. (1972) *Italy: The Politics of Uneven Development*. Hinsdale, Ill: Dryden Press.
Zülich, R. (1973) *Von der FDP zur FDP*. Meisenheim: Anton Hain.

Index

age, and small party support 159, 161–2
Agrarian Liberal Party, Denmark 96, 97, 100, 101, 107
agrarian parties
  classification 4, 19, 58, 69–70, 118
  electoral support 61, 153
  large 59
  research 21
Agrarian Party of Greece (AKE) 195–6
'Alliance of the Left and Progress', Greece 176, 182–3, 185, 196, 197
Allum, P.A. 88
Anti-Revolutionary Party (ARP), Netherlands 53, 67, 133
'anti-system' parties 32, 73, 87, 91, 103, 108, 122–3, 166, 188–9
approaches, *see* research
Austria
  changing electoral support 52–3, 56, 63
  electoral system 55
  party system 8, 9, 31, 45–7, 65
  research 21
authorization threshold 10, 23, 98, 99, 100–1, 121, 157, 176

Barnes, S. 161
Basque Nationalists, Spain 38, 68
Belgium
  changing electoral support 53, 56, 63
  historical background 136–40
  impact of small parties 8, 12
  new parties 62, 65 n. 11
  party system 6, 9, 13, 33, 34–5, 38, 45, 48, 65, 135–46, 149–50
  see also language and politics
Bille, L. 114 n. 25
'blackmail potential' 7, 8, 26–7, 28, 116, 165–6
  Denmark 109, 112
  Greece 175–6, 179, 188–90, 192, 194
  Italy 73, 87–8
  of third parties 31
Blondel, J. 26, 30
Boerenpartij (Farmers' Party), Netherlands 118, 132
  electoral support 120, 128
  as extreme right party 118
  membership 131
  as mobilizer 126

  and other parties 125
  and the state 122, 123
Britain
  changing electoral support 53, 56, 63
  electoral system 29, 54–5, 152–6, 157, 171–2
  party system 9, 13, 23, 29–30, 45–7, 69, 152
  research 6, 22
  role of small parties 154–70
Brussels Liberals, Belgium 65

Caciagli, M. 94 n. 1
case studies, national 4–5, 6, 12, 13
Castles, F.G. and Mair, P. 107
Catholic People's Party (KVP), Netherlands 45, 53, 115, 134
Centre Democrats, Netherlands 129
Centre Democrats, Portugal 68
Centre Democrats (SD), Denmark 65, 119
  classification 118
  electoral support 104
centre parties
  Britain 165–6, 171
  Denmark 109–10
  Greece 196
  Italy 74–6, 82–3, 85–6, 89–90, 91
  research 6
Centre Party, Netherlands
  classification 118–19
  as detached party 118, 132
  electoral support 116, 120, 129
  as mobilizer 126
  and other parties 126, 134
  and the state 121
Centre Party, Norway 67
Centre Party, Sweden 68
Centrumdemocraten, Netherlands 133
challenger parties 126, 132, 161–3, 168
change, *see* volatility
Christian Democracy, Greece 195
Christian Democratic Appeal, Netherlands
  electoral support 43, 125, 127–8
  and large parties 45, 53, 124–5
  and new parties 115, 116, 127
  and small parties 35, 126, 134
Christian democratic parties, research 1

Christian Democratic Party, Belgium
  140, 149
Christian Democrats (CDU), West
  Germany, and party system 30–1
Christian Democrats (DC), Italy
  decline 72
  and party system 32, 33, 74, 78–9, 88–90
Christian Democrats, Sweden 68
Christian Historical Union, Netherlands
  53, 67, 134
Christian League, Finland 66
Christian parties
  classification 4, 17, 58, 70
  electoral support 9, 59, 61
Christian People's Party, Denmark 65
Christian People's Party, Norway 67
Christlich-Soziale Union (CSU), West
  Germany
  and party dominance 28
  and third parties 31
Clann na Poblachta, Ireland 66
Clann na Talmhan, Ireland 66
class, social, and party support 43, 80,
  92, 103, 127–9, 158–63, 187
classification 8, 9, 24, 25, 26–36, 42–9,
  63–4
  of Belgian parties 142–6
  by country 65–9, 135
  by family 3–4, 69–70, 118–19
  of Dutch parties 118–19
  of Italian parties 72–3
  and party systems 47–8, 198
cleavages 43, 108
  Belgium 136–42, 149–50
  Britain 158–63
  Greece 178, 187, 198, 201 n. 1
  Italy 79–80
  Netherlands 126–31
clientelism 181, 182, 194, 196, 198
clusters, small-party 33–4
'coalition potential' 35, 116
  Belgium 145, 147, 150
  Britain 165, 166, 167–8, 170, 171
  communist parties 37
  Denmark 109, 112
  detached parties 36, 38
  Greece 176, 179, 182, 188–9, 191–2
  hinge parties 36, 37
  Italy 73, 87–8
  marginal parties 36, 37, 108
  and party system 7, 8–9, 26–7, 28–31
  of third parties 30–1
coalitions 4, 10, 158
  Belgium 34–5, 145–50
  Denmark 32–3, 37, 96, 105, 108–9,
    111

Finland 34
fragile 32, 63
Greece 174, 176, 183, 200
Italy 32, 72, 74, 82, 83–90, 93
Netherlands 121–2, 124, 130, 133
West Germany 30–1
committee, parliamentary, Denmark 96,
  102, 105–6
communist parties
  classification 3, 14–15, 69
  coalition potential 37
  electoral support 59, 61
  as large parties 59
  research 1, 5, 20
Communist Party, Austria 65
Communist Party, Belgium 62, 65,
  145–6, 151
  electoral success 140–1
Communist Party, Britain, electoral
  support 152
Communist Party (DKP), Denmark 65
  electoral success 102, 109–10, 111–12,
  114 n. 20
Communist Party, Finland, and party
  system 34
Communist Party (KKE), Greece 66,
  176, 179–81, 184, 195, 201 n. 4
  coalition potential 191
  electoral support 182–3, 185, 190, 196
Communist Party of the Interior
  (KKE-es), Greece
  classification 66, 177
  electoral support 196
  leadership 185
  and society 179, 184–6, 189–90
Communist Party (PCI), Italy
  and coalitions 85
  decline 72, 86, 90
  as marginal 38
  and party system 32, 63, 74, 78–9, 89
Communist Party (CPN), Netherlands
  67, 132, 134
  classification 118, 119
  electoral support 120, 124, 128
  organization 130–1
  and the state 122, 124
  and values 129, 132
Communist Party, Norway 67
Communist Party, Spain 68
Communist Party, Sweden 68
Communist Party, Switzerland 69
comparative approach
  methods 7–13, 24, 135
  research findings 1–6
competition 29, 35, 41, 106–8, 116,
  124–6, 158, 165, 171

centrifugal 7, 27, 30, 73, 74, 109, 165–6, 188, 192
centripetal 27, 30, 39, 166
  Greece 179–82
conscience, external 123, 126
conservative parties 1, 58, 70
  electoral support 61
Conservative Party, Britain 30, 153, 156, 160, 165, 167–9, 173 n. 3
Conservative Party, Denmark, and party system 32–3, 65, 97, 101, 107
Conservatives, France 66
Conti, G. 94 n. 1
convergence, political 74–6, 89, 165
Convergence and Unity, Spain 68
Corbetta, P. and Parisi, A. 94 n. 1
culture, political 5, 79, 132, 177, 187

Daalder, H. 6
Damgaard, E. 106
Danmarks Retsforbund, electoral success 102
Dansk Samling, electoral success 102
declaration threshold 10, 98–100, 121, 156, 176
definitions
  of political party 98–9
  of small party 9, 12, 23–5, 42, 43–4, 72, 95–7, 115–18, 135
Degrelle, Léon 138
Democratic Social Party, Netherlands
  classification 119
Democratic Socialists '70, Netherlands 67, 132, 134
  as challenger 126
  classification 119
  in coalition 122
  electoral support 120, 121
  as hinge party 118
  and ideology 130
  membership 131
  and other parties 125, 133
Democrats '66, Netherlands
  as coalition partner 122, 124–5, 133
  electoral support 120, 121–2
  ideology 118
  membership 131
  as mobilizer 126
  and party system 35, 41, 67, 116, 118, 134
  and the state 124
  and values 129, 132
Democrats, Switzerland 69
Denmark
  changing electoral support 53, 56, 63
  electoral system 95, 101

impact of small parties 8, 95–113
new parties 41, 62
party system 9, 13, 32–3, 45, 47, 65, 95–6, 99, 106–9
research 6, 21
socialist success in 59
Deschouwer, K. 135–51
detached small parties 8, 36, 37–8, 39, 77, 118, 165, 171, 187
Deth, J.W. van 129
Di Lalla, M. 94 n. 1
DIANA ('Democratic Renewal'), Greece 177, 183–4, 195, 197
differentiation of small parties 57–63
dissatisfaction, programmatic/organizational 42
distribution 36–8, 43, 45–7
diversity, Britain 171–2
DNSAP, Denmark, electoral success 102
Doens, A. 189
dominance, party 27–8, 31–2, 74–6, 95, 179, 200
  hard/soft 28
Dutch Middle Class Party, electoral support 128–9, 134
Duverger, M. 29, 113 n. 1

EAR (Greek left)
  blackmail potential 190
  and society 184–6
ecology parties, see green parties
Ecology Party, France 66
ecumenicals, Netherlands 115, 118, 124–5, 133
EDA (Unitary and Democratic Left), Greece 178–9, 195–6
EDIK, Greece 179–81, 195
Einaudi, L. 86
EK-ND (Centre Union-New Forces), Greece 179
electoral system
  disproportionality 54–5
  as variable 13, 35, 54–5, 80–1, 83, 93, 95, 157–8
environmentalism, see green parties
Epstein, L.D. 176
ESPE, Greece 195–6
ethnicity and politics 8, 80, 129
Eurocommunism, Greece 177, 179, 182–3, 184, 189–90, 196–7
European elections
  Britain 153
  Greece 196–7
  Netherlands 124–5, 129

Evangelical People's Party, Netherlands 69, 119, 125, 127, 134
  as challenger 126
Extreme Right Party, Greece 66

Faelleskurs, Denmark, electoral support 104
families, large party 58–9
families, small party 3–5, 9–10, 12, 14–21, 43, 118–19, 187
  differentiating 57–63
Farmers' Party, Netherlands, see Boerenpartij
Farneti, P. 74, 76, 78, 79–80
Feltrinelli, Fondazione 94 n. 1
Feminist Alliance, Iceland, and new politics 38
feminist movements 91, 131
finance
  Britain 164
  Denmark 101, 105, 109
  Netherlands 122–3
Finland
  changing electoral support 53, 56, 63
  party system 9, 33–4, 43, 47, 66
  research 6
Finnish Centre Party 59
Finnish Rural Party 66
Fisher, S.L. 2, 175
Flemish Christian Democrats (CVP), Belgium 45, 53, 135, 142–3, 147–9, 150
Flemish Frontpartij, Belgium 136–8
Flemish Green Party, Belgium 142, 149–50, 151
Flemish Liberals, Belgium 53, 65, 144, 148–9, 151
Flemish National Union (VNV), Belgium 138, 146–7, 149, 151
Flemish Socialists, Belgium 53, 65, 148–9, 151
France
  changing electoral support 52–3, 56, 63
  electoral system 54–5, 66
  party system 9, 48, 62
  research 6
Francophone DF party, Belgium 65
Free Democrats (FDP), West Germany, as third party 30–1, 65
Freedom Party (FPÖ), Austria 65
  coalition potential 31
Frie Folkeparti, Denmark, electoral success 102
Frisian National Party 119, 128

Front des Francophones, Belgium 139, 140, 144, 146–8, 151
FRP, Denmark, electoral support 104

Galli, G. 74
gender, and small party support 159
German Party, West Germany 65
German Reich Party, West Germany 65
Germany, West
  changing electoral support 52–3
  electoral system 55
  and party dominance 28
  party system 8, 9, 30–1, 38, 46–7, 65–6
  research 6, 21–2
Glistrup, M. 2
government, and British small parties 163–6
Gramsci, A, 187
Greece
  electoral system 179, 182, 183, 193–4, 196–7, 199
  as new democracy 48–9, 174, 178, 186, 191, 199, 201 n. 1
  origins of small parties 198–9
  party system 13, 66, 174–200
Green Left alliance, Netherlands 125, 127
green parties
  classification 4, 19–20, 58, 70, 118–19
  electoral success 9, 59, 61
  impact 2, 12, 38, 41, 42–3
  research 5–6, 21
Green parties, Belgium, and party system 35, 65, 140, 142, 144, 149–50
Green Party, Austria 8
Green Party, Britain, electoral support 153
Green Party, Greece 184, 197
Green Party, Italy 75, 76, 90
  and cleavages 80
  ideology 79
Green Party, Netherlands 118
Green Party, West Germany 8, 31, 66
  and competition 38
Grimond, J. 164
growth, small parties 53–7, 102, 171, 197–8

Hanning, J. 79
Heath, E. 168
Herri Batsuna, Spain 68
Herzog, H. 5, 123
hinge small parties 8, 36, 37, 39, 77, 118, 122, 132, 165
Humanist Party, Netherlands 127

Index 225

Iceland, new politics 38
ideology 74, 78–9, 89, 109, 112, 115, 116, 118–19, 123, 129–30
impact
  on large parties 6, 8–10, 26, 39–40, 89–90
  on policy 3, 13–14, 82–3, 86–8, 116, 132–3, 145–50
  on public 123
Independent Republicans, France 66
Independents, Denmark 65
Independents' Party, Switzerland 69
industry, support of small parties 91
information, availability 2–3, 23, 71–2, 94 n. 1
Inglehart, R. 129
integralists, Netherlands 115, 116, 125, 126, 131–3
integration parties 130
interest groups 104, 108, 130
Ireland
  changing electoral support 52–3, 56, 63
  party system 9, 47, 66
  research 6, 22
Ireland, Northern, and party dominance 28
issues, new 2, 4, 5, 40, 53, 162–3, 169
Italy
  changing electoral support 52–3, 63
  cleavages 79–80
  electoral system 80–1, 83, 93
  ideology 78–9
  impact of small parties 8, 12, 71–93
  new politics 38
  party history 72, 76, 78
  party system 9, 13, 31–2, 41, 47, 67, 74–8, 93
  research 6, 22, 71

Janda, K. 111
Justice Party, Denmark 65, 111, 112, 114 n. 28

Karamanlis, K. 179
Katsoudas, D.K. 174
King, A. 170
Kirchheimer, O. 39
KKE, see Communist Party, Greece
KKE-es, see Communist Party of the Interior, Greece
KODISO (Party of Democratic Socialism), Greece 195–6
Koekoek, Mr 128, 131, 132
Kristeligt Folkeparti, Denmark, electoral success 102
Kyrkos, L. 185

La Malfa, U. 82, 86–7, 89, 91
Laakso, M. and Taagepera, R. 191
Labour Party, Britain 160, 165–70, 173 n. 3
  and Liberal Party 29, 167–9
  and regionalist parties 30, 37–8
  and SDP 156–7
Labour Party, Ireland 66
Labour Party (PvdA), Netherlands 115, 116–18, 124–5, 127, 129–30, 132, 134
Lagasse, A. 6
Lane, J.-E. and Ersson, S. 75
language, and politics 35, 38, 45, 53, 129, 136–8, 140, 146, 150, 163
Lanzalaco, L. 71
Larsen, D. 100
lay-socialist pole 76, 90, 93
leadership 82–3, 86, 91, 93, 104, 118, 162, 185, 189, 199
left, extreme, classification 118, 122
Left Socialists, Denmark
  electoral support 111, 113 n. 20
  and new politics 41, 65
Left Socialists, Norway 41, 59
left–right axis 4, 36–8, 39–40
  Denmark 107
  Greece 187, 192
  Italy 79, 89
  Netherlands 119
Leonardi, R. 94 n. 1
Liberal Centrum, Denmark 100, 104
Liberal Conservatives, Switzerland 69
Liberal Democratic Party, Britain 173 n. 3
Liberal Democrats, USA 132
liberal parties
  classification 3–4, 16–17, 58, 69–70, 118
  electoral support 9, 59–61
Liberal Party, Belgium 53, 65, 140
Liberal Party, Britain 29, 69, 132
  as challenger 162, 168, 172
  electoral support 152, 157, 160–3
  ideology 153, 172
  lifespan 156–8
  as mobilizing party 162–3
  and other parties 167–9
  and postwar consensus 165
  and social class 158–9
Liberal Party, Denmark 58, 65
Liberal Party (PLI), Italy 67, 75, 76
  and cleavages 80
  in coalitions 82
  electoral support 92, 93
  history 78

ideology 79, 89, 90
leadership 82, 93
membership 90–1
and the state 83–6
Liberal Party (VVD), Netherlands 67, 134
 as coalition partner 124–5
 electoral support 116–18, 127
 and values 129
Liberal Party, Norway 67
Liberal People's Party, Finland 66
Liberal–SDP Alliance, Britain, representation 29, 157, 159, 166, 167–8
lifespan, party 10–11, 12, 24–5, 97–105, 109–12, 120–2, 156–8
List for Trieste ('Melon'), Italy 77
Longo, P. 82, 87
loyalty, voter 14, 161; *see also* volatility, of electorate
Lucardie, P. 64 n. 8, 115–34

Mackie, T. and Rose, R. 64 n. 2
Mair, P. 2, 9, 11, 25, 41–70, 115–16, 142, 152–3, 174–5
Malagodi, G. 76, 82, 86, 89
Malta, two-party system 29
Marcuse, H. 123
marginal small parties 8, 36, 37, 39, 77, 108, 116, 118, 120, 122–3, 165
 Greece 184, 185–7, 199
Market Opinion and Research International (MORI), opinion polls 159
Mavrogardatos, G.Th. 191
media
 access to 100–1, 105, 157
 influence 82, 92, 121
membership, Italy 90–1
micro-parties 44, 49, 57, 116, 158, 160, 167, 175
middle ground, role of 39
Mitsotakis, C. 181–2, 189
mobilization potential 123, 126, 132, 161–3, 171, 181, 184, 193
Moderate Unity Party, Sweden 68
Monarchist Party, Italy 67
mortality rate, party 111–12
MRP, France 66
MSI/DN, *see* Neo-Fascists
Müller-Rommel, F. 1–22, 97

National Action, Switzerland 69
National Coalition, Finland 66
National Front, Britain, electoral support 152

National Front, France, as marginal 37
National Front, Greece 177, 179–81, 188, 194
National Party of Greece 178
National Party (NPD), West Germany 2
nationalist parties
 Belgium 136–8, 142, 147–50
 Britain 153, 168–70, 172
 classification 4, 5, 18–19, 119
 electoral success 59, 61
 Spain 191
Neo-Fascists (MSI/DN), Italy
 classification 67, 73, 75
 history 78, 81
 ideology 79, 83, 89
 and the state 87–8
 trade union support 91
Neo-Liberal Party, Greece 177, 181–2
 ideology 181
 leadership 189, 194
Netherlands
 changing electoral support 52–3
 cleavages 126–31; *see also* religion
 electoral system 35, 132–3
 impact of small parties 8, 43
 new parties 62–3
 party system 9, 13, 33, 35, 41, 45, 47, 67, 115–19, 124
 research 6, 22
Netherlands People's Union, and the state 121
New Democracy (ND), Greece 174, 177, 179, 182, 189, 194
 and dissent 195
 electoral support 183–4, 188, 196, 200
'new left' 76, 79, 118, 130, 132, 186, 189–90, 195
new parties 42–3, 45, 53, 61–3, 76, 93, 99–105, 121
new politics parties 42, 43, 61, 115, 118–19, 129–30, 132
Norway
 changing electoral support 52–3
 new politics 41
 party system 9, 47, 67
 research 6, 22
 socialist success in 59
 numbers of small parties 26, 45, 46, 49–50, 64 n. 5

Official Unionist Party, *see* Ulster Unionist Party
Opello, W.C. Jr 201 n. 5
organization 71, 77, 102, 106
 Belgium 147
 Italy 91–2

Netherlands 130, 132
organization theory 98
origins, small parties 198–9
Owen, D. 152, 164

Pacifist Socialist Party (PSP), Netherlands 67, 118–19, 132, 134
 electoral support 128
 as mobilizer 126
 and the state 122, 123–4
 and values 129, 132
Panebianco, A. 72
Pannella, M. 82
Papadopoulos, Y. 174–202
Papandreou, A. 179, 184, 190
Parisi, A. and Varni, A. 94 n. 1
Parisi, A. et al. 94 n. 1
PARKE, Greece 195
parliament, small parties in, Denmark 105–12
participation, electoral 41, 53, 55–7
Party of Proletarian Unity (PdUP), Italy 76
party systems
 classification 47–8
 crisis 51–2
 intermediate 9, 34, 47–8, 89
 large 9, 47–8
 multi-party: research 6, 8; undifferentiated 8, 33–6, 39, 115
 multi-party dominant 8, 31–3, 73, 74, 95, 142–3, 145
 one-party dominant 8, 27–8
 small 9, 47
 transitory 9, 48
 two-and-a-half-party 8, 30–1
 two-party 8, 28–30, 31, 152, 171–2, 178–9, 182, 190–2, 195, 198–200; imperfect 75
PASOK, Greece 174, 175, 179–81, 183, 184, 201 n. 4
 electoral support 182, 185, 186, 188, 190, 196, 197
 and electoral system 193, 196, 199
 ideology 195
 as mobilizing party 194
Pasquino, G. 77
peace movements 91, 131
Peasants' Party, Netherlands 67
Pedersen, M.N. 3, 10–11, 56, 95–114, 120
pentapartito formula, Italy 75, 82, 85
People's Party for Freedom and Democracy, Netherlands 134
People's Party, Sweden, defined as small party 44, 58, 68

People's Union, Belgium, *see* Volksunie
persistence, small party 40, 78–83, 93, 109–12
personalism 176, 177–8, 181–2, 193, 198–200
Plaid Cymru (Welsh Nationalist Party) 153
 electoral support 158, 160, 163
 and government 164
 lifespan 156
 and other parties 168, 169, 170
 separatism 166
pluralism
 centripetal 74–6, 93
 limited 191
 polarized 75
 social 13
Political Party of Radicals, Netherlands
 as challenger 132, 133
 electoral support 128
 as hinge party 118–19, 121, 122, 127, 132, 134
 as mobilizer 126
 and values 129, 132
politics, 'new' 38, 40, 41
Popular Alliance, Spain 68
Popular Democratic Union, Portugal 68
Portugal
 as new democracy 48–9, 178
 party system 68
post-materialism 38
 Britain 162
 Greece 187
 Italy 79, 80
 Netherlands 129, 132
Pridham, G. 11, 71–94
privy councillors, Britain 164
Progress Party, Denmark 2
 electoral success 59, 108, 111
 as marginal 37
 and party system 33, 65, 109
Progress Party, Norway 59, 67
Progressive Organizations, Switzerland 69
Proletarian Democracy, Italy 67, 76, 81
proportional representation 13, 54, 72, 80–1, 93, 96, 101–2, 105, 137–8, 169
proto-parties 99, 175–7
public opinion, effect 2, 40

race, and politics 129
Radical Liberal Party, Denmark 65, 108, 114 n. 24
Radical Party (PRI), Italy 67, 73, 75, 186
 electoral support 77–8, 92
 and electoral system 80

history 76, 78, 81
ideology 79
leadership 82–3
membership 90–1
and new politics 38, 41, 76–7, 90, 93
organization 92
and the state 87, 88
Radical Party, Netherlands 67
  and large parties 124
  and the state 124
Radical Socialists, France 66, 132
Rae, D. 191
Rasmussen, J. 152–73
Rassemblement Wallon, Belgium 65, 139, 146–7, 151
realignment, political 41–2, 49–53, 63
  Britain 161–3
  Italy 92–3
  Netherlands 116, 120, 122
recognition, threshold 23, 25, 72
reference parties, Netherlands 123–4, 124–5, 132
reform, electoral, Italy 81, 93
Reformed Political Association (GPV), Netherlands 119, 131–2, 134
  and large parties 124–5
  as mobilizer 126
  organization 130
Reformed Political Federation (RPF), Netherlands 119, 120, 126–7, 131, 134
  and large parties 124–5
  as mobilizer 126
  organization 130
Reformed Political League, Netherlands 67
Reformed Political Party (SGP), Netherlands 67, 119, 120, 126, 131, 134
  and large parties 124–5
  organization 130
regionalist parties
  classification 4, 5, 18–19, 119, 150
  as detached 8, 37–8, 165, 171
  electoral success 59, 61, 80, 129, 153, 158, 159
  and electoral system 29–30, 77, 136–40, 143–5, 146–7, 165, 169, 172–3
relationships, inter-party
  Belgium 145–50
  Britain 166–70
  Greece 195–6
  Italy 88–90, 93
  Netherlands 124–6
relevance
  Belgium 145, 148–9

Britain 158, 163–4, 165–73
Denmark 96–7, 108–9, 112
Greece 175–6, 177, 190–2
Italy 72–3, 78
Netherlands 121
  and party system 7–8, 26–36
  as threshold 5, 10, 24, 42, 72, 98
religion
  in Belgium 137, 139
  influence 43, 79–80
  in Netherlands 35, 119, 120, 123–5, 126–7, 130, 131
  in Northern Ireland 160
representation threshold 10, 25, 29, 80–1, 96, 98, 101–2, 104–5, 108–10, 112, 120–1, 138, 157–8, 171
Greece 175–6, 182
Republican Party (PRI), Italy 67, 72, 75, 76, 132
  and cleavages 80
  in coalitions 82
  electoral support 77, 92
  history 78
  ideology 79, 89
  leadership 82
  organization 92
  and the state 83–8
research
  case studies 4–5, 6, 12, 13
  comparative 1–6, 98
  conceptional definitional approach 7–9, 10, 11
  cross-national 5–6, 9, 20–1, 41–60, 71–93
  diachronic approach 7, 10–11
  numerical, party family approach 7, 9–10, 11, 142–5, 150
  systemic approach 7, 11–12, 145–50
Respect for Work and Democracy, Belgium 142, 151
REX, Belgium 138
right, extreme
  classification 4, 5, 17–18, 70, 118
  electoral success 59, 61, 181, 187–8, 196–7
  research 20
Rochon, T.R. 126, 132
role of small parties 38–40
Roman Catholic Party of the Netherlands 119, 127, 134
  as challenger 126
Rose, R. 199
Rose, R. and McAllister, I. 39
Rosenstone, St. et al. 160
Rural Party, Finland, and party system 34

Saragat, G. 82, 86
Sardinian Action Party (PSdA), Italy 77, 80, 81
Sartori, G. 7, 26–7, 29, 42, 72–3, 74, 88, 96–7, 109, 188–9, 191–2
satellite parties 175, 177, 183, 198, 199
scope, political, maximization 76
Scottish National Party (SNP) 153
  electoral support 157, 159–60, 162–3
  and government 164
  lifespan 156, 158
  and other parties 30, 37–8, 168–9, 170
  separatism 166
Seferiades, S. 192
Seiler, D.-L. 130
separatism 38, 166, 171
Sforza, C. 86
significance, party 26–7, 28
Sinn Fein, Ireland 66
size
  and classification 9, 25, 26, 42–9, 63–4, 135, 142–5
  effects 5, 7, 28, 63
Sjoblom, G. 88
Smith, G. 7–8, 10, 11, 23–40, 42, 73, 77, 118, 132, 165, 175
Social Democratic and Labour Party (SDLP), Northern Ireland 153
  electoral support 158, 160, 163
  and government 164
  lifespan 156
  and other parties 169
  separatism 166
Social Democratic League, Finland 66
social democratic parties, research 1
Social Democratic Party (SDP), Britain 2, 69, 119, 152, 166
  as challenger 162
  electoral support 159
  lifespan 156–8
  and other parties 167–8
Social Democratic Party, Denmark, and party system 32–3, 95–7, 101, 107–9
Social Democrats (PSDI), Italy
  classification 67, 75
  and cleavages 80
  in coalitions 82
  electoral support 92, 93
  history 76, 78
  ideology 79, 90, 119
  leadership 82
  membership 90–1
  and the state 83–7
Social Democrats (SPD), West Germany
  and party dominance 28, 38

and party system 30–1
Social and Liberal Democratic Party, Britain, *see* Liberal Democratic Party
socialist parties
  classification 3, 15, 58, 69–70, 119
  electoral support 9, 59, 61
  research 1, 6, 20
Socialist Party (SPÖ), Austria, and party dominance 28
Socialist Party, Belgium 45, 139, 140, 146
Socialist Party, Greece 195
Socialist Party (PSI), Italy 67, 75, 76, 77, 79, 90
Socialist Party, Netherlands, electoral support 128
Socialist Party, Norway 67
Socialist People's Party (SF), Denmark 59, 65, 97
  electoral support 104, 109, 112, 114 n. 20
society, relationships with 12
  Denmark 97
  Greece 177–87, 198
  Italy 90–3
  Netherlands 126–31
South Tyrol People's Party (SVP), Italy 77
  coalition potential 38
  electoral support 80
Spadolini, G. 72, 82, 83, 86–7, 91–2, 94 n. 1
Spain
  as new democracy 48–9, 191
  party system 68
specialization 106
Staphorst coalition, Netherlands 125
state, relationship with 12, 83–8, 122–4, 149–50, 163–6, 192–8
Stephanopoulos, C. 183
Stewart, D. 164
structure, party, Italy 91–2
support, electoral
  accounting for 53–7
  decline 49, 50, 52–3, 56–7, 62
  and definition 43–7
  Denmark 102–5
  increased 42–3, 50–3, 56, 62–3, 77
  Italy 83, 90–3
  large parties 50–3, 56, 63, 77
  time trends 49–53
Sweden
  changing electoral support 53
  party system 9, 47, 68
  research 6

Swedish People's Party, Finland, and party system 34, 38, 43, 66
Swiss People's Party 69
Switzerland
 changing electoral support 53
 communist party 3
 party system 9, 33, 48, 69, 192–3

Tanassi, M. 82, 87
Tarrow, S. 79
Teodori, M. et al. 94 n. 1
terrorism, Italy 91
Thatcher, M. 165, 169
third parties 30–1, 37, 148
Thomsen, S.R. 114 n. 27
Thorpe, J. 168
Tindemans, L. 146
trade unions, support of small parties 91, 131
turnout, electoral 56–7

Ulster Unionist Party, Northern Ireland 69, 153
 electoral support 28, 158, 160, 163
 and government 164, 166
 lifespan 156
 and other parties 166–7, 168
Unified Socialist Party, France 66
Union of Democratic Centre, Spain 68
Union Valdotaine (UV), Italy, electoral support 80, 81
United Left alliance, Greece 179
United States
 party system 171

relevance of third parties 169–70
support for small parties 160

values and politics 79, 129–30, 132
Vegleris, Ph. 193
Ventresocialisterne (VS), Denmark, electoral support 104
visibility 72, 80, 81, 82–3, 92, 185
Vlaams Blok, Belgium 65, 138, 146, 151
volatility
 of electorate 9, 38–40, 41–2, 55–7, 77, 109–10, 112, 186
 in party systems 13, 14, 72, 76–7
Volksunie Party, Belgium 65, 138, 146–7
voting
 exchange 77
 opinion vote 77, 83, 90, 92
 voto di appartenenza 77

Walloon Christian Democrats, Belgium 53, 65, 147–9, 151
Walloon Green Party, Belgium 142, 149–50, 151
Walloon Liberals, Belgium 53, 65, 148–9, 151
Walloon Nationalist Party, Belgium 144
Walloon Socialists, Belgium 45, 53, 148–9, 151
Wilson, F.L. 192
Wolinetz, St.B. 193
Workers' Party, Ireland 66
workload, Denmark 105–6

Zanone, V. 82, 86, 89

Index compiled by Meg Davies (Society of Indexers)

Notes on the Contributors

Kris Deschouwer is Professor of Politics at the Free University of Brussels. His research and publications are concerned with political-party theory and party organization. His publications include *Politieke partijen in Belgie* (1987), and he has written on the Belgian Greens in *New Politics in Western Europe* edited by F. Müller-Rommel (1989).

Paul Lucardie is Research Associate at the Documentation Centre on Dutch Political Parties at the University of Groningen, the Netherlands. He obtained a PhD in political studies at Queen's University at Kingston, Canada.

Peter Mair is a member of the Department of Political Science at the University of Leiden. He is author of *The Changing Irish Party System* (1987), co-author of *Identity, Competition and Electoral Availability: The Stabilization of European Electorates, 1885–1985* (1990) and editor/co-editor of *Western European Party Systems* (1983), *Party Politics in Contemporary Western Europe* (1984), *Understanding Party System Change in Western Europe* (1990) and *The West European Party System* (1990). He is currently engaged in a major cross-national research project on party organization.

Ferdinand Müller-Rommel is Akademischer Rat in Comparative Politics and Methodology at the University of Lüneburg, Federal Republic of Germany. Among his books are: *Empirische Politikwissenschaft* (1979), *Innerparteiliche Gruppierungen in der SPD* (1981), *Grüne Parteien in Westeuropa* (forthcoming) and *New Politics in Western Europe*, editor (1989); he is co-editor of *Vergleichende Politikwissenschaft* (1987) and *Cabinets in Western Europe* (1988).

Yannis Papadopoulos is Professor of Political Science, University of Lausanne, Switzerland. He is author of *Dynamique du discours politique et conquête du pouvoir – le cas du PASOK (Mouvement socialiste panhellénique): 1974–1981* (1989) and of articles on Greek politics. His interest in political theory is reflected in a number of essays on party ideologies. His current empirical research concentrates on referendary democracy.

Mogens N. Pedersen is Professor of Political Science at the University of Odense, Denmark. He has published widely on comparative politics, legislative and electoral behaviour, on party systems and on Danish politics in particular. Since 1980 he has served as editor of the *European Journal of Political Research*.

Geoffrey Pridham is Reader in Politics and Director of the Centre for Mediterranean Studies at the University of Bristol. Among his books are: *Transitional Party Co-operation and European Integration* (1981), *The New Mediterranean Democracies*, editor (1984), *Coalitional Behaviour in Theory* *and Practice*, editor (1986), *Political Parties and Coalitional Behaviour in Italy* (1988); and, *Securing Democracy: Political Parties and Democratic Consolidation in Southern Europe*, editor (1989).

Jorgen Rasmussen is Distinguished Professor of Political Science at Iowa State University, USA. He has served as the Executive Secretary of the British Politics Group, an international organization of scholars specializing in the study of British politics, since its founding in 1974. His scholarly publications have concentrated on the Liberal Party, the role of women in electoral politics and legislative–executive relations.

Gordon Smith is Professor of Government at the London School of Economics. He is the author of *Politics in Western Europe* (5th edn, 1989). Most recently he has co-edited *Developments in West German Politics* (1989). He is also the joint editor of the journal *West European Politics*.